THE DIPLOMACY OF THE GREAT WAR

THE MACMILLAN COMPANY
NEW YORK · BOSTON · CHICAGO · DALLAS
ATLANTA · SAN FRANCISCO

MACMILLAN & CO., LIMITED
LONDON · BOMBAY · CALCUTTA
MELBOURNE

THE MACMILLAN CO. OF CANADA, LTD.
TORONTO

THE DIPLOMACY OF THE GREAT WAR

BY

ARTHUR BULLARD

AUTHOR OF "PANAMA, THE CANAL, THE COUNTRY AND
THE PEOPLE," "THE BARBARY COAST,"
"A MAN'S WORLD," ETC.

New York
THE MACMILLAN COMPANY
1916

All rights reserved

COPYRIGHT, 1916
By THE MACMILLAN COMPANY
Set up and electrotyped. Published January, 1916.

PREFACE

THE object of this book is limited. It has the same relation to a treatise on diplomacy that a high school "algebra" has to a text-book in "celestial mechanics."

Very little has been written in America on European diplomacy. We have not been interested in the subject. Suddenly the roar of cannon has broken in on our ordinary life and month by month as the War drags on the vital necessity of knowing more about Europe becomes apparent. Many people ask: "What is it all about?" The more determined ask: "Where can we find out about it?" In our larger public libraries there is a great deal of material, but interest in such matters had been so slight that this material was not fully catalogued. What the libraries have to offer in our own language is mostly from English sources and as Great Britain is a party to the dispute it is unadvisable to hear only one side.

A general wish is evident among us to do something towards a settlement of the conflict, not merely to hasten the cessation of hostilities, but especially towards the establishment of decent relations between our European cousins after the War. All chance of success in this direction depends on our having some conception of the issues at stake.

So it has seemed to me worth the effort to attempt an introductory text-book, a first-year course in European diplomacy, more especially, as for many years the subject has fascinated me.

Sooner or later the War will burn itself out. The diplomatists will gather around their traditional "green table" to see what they can save from the general bankruptcy. The news of their proceedings will come to us in fragments, cablegrams to our daily papers, articles on one or another phase of the situation in our magazines. This information will seem chaotic and often petty. One morning we will read of acrimonious debates about Walfisch Bay in South West Africa, the next of a wrangle over the harbor dues of Trieste. There will be suave but virulent discussion over whether the name of the capital of Galicia should be spelt after the German or Russian, Polish or Ruthenian fashion. There will be apparently undue excitement over the question whether the majority of the population of the little town of Temesvar is Roumanian or Magyar or Serb.

I have tried to draw a sketch map into which such isolated details will fall naturally and intelligibly.

The book is divided into four sections. The first is an account, almost stenographic in its condensation, of the development of international politics in Europe since the Congress of Berlin in 1878. This period is too recent to admit of definite history. There are few important events on which there is any general agreement. The more nearly we approach the present the greater becomes the difficulty. I have tried to meet it by a study of as many and as various documents where there is no definite consensus of opinion.

In Part II. there is a consideration of the new ideas which have grown up about the functions of diplomacy during the last generation.

Part III. is pure hypothesis. I have suggested a solution which may, but probably will not, result from this War. This suggestion is not a prophecy but simply a means by which to display how these more modern ideas of diplomacy would apply to problems raised by this War. In so far as the actual results differ from the outcome I suggest it will be possible to judge how far these new ideas of diplomacy have prevailed.

Part IV. deals with the diplomatic relations between the United States and Europe. This War is an important point, perhaps a turning point in our history. We may continue along our traditional policy of non-interference in the disputes of Europe, or we may be drawn into active participation in world politics. Few decisions which face our generation will have more effect on those to follow.

As my object is essentially elementary, I have not burdened the text with foot notes. These thumbmarks of erudition would have small value to any but specialists, residing in Europe, for most of the sources to which they would refer are not easily available to American readers. I have appended a condensed and critical bibliography of the books I have found most valuable. The amount which has been printed on the various phases of the subject is stupendous. The official publications of the different foreign offices—Yellow Books, White Papers, etc., are voluminous. Thousands of books of all value and from all points of view and in every language have been issued. And of most importance is the endless flow of articles in reviews and daily papers of Europe.

The one common note of all this mass of material is its partiality, its partisanship. The War itself becomes more comprehensible as one discovers the fanatically patriotic bias of learned historians.

The memories of my childhood have, I think, helped me somewhat to meet this difficulty. I was born and bred in a "border state" and the wounds of our great war were only half healed. I remember a schoolmate telling quite seriously how the Yankee soldiers had wrecked the plantation of his grandfather on Sherman's march and of the abominations they had committed. "All the Yankees are like that," he said, and he believed it. I could not. My father was a Yankee and I knew he was a very decent sort of person. Quite as often I heard equally vindictive denunciation of the "Rebs." But I knew too many Southerners to believe these stories either. One of my friends went to a school where he was taught that the Confederate Army won the Battle of Gettysburg. We fought the battle over again several times and although I was bigger than he, I never convinced him that the North really won.

In rather vague terms our Bible promises us that the

Messiah will come again to marshal the forces of light in a last great war against the powers of darkness. There is small chance that, in any combat with merely human generals, the lines will be so sharply drawn. Until it comes to that last, stupendous struggle the student of history will be surprised and a little sceptical if his researches show him an army commanded by a real saint or a nation led by a thorough-going villain—or blood being shed in a spotless cause. We may be very sure that leading figures in the history which our times are making are quite like their predecessors in times past. The more closely we study them the more surely we will find them human beings with aspirations and efforts and defects and pettinesses very similar to our own.

Almost the first act of the Congress which was elected with Lincoln was not to free the slaves but to revise the tariff upwards. The records of the Crusaders, of their intrigues, their treasons, their love of spoils, show that the Holy Sepulchre was only one of their preoccupations and not always the principal one. And more than one of King Arthur's knights turned aside from the quest of the San Graal to kiss a pretty girl or pick up a bit of loot.

So, not expecting to find superhuman virtue or vice on either side, I have tried to be impartial. But I must confess to a very definite fondness for France. If I could not enjoy our American privilege of being misgoverned by American citizens of foreign descent (from the *Mayflower* to the latest immigration); if I had to submit to "foreign domination" I would rather be ruled by the French than by Germans. Unfortunately the choice is not so simple. The Allies of France make it somewhat easier for me to persuade myself of a large degree of impartiality.

Undoubtedly the fact that my mother tongue was English, that I have chanced to live much more in France and Russia than in Germany, has given my impression a certain unavoidable bias. My judgment might also be changed on many points if I knew the Hungarian and Slav languages, and if I could read German as easily as French. But I have done my best to see straight and I certainly am not tempted to partisanship as much as are the patriots of the various belligerent nations.

The book will have met its purpose if it helps the American reader to understand the moves on the diplomatic checker board after the War.

The chapters in Book IV. are based on articles which appeared in *The Century Magazine*.

It would be quite impossible to acknowledge in detail my personal indebtedness to the many European friends who during the recent years have so often helped me with their advice and their special information.

TABLE OF CONTENTS

	PAGE
PREFACE	v

BOOK I

THE STRUGGLE OF A GENERATION

CHAPTER
- I. The Congress of Berlin, 1878 3
- II. The Europe of Bismarck 13
- III. Das Deutschtum 24
- IV. The Resurrection of France 36
- V. The Anglo-German Friendship Cools 54
- VI. L'Entente Cordiale 69
- VII. The Algeciras Crisis 84
- VIII. Eight Years of Tension, 1906–1914. A. Morocco-Bosnia 102
- IX. Eight Years of Tension. B. The Balkans 124
- X. The Fatal Year 150

BOOK II

THE NEW ELEMENTS OF DIPLOMACY

- XI. The Rights of Nations 163
- XII. Dollar Diplomacy 178
- XIII. The Colonial World 190
- XIV. The Growth of Public Opinion 206

BOOK III

THE LIQUIDATION OF THIS WAR

Chapter	Page
XV. The Military Outcome	219
XVI. Diplomatic Tactics	228
XVII. The Demands of the Entente	235
XVIII. The Division of the Spoils	241
XIX. The Fate of Turkey	248
XX. If Germany Wins	257
XXI. The Problems of Power	262
XXII. Democratic Control	270

BOOK IV

THE UNITED STATES AND EUROPE

XXIII. Our Traditional Policy	281
XXIV. The Problems of the War	291
XXV. National Defence	305
XXVI. The United States and Peace	313
Bibliography	325
Index	335

THE DIPLOMACY OF THE GREAT WAR

BOOK I

THE STRUGGLE OF A GENERATION

THE DIPLOMACY OF THE GREAT WAR

CHAPTER I

THE CONGRESS OF BERLIN, 1878

Some writers on the history of diplomacy begin the "Modern Epoch" with the founding of the German Empire after the Franco-Prussian War. The Treaty of Frankfort which ended that war—10 May, 1871—took Alsace-Lorraine from France and struck at the industrial life of the Republic by a colossal war indemnity. Some of the seeds of hatred which are bearing fruit now were planted then. But the Congress of Berlin, seven years later, gives a more convenient starting point for a brief review of recent diplomacy.

The Congress of Berlin was the last of the kind. It followed the traditions of the *ancien régime*. It was essentially monarchial. The delegates, when they had finished their work, had to report not to their peoples but to kings. They were free to intrigue and conspire without any fear of democratic publicity.

Disraeli, the British Premier, returned to London in triumph. "Peace with honor," he announced. Under the sinister tradition of secrecy, all the other delegates could make the same claim and the nations they were supposed to represent could not know whether the peace they brought home was honorable or not.

A number of ideas, then hardly born, have grown amazingly in Europe since 1878. Perhaps the most important—an incident of the general progress of democracy—has been the idea that the people have a right to know what the diplomats are doing in their name. The Congress of Berlin was the last important diplomatic conference which entirely ignored public opinion. It was the end of an epoch.

Also from quite another point of view this congress furnishes a good starting point. It was the last great victory of Prince Bismarck. It was the apotheosis of his career.

The congress was summoned to settle the Near Eastern question. Russia's victorious war against Turkey had once more brought up the thorny problem of the Balkans.

The malady of the Sick Man was of the purulent kind, which had made a stench in Europe for many years. With rather monotonous persistence, various doctors had proposed cures, but their jealousy—the traditional hostility of the Great Powers—had prevented any effective treatment. For some unaccountable reason, after a long series of unspeakable atrocities, the Bulgarian massacres especially caught the attention of Europe. Everyone agreed that something ought to be done about it. But everybody suspected everybody else and for many months nothing was done beyond exchanging diplomatic notes.

Russia, claiming a vague sort of protectorate over all christians of the orthodox church, professed a special interest in the fate of the Balkan Slavs. But rightly or wrongly—probably rightly—the English felt that the Tsar cared very little for "bleeding Bulgaria" and a great deal for a good excuse to conquer Constantinople. Austria, feeling that she had "legitimate aspirations" and a "manifest destiny" in the Balkans, was opposed on principle to any increase of Russian influence in that quarter. So the statesmen of London and Vienna blocked the Tsar's efforts to get some united action out of the Great Powers on behalf of the Bulgars.

At last, after much muttering and many threats, the Russians lost patience and decided to go in and settle the matter alone. In those days the fighting qualities of the Turks were ranked very high. All Russia's enemies, hoping for her defeat, urged her to go ahead.

THE CONGRESS OF BERLIN, 1878

Before Russia opened hostilities she arranged some sort of a treaty with Austria at Reichstadt. It was typical of the way things happen in diplomacy. The text has never been published. All we know about it is from occasional allusions to it and shrewd guesses. Russia wanted to be sure that Austria would not jump on her back in the midst of her struggle with the Turks. And as payment for this promise of benevolent neutrality she recognized Austria's claim to a predominant interest in the two Turkish provinces of Bosnia and Herzegovina.

Russia started her campaign by sending a notice to the little country of Roumania that her armies were going to pass that way and that the Roumanians must not object. The Roumanians—unlike the Belgians in 1914—did not object.

At first it looked as if the general expectation would prove right and that Russia would be defeated. As usual she was slow in getting started, her army was poorly organized, her generals inefficient and corrupt. But after months of reverses, the campaign was saved by the Roumanians, who decided to change from benevolent neutrality to active coöperations. These new reinforcements arrived before Plevna at the critical moment. The Turkish military power was crushed. The christian armies marched to the very walls of Constantinople (they were kept from entering by the fear of European intervention). In the little suburb of San Stefano the Sultan was forced to sign a humiliating treaty.

By this treaty most of the Balkan christians were freed from Turkish rule, but its main feature was the creation of a large independent principality of Bulgaria. It was generally assumed in Europe that this new nation—a unit composed of Slavs—would be an adjunct of Russia, in reality a new province. Such undoubtedly was the expectation of the Tsar. Although Constantinople and the control of the Straits were left to the Turks, Bulgaria was to have ample ports on the Ægean Sea, and if Bulgaria was only another name for Russia, it meant that at last the great empire of the North had reached warm water. British naval control of the eastern Mediterranean was threatened. Of course the Austrians were equally displeased to find that they had guessed wrong and that the war, instead of ruining Russia, had greatly increased her hold on the Balkans.

So London and Vienna joined in claiming that the fate of Turkey was not a private quarrel between Tsar and Sultan, but a matter of European interest. The affair could not be "localized," it was of such importance that it could only be settled by an international congress.

Germany was in a delicate situation. Bismarck would have preferred to keep on good terms with both Russia and Austria. There was an ancient tradition of friendship between the Hohenzollerns and the Romanovs. During the long struggle between Prussia and Austria for predominance in the German federation and more recently during the war with France, Bismarck had made this Russian friendship the foundation stone of his policy. But he was no longer merely the prime minister of Prussia, he was now chancellor of the German Empire. And from this new point of view the friendship of Austria was more valuable to him than that of Russia.

This was plainly a crisis where it was necessary to be "realistic." So Bismarck secretly pledged his support to Austria and reassured Russia by protestations of undying affection. And Russia, relying on the debt of gratitude which the kaisers undoubtedly owed to the tsars, came to the congress—like a sheep to the shambles.

The Congress of Berlin was the most brilliant ever held. Ordinarily such affairs are settled by mere ministers plenipotentiary and ambassadors extraordinary. But three prime ministers—of the three great empires—were present. Bismarck presided in person, Lord Beaconsfield (Disraeli) represented Great Britain, and Prince Gortschakov headed the Russian delegation. Austria, Italy and France sent their ministers of foreign affairs—Count Andrassy, Count Corti and Monsieur Waddington. Most of these gentlemen were in uniform. All of them were bejewelled with decorations.

The seances were held in the rather gaudy ball-room of the Chancellerie. In the middle of the great room a long table was covered with the traditional green cloth of diplomacy. The head of each delegation had a highbacked chair. Lesser chairs were provided for the lesser lights. And down at the far end of the table a space was reserved for the Turkish delegates, whose red fezzes gave an added touch of color to the brilliance. Close by was a buffet where the hospitable German government offered endless supplies of port wine and sandwiches.

A great many books have been written about the Congress of Berlin—objective criticisms and personal memoires by the participants. It is clear from all of them that very little happened about the "green table" which really mattered. The work of the congress was not done publicly. The important deals were put through in secret. It was an almost perfect example of what ordinarily decent men would agree an international congress should not be.

In the weeks preceding the opening—13th June, 1878—at least a dozen secret agreements had been arranged by the different parties. Bismarck, while posing as a disinterested presiding officer, had pledged his support to everybody.

England and Russia had signed a "convention" on 30th of May, which in the course of the congress they both tried to break. And on the 4th of June, England had signed a secret treaty with the Sultan. Disraeli was primarily interested in checking the Russian advance, but he persuaded the Sultan that it was only out of his great love for Turkey that he had insisted on revising the treaty of San Stefano—and in return for this disinterested service he demanded Cyprus. This treaty was secret but Disraeli communicated it to Austria, so it got out. For some days the Turkish delegates—at the foot of the table—were the only people at the congress who did not know of its existence! And in the corridors, during the congress, Disraeli, in spite of this defensive alliance with the Sultan, secured the French vote by offering them the Turkish province of Tunisia—which, by the way, the Italians thought was being promised to them. All through the congress Austria and Russia were trying to tear up the treaty they had signed at Reichstadt.

Anyone who is inclined to doubt that such honorable gentlemen could lend themselves to such sinuous doubledealings, should read Bismarck's "Memoires." The threads of most of these intrigues were in his hands and he stands out distinct from other statesmen and diplomats by his amazing frankness. Machiavelli was only a theoretician. The Iron Chancellor tells us simply and naïvely just how he practised politics.

Even more interesting sidelights on the congress are furnished by the *"Souvenirs inédits"* of Caratheodory Pasha, the chief of the Turkish delegation.

"We were already in the third week of the congress when the bomb was exploded"—*i. e.*, the news that the English were preparing to repudiate the Anglo-Russian convention, which was favorable to the Turks. "Broken-hearted by the news, I reminded the Marquis of Salisbury that he had given his signature and begged him to honor it. The foreign secretary admitted the binding nature of the engagement but told me he would get around this. He would resign, so that he could be replaced the next day by another minister of foreign affairs, who would not be bound by his signature."

But the most impressive part of this Turk's account of the congress is where he tells of the insults he had to swallow. Not knowing of the Anglo-Russian agreement, Caratheodory Pasha was unprepared for the discussion which followed its announcement. He asked for time to consult his government. "The Prince Bismarck spoke to the

Ottoman delegation with extreme harshness: 'If the plenipotentiary has anything to say, he must say it at once and without delay, and even if he wishes to take the floor immediately I cannot permit him to use his opportunity to make objections.'"

"The Prince Bismarck," he writes in another place, "did not miss any occasion to point out that the Oriental question, in so far as it concerned the peoples and forms of government which are outside the circle of European civilization, ought not to interest Europe except for the effect it might have on the relations between the Great Powers. It was only on this count that he deigned to interest himself in us."

The very existence of Turkey was at stake. But no one paid any attention to what the Ottoman delegates had to say.

Next to the Turks, the people most intimately affected by the decisions of the congress were the various christian nations of the Balkans. They were not even allowed to have a voice in the discussions. Delegations of Serbs and Montenegrins, of Roumanians and Greeks hung about in the anterooms of the Chancellerie, longing to lay their grievances and their hopes before this high court of Europe. They were treated like troublesome children.

Quite as shocking as the plenipotentiaries' lack of interest in the human aspect of their task, was their almost unbelievable incompetence. They had not taken the trouble to study the problems they met to solve. The Near East offers a most complicated question in ethnology. Not one of them was an ethnologist. A large part of their work consisted in drawing frontiers. There was not a geographist among them. And of course they knew nothing about economic problems. They were lordly gentlemen—not business men.

They were diplomats, but some of them at least did not even know their own profession. The incident of the Caucasus frontier was worthy of comic opera. It is sufficiently amusing—and typical—to warrant a rather long quotation from the unpublished memoirs of Count Schouwalov, who was the second Russian delegate.

"I do not exaggerate in saying that he (Prince Gortschakov, the Russian prime minister) was incapable of pointing out on a map, even approximately, the different countries of the Balkan Peninsula or, for example, the location of Kars and Batoum." . . . "So I was considerably disturbed one morning when the Prince told me that he left all other questions to me but that he reserved especially for himself the case of Batoum" (and the Caucasus frontier).—"He would treat directly with Lord Beaconsfield about that." Count Schouwalov told Lord Salisbury, the second English delegate, about this decision of his chief. "He replied to me in vexation: 'But, my dear Count, Lord Beaconsfield cannot arrange that. He has never even seen a map of Asia Minor.'"

The matter dragged along till the end of the congress. Prince Gortschakov and Lord Beaconsfield could not come to terms. It looked for a while as if negotiations would be broken off and war result. But at the last moment it was announced that an accord had been reached.

Count Schouwalov explains that the Russian general staff had prepared a special confidential map for them on which was drawn two frontiers. One represented the border as arranged between Turkey and Russia by the treaty of San Stefano. But some concessions would certainly be necessary, so the general staff had drawn a second frontier considerably further back, which represented the utmost they were willing to give up. The delegation was instructed to demand the San Stefano frontier and to concede, if necessary, mile by mile back to this ultimate line. Russia was prepared to go to war rather than give up more. Of course these maximum concessions should have been guarded as the most strict secret of state.

"This last session, consecrated to the question of Asia, had an air of solemnity. On its issue depended peace or war for Europe. The president asked the two negotiators, Lord Beaconsfield and Prince Gortschakov, to take places side by side and explain the nature of their accord. The two gentlemen sat down and each spread out a map specially drawn for the occasion. The rest of us, standing up, formed a group behind them. At once I saw the terrible confusion which was coming. The map of Prince Gortschakov contained a single frontier, that of San Stefano, and the Prince declared with emphasis that 'my lord' had accepted it. He, on the contrary, replied to each word of the Prince by a laconic 'No.' And he indicated on his map the frontier they had agreed upon. And, to my great surprise, this line, with all its twistings and turnings, was exactly the one we were authorized to accept as the extreme concession.

"The denials, which the two plenipotentiaries exchanged, began to envenom the discussion. Each one insisted bitterly on his frontier. At last Prince Gortschakov stood up and gripped my hand. 'There has been treason,' he said to me, 'they have had the map of our general staff.'

"I found out after the session that the evening before Prince Gortschakov had asked for a map of Asia Minor. Some one had entrusted to him the confidential map with the two frontiers. He not only showed it to Lord Beaconsfield but had lent it to him for a few hours so that Lord Salisbury could see it."

The results accomplished by these diplomats, with their incompetence and their spirit of intrigue, was—what could be expected.

Bénoit Brunswik, in his careful analysis of their work, "Le Traité de Berlin," gives a judgment which is on the whole the kindest I have found in all the literature on the subject. In his introduction he admits that the work of the congress has been severely criticised. " . . . this treaty does not give satisfaction to any interest, does not respond to any aspiration, does not condemn any ambition . . . it touches many questions and does not satisfy any. Its decisions are based on contradictory motives, are opposed to sane logic, indifferent to justice and insensible to honor." But the alternative to accepting this sorry patchwork was a general European war. "The treaty," he writes, "is the result of a compromise between the English fear of a Slavic advance and everybody else's fear before the threatening war. It is a document of opportunism, the fruit of hostile rivalries."

Unfortunately, the history of diplomacy is full of such documents.

"Peace, with honor," Lord Beaconsfield could report. It is not fair to charge him with hypocrisy. The brand of chicanery, which we would now call disreputable, in those days came within the definition of diplomatic honor.

That is why I choose the Congress of Berlin as the starting point for modern diplomacy. Our more recent times have not been free from similarly disgraceful intrigues, but prime ministers no longer call them honorable. All the world—or at least a large majority—has changed its ideals of common decency in such matters, since 1878.

CHAPTER II

THE EUROPE OF BISMARCK

A STUDY of the Congress of Berlin is a sad matter for anyone who likes to believe that honesty is the best policy. Bismarck, whose sinister genius for intrigue inspired most of the crookedness, accomplished exactly what he wanted.

Territorial expansion was not at the moment his ambition. He wanted—and secured—two things from this crisis.

First of all he wanted an ally. Under his guidance Prussia had fought three successful wars, against Denmark, Austria, and France. Germany had ceased to be a mere geographical expression and had become a great empire. But Bismarck was shrewd enough to realize that grandeur acquired by such strong-arm methods does not make one popular. And immediately after the war with France he began to be haunted by his "coalition nightmare." He feared that Europe would unite against him, as a few generations before it had united against the great Napoleon. His "Memoires" show that his principal worry was the danger of an Austro-French alliance. These two nations, whom he had so recently humiliated, seemed logical allies. To guard against this hostile combination it was necessary to make friends with one of them. Of the two, he chose Austria, and in order to make Austria forget her anger over her recent defeat it was necessary to render her some resounding service.

The domain of the Hapsburg was in a precarious position. On its southwestern frontier was the new kingdom of Italy—made up of recently revolted provinces. On the north was this young German nation which had shattered her armies at Sadowa: and on all other sides, north, east and south, were Slavs.

The Congress of Berlin gave Bismarck the chance to step in gracefully and say: "I will save you from Russia. See what a powerful and valuable friend I can be!" It still took some time to overcome the "traditional" hostility between Austria and Prussia, but the foundations of the present Germanic alliance were laid at this Congress of Berlin.

It was not till the next year—7th October, 1879—that the alliance was signed. It was at first kept secret, but part at least of it has since been published. It was a defensive alliance directed principally against Russia. Although its terms imply perfect equality it was really a case of Germany promising to protect Austria. What Bismarck gained was the assurance that Austria would not unite with France against him.

The second result which Bismarck sought from this congress over the affairs of the Near East was the chance for a new and more emphatic assertion of German supremacy on the continent of Europe.

The spokesmen of the entente—in the present crisis—frequently state that they are fighting to prevent German hegemony. It would be nearer the truth to say that Germany is fighting to maintain—or, better, to regain—her supremacy. While Bismarck was chancellor no one had any doubt about who was master of Europe.

Caratheodory Pasha was not the only one to whom Bismarck spoke sharply. The Turkish delegate records his surprise that not even the British prime minister showed enough spirit to resent the chancellor's dictatorial manner. The Great Powers of Europe docilely performed his goose-step in honor of the Man of Blood and Iron. There was not the slightest indiscipline.

Besides their marvellous mechanics, and their manifold conquests over the material world, the Germans have a large measure of high—perhaps extravagant—idealism. Their Fatherland is not only of this world. Much of it is in the clouds—where they were said to live before Bismarck taught them victory. And the French, whose imagination deals with things concrete, and the matter-of-fact Englishmen find this strange idealism the hardest part of the German character to understand.

Over and above the *Deutschland*—the geographical section of the globe where their flag flies—hovers a mystic ideal,—the "Deutschtum". It is an expression impossible to translate into English.

It is the force of this ideal which has made Germany what it is. It has amalgamated scattered dukedoms and petty principalities into a great, coherent, forward-pushing nation. It has performed a miracle of psychology. It furnishes the most striking example in history of how to change human nature. Whether you consider it a regeneration or a malignant degeneration, it is impossible to dispute the amazing change which has come over the German people since the days of Goethe or Kant.

To Germans, this ideal is entirely beneficent. It means orderly comfort. It means everyone finding the niche they fit. It means mutual, well-organized effort, a harmonious striving together—a force of progress which is irresistible. And in their faith that this life-giving discipline is to spread abroad and regenerate all the earth there is something a great deal finer than gross political or economic greed. To their minds it is almost, if not quite, synonymous with the millennium. There is a very marked messianic note in some of Bismarck's speeches.

The ordinary Latin or Anglo-Saxon, who studies his life, is forced to the conclusion that he ought to have been locked up. He was a magnified brigand—a robber baron of the Dark Ages strayed into the nineteenth century. No jury—after reading the confessions in his "Memoires"—would acquit him. And yet Bismarck was undoubtedly an idealist!—every bit as much as Torquemada. The Inquisitors burned heretics at the stake—for the greater glory of God. And Bismarck, in a similar state of cold-blooded exaltation, falsified telegrams, lied copiously and unchained the dogs of war for an ideal, which seemed to him equally holy—the greater glory of the Deutschtum.

Never in history has the ideal of the Deutschtum seemed so near realization as at the Congress of Berlin. Everything in Europe was at sixes and sevens; a general war was imminent. Bismarck rapped on the table and all the Great Powers stopped their disorderly noise. Sitting at the head of the green table, Bismarck—his armor laid aside and rather after the manner of an irritable but kindhearted school-master—told them how to behave, and not one of his unruly flock dared—under his eye—to question his will. A sort of Pax Germanica reigned in Europe. It was the great moment of Bismarck's career. It was a proud moment for the young German nation.

The international relations of Europe since 1878 have been immensely complicated. They are hopelessly confused, unless one starts out with the idea that Bismarck had—past any doubt—established the supremacy of Germany in the continent of Europe. In the seventies and eighties no one thought of questioning this proposition—except a French officer named Boulanger, who gathered a certain following in France by preaching that it was better to die fighting than to live on ignobly under the almost ceaseless insults from across the Rhine. In all the diplomatic correspondence of those years—White Papers, Blue Books, etc.,—it is hard to find a single document which does not accept the German predominance as the basis of European politics. No one of the continental powers dared to dream of a different order.

Without doubt Bismarck and the Germans enjoyed the sensation—for so many years their race had been ignored and despised! Many of their acts can be explained on no other basis than that they liked to remind others—and themselves—of the power of the Deutschtum.

This idea that at last they had come into their own—that the superiority and preëminence of the German race was recognized by all the world—became a national possession the loss of which would be as heart-breaking to them as the cession of Alsace-Lorraine had been to France.

There was only one of the European powers which did not admit that Berlin was the center of the world—the British empire. But Great Britain is not a continental country. In those days its island situation allowed it a splendid isolation. More important than this matter of geography was the fact that English and German interests did not clash. On all the continent of Europe the only British soldiers were at Gibraltar. They would have had to march across the length of Spain and breadth of France to meet the Kaiser's army. And in most other matters they were equally far from points of conflict.

So long as Britons ruled the waves the English were quite content to let the Germans rule the land. The British interests were overseas—colonial—and Bismarck was not inclined to colonial adventure.

Later in life he was forced by the growing commercial and industrial classes to devise a colonial policy, but from his "Memoires" it is clear that his interest in these projects was not keen. Colonial matters attracted his attention principally as they furnished an endless supply of apples of discord to toss among his rivals. The more England quarreled with Russia in Asia and with France in Africa, the less likely they were to trouble him. He was forever urging his possible enemies to squander their energy in distant parts. And even after he half-heartedly launched his own colonial enterprises he was careful to avoid friction with England. This policy worked to perfection and it became a maxim of diplomacy that England and Germany had the same enemies.

Always the Chancellor of Iron and Blood was shivering with fear of a hostile coalition. He himself called it his "nightmare." His clever and unscrupulous manipulation of the Congress of Berlin had increased the cordiality of the English and had resulted in the alliance with Austria. But this did not content him.

By approving England's offer of Tunisia to France at the Congress of Berlin, Bismarck had seriously hurt the feelings of Italy. But he needed Italy in his system, so he set to work to draw her in.

The brand new nation of Italy was in an uneasy and precarious position. Above everything else she needed a period of peace for internal reorganization. But in the first decades of her national life hardly anyone believed that she was destined to enjoy forty years of peace. She was threatened on both her land frontiers.

Austria was the "traditional" enemy. The story of the Italian struggle for national unity is very similar to the recent history of Servia. The kingdom had been built up by provinces snatched from the patchwork empire of the Hapsburgs. The work was not completed. There were still many thousand "unredeemed" Italians under the Austrian yoke in Istria and the Trentino. And the Hapsburgs were not reconciled to the loss of the fair Italian provinces. They would never have given up the struggle to hold them if it had not been for the crushing defeat they received from Prussia. A new Austro-Italian war was chronically imminent.

The second menace came from across the French frontier. Napoleon III. had—off and on—favored the Italian nationalist movement. And for what aid he had given he had claimed as his price the province of Nice. The republic was unenthusiastically friendly. During the presidency of Marshal MacMahon the French were too torn by internal dissension to be of any help to Italy even if they had wanted to be. Paris was aflame with Royalist conspiracies. Not even the Republicans were sure of their victory. A monarchical restoration was always possible—the danger became acute in the late seventies—and the Royalists were good catholics. No king could reign in France without the support of the clericals, and they made it very clear that if ever they won to power their first demand would be for war against the impious Italians who had deprived the Pope of his temporal power. Fear of a possible attack from catholic France seems to have been the chief motive which led Crispi to seek an alliance with protestant Germany.

Bismarck met Crispi's advances with calculated coyness. Italy needed his help a great deal more than he needed Italy.

There had been some rumors of an Italian-Russian alliance. In case the Tsar went to war against the two Germanic empires there was danger that the Italians might attack Austria in the back. The prevention of this complication was the one advantage which Bismarck hoped for from the Italian alliance. He was very contemptuous of their military power. He did not expect them to help him in his work for the Deutschtum, he wanted to make sure that they would not hinder him. So the only terms he would offer Italy was a chance to enter the existing Austro-German alliance. Crispi had been one of Garibaldi's "Thousand." He would not hear of making friends with Austria. So, for the moment, the negotiations fell through.

But in 1881 France clashed in on the promise of the Congress of Berlin and declared a protectorate over Tunisia. This infuriated the Italians. They were too weak—too young a nation—at the time to risk colonial adventures, but from historical and economic reasons they claimed "rights" in Tunisia, which the French action violated. It was Bismarck's opportunity. Crispi had fallen from power. A new Minister signed the Triple Alliance at Vienna. The date is uncertain, but it was near, if not on, the 20th of May, 1882.

Once more Bismarck had had his way. But he was not content.

He foresaw the danger of a Franco-Russian alliance. It was something which everyone foresaw. The three nations of central Europe had united. The island empire of Britain was friendly to this alliance. The two other powers had to unite or be crushed separately. Sooner or later the autocracy and the republic would be forced into each other's arms. And all the last years of his official life Bismarck dedicated to preventing this occurrence which everyone felt was "logical." Once more he succeeded.

As, after the Congress of Berlin, he had tried to checkmate an Austro-French alliance by making friends with Austria, so now he tried to prevent a Franco-Russian alliance by making the Tsar forget the sorry trick he had played on him in 1878.

Russia was engaged in that stage of her expansion which gave her Transcaspia, Boukhara, and a predominance in central Asia. Her advance guards were in Afghanistan on the frontier of India. The English were much worried by what Kipling called "the bear who walks like a man." When the Tsar's forces occupied the Oasis of Merv all England shook with what *Punch* called "mervousness." The only thing which prevented an Anglo-Russian war was the obvious fact that Moscow could not be captured by a fleet. The English articles on international politics of the day showed a certain peevishness over Russia's lack of a vulnerable sea-board.

But the Russian Bear was more afraid of the British Whale than it had any reason to be. Worry over this quarrel with England induced the Tsar to bury the grudge he had against Germany for the betrayal at the Congress of Berlin, and once more to listen—with attention, if not with enthusiasm—to the siren-song of Bismarck.

So, in spite of every probability against it, Bismarck was able to sign a new treaty—21st March, 1884—at Skiernowice, between the emperors of Germany, Austria and Russia. This amazing agreement—it must be remembered that Austria and Germany had an anti-Russian alliance—is generally called "the counter-assurance."

The text of the "Dreikaisersbund" was kept secret. But its purpose was evident. Bismarck wanted to make it impossible for Russia and France to unite, and this bizarre treaty served his purpose. But no one less clever than Bismarck at making black seem white could have managed to persuade Russia that this alliance was in her interest. It did not outlive his term of office.

Great Britain had not at that time started the fashion of Oriental alliances or Bismarck would certainly have re-countered or anti-countered his insurance by seeking a treaty with the Great Mogul or the Grand Llama.

A notable point about this intricate network of Bismarckian treaties is, that France was left out. The Iron Chancellor's policy towards the Republic was simple to a degree. France ought to be eliminated. He told his friends that the greatest mistake of his career had been in fixing the indemnity after the War of 1870 too low. He had thought that five milliard francs—a thousand million dollars—would "bleed France white." When she paid this immense sum within three years he was so chagrined that he wanted to "begin again" and "finish with her."

It is a well-established fact that nothing but the energetic intervention of Russia and England saved France from a new invasion in 1875. A second war would probably have been the end of France. While these two powers— England and Russia—had not objected to the crushing of Napoleon III. they did not want to see the French nation entirely rubbed out. Of even more importance—for altruism has small weight in international politics—they were beginning to feel that Germany was growing over fast.

Although Bismarck reluctantly decided that it would be unwise to indulge in a new war, he rarely neglected an opportunity to humiliate his victim. The Schnaebelé incident in 1887 was only the most marked, the most inexcusable of the long series of Franco-German crises which marked Bismarck's *régime*.

The Chancellor was trying to force a new and very expensive military law through a reluctant Reichstag. It was necessary to find a menace of war in order to justify the new taxes. In the same cynical manner in which he had twisted the Ems telegram he manufactured this "incident."

A French custom official, Schnaebelé, was invited by his German colleague to cross the frontier to straighten out some accounts. He had scarcely put his foot on the German side of the line when he was arrested. The news was spread in France that the German police had arrested this official on the French side of the line, and so Bismarck was able to read to the Reichstag excited extracts from the French newspapers. No one knows, even today, exactly what happened. Only one thing is sure, nothing happened which was serious. But Bismarck had engineered the entire affair to facilitate the success of his internal policies. It is possible that he did not realise that such action would embitter the French. It is more probable that he did not care. He pretended to blame the French for not forgetting the loss of Alsace-Lorraine. But he was forever opening again the old wound.

After he had given up his project of a second war in 1875, his guiding principle towards France was to encourage her in colonial adventure. This, he held, would use up and scatter her forces, keep her mind off revenge and embroil her with England. He seems to have never given up hope of an Anglo-French war.

But even geniuses grow old, and, in 1890, the impatient young Kaiser, Wilhelm II. dropped the old pilot.

The heritage which Bismarck left to his people was imposing. Very rarely has such stupendous growth been achieved in one man's watch at the helm. Of all the great ministers from Richelieu to our day none have accomplished so much for their sovereigns.

But this heritage was not all rosy. A Chinese proverb tells us that while it is easy to lie, it is exceedingly difficult to lie well. Bismarck left to his nation a tradition of statescraft which only genius could manage. His technique in the hands of lesser men has not worked so smoothly.

And perhaps of even greater detriment to his people is

the legacy of hate which he left. People feared the Germany of Bismarck, some admired it, but nobody loved it.

The new *régime* in Germany seems to have tried to establish better relations with its neighbors, to build up a better reputation. But the tradition of Bismarck was too strong. Nobody trusted it.

CHAPTER III

DAS DEUTSCHTUM

To pretend, as so many of their present enemies do, that the Germans are simply retrograde barbarians engaged in a reckless military raid for spoils, is to vastly and dangerously underestimate their force. They are a great and intensely modern nation; they are moved by an ideal.

It is extremely difficult for an American to grasp what the Germans mean by the "Deutschtum." It is something so foreign to our habits of thought that it inevitably seems extravagant and fantastic.

Here we are faced by a psychological situation the importance of which cannot be over emphasized. Some people find it easy to laugh at the German pretensions—more are angered by them. But it is impossible to have any understanding of recent history—or the present crisis—if one ignores this ideal, or believes that when Germans speak of the Holy Mission of the Deutschtum it is arrant hypocrisy to cover gross greed and love of gore.

The Germans may be insane—but they are not insincere. The amount of devotion they have given to their ideal—and are giving—is stupendous. There has probably never been a time in history when so large a number of individuals have given so large a share of their energy to a common ideal as has been the case in Germany during the last generation. College professors, historians, and philosophers—after the manner of Peter the Hermit—have infused into the people an ardor which is not of this world. It is a fact of social psychology which must not be ignored. The Deutschtum is a crusade.

It is well to remember that such national spasms are not unknown to history. Just about a century ago the

French suffered from a somewhat similar frenzy. The barefooted soldiers of the First Republic went out crusading on behalf of "Liberty, Equality, Fraternity." "*Le chant de départ*," their recruiting song, shows clearly how they were thrilled by a passionate desire to impose their ideal on all the world.

> D'anéantir les oppresseurs!
> En tous lieux, dans la nuit profonde,
> Plongeant l'infâme royauté.
> Les français donneront au monde
> Et la paix et la liberté.

> (To annihilate the oppressors!
> In all places, hurling into the profound night,
> The infamous royalty.
> The French will give to the world
> Both Peace and Liberty.)

The further the French marched the more they strayed away from their ideal and eventually they were defeated by people who—as they said—preferred to be slaves.

The Germans of today feel towards their crusade very much as French revolutionaries did towards theirs. It is quite aside from the point to discuss which ideal is the better. I, personally, prefer the French. But it is an ostrich policy, a refusing to look danger in the face, to pretend that the Germans are mere bandits. They are people on fire—exalted by a stupendous ideal.

Professor John Dewey's admirable book "German Philosophy and Politics," traces the genealogy of this ideal back to the beginning of the last century. Out of the ruin which was brought to the scattered peoples of central Europe by the vast adventure of Napoleon there arose here and there prophets who foresaw the imposing strength which would come to the Germans, if only they would unite. Poets sang, philosophers discoursed, statesmen intrigued, and soldiers fought to this end.

The program for this mighty reconstruction was formulated by the philosopher Fichte in his "Address to the German Nation." (1807.)

"Elevate the German name to that of the most glorious among all peoples, making this nation the regenerator and restorer of the world."

He tells the people of his generation how their ancestors had by the Reformation saved the race from the suffocating traditions of Roman obscurantism, but "yours is the greater fortune: you may establish once for all the kingdom of the spirit and of reason."

Fichte believed—or he could not have preached it so passionately—that the Germans were a chosen people. There is something sublime in the faith he showed in those days when Napoleonism was triumphant. But his crusade was no merely selfish joy of dominion.

"The great promise of a kingdom of right, reason, and truth on earth must not become a vain and empty phantom; the present iron age is but a transition to a better state." He had no hope except in the Germans. "There is no middle road: if you sink, so sinks humanity entire with you, without hope of future restoration."

And for the great task—the reconciliation of all the warring branches of the Teuton family, their coördination in a supreme effort to overthrow Napoleon, the binding of them all together in a unified state—some surpassing inspiration was necessary. The apostles of Germanism found it in "pride."

Historians delved into the records of the past for items to feed their new and dynamic pride. Poets revived—and invented—folklore of the glorious antiquity. The legend of Barbarossa—who, like the Messiah, was to come again—was popularized. It was discovered that Charlemagne's real name had been Karl der Grosse. The goal which these apostles of the new order set before them was that no one would boast of being a Hessian or Prussian, or Bavarian, but to find a greater pride in being a German.

It is delicate business criticising ideals. There is so much to be said for the proposition that any ideals are better than none. And also, if someone else's ideals are not pleasing, it is so easy to call them base. This is what most writers are doing in Europe in the fervor of the present war. Tons of such uninteresting invective have been published during this last year. If the Germans have called their neighbors scurrilous and puerile names because they refused to bow down before the Deutschtum, it is every bit as true that the self-styled "intellectuals" of France and Russia and England have been just as childish in their vituperation.

It is also necessary to bear in mind the staggering force of what has been called "mob psychology." Auguste Comte said that there was more of past generations in us than of ourselves. It is equally true that there is in us a very large—if not predominating—element of this generation. The most objective philosopher cannot escape from the influence of the social mind. It is entirely normal for our thinking—chameleon-like—to take in color from our environment. The guardians of insane asylums often go mad. It is easier to be gentle among gentlefolks. To the Mohammedans it seems the most natural thing in the world to believe in Allah. And we, in America, are republicans, very little because of a reasoned antipathy to monarchy, much more because the chance of birth arranged to have us grow up in a republic. If the crane had dropped us in Tibet, we would have kowtowed to the Grand Llama without the slightest idea that government rests on the consent of the governed and that taxation without representation is iniquitous.

There is every reason to believe that the English and Frenchmen, who are now most loudly denouncing the German idea of Kultur, would, if they had been born in Germany—if they had grown naturally into a habit of disciplined life, if they had seen at close quarters how all these rigid laws, these *Verboten* signs, lead to order and peaceful progress and *Gemüthlichkeit*—be among the most ardent apostles of the Deutschtum.

The Germans do not see anything outrageous in their ideal. In fact they can bring forward an impressive mass of evidence to back up their belief in its beneficence. One who cared to defend the German position could build a very strong case for them from the books and magazine articles which were written in English before the outbreak of this war. It was the fashion, not so very long ago, to admire the stupendous progress which the Germans have made in science, in industry, above all in education and various forms of social legislation.

It is no sentimental sympathy for the under dog which makes me emphasize the marvellous achievements which the Germans have won under the impetus of such passionate idealism as that of Fichte. Personally I have always felt (having had the good fortune to have been born and bred on the other side of the world) less sympathy for them than for any people on earth. But private likes and dislikes are of small moment: the important thing is to try to understand what they think about themselves. And nothing is more evident than that they do not feel the same distaste to their theory and manner of life that I do.

The charge most often brought against them is that they have sacrificed all personal liberty to their grandiose ideal—which, whether they admit it or not,—seems, to an outside observer, to have been very closely synonymous with the grandeur of the Hohenzollern dynasty. This charge they indignantly deny. The German who is sufficiently educated to discuss such matters—and to our shame we must admit that there is a larger percentage of such people in Germany than with us—believes passionately and sincerely that they have more real freedom than we. They believe that it pays—in terms of freedom—to be obedient and orderly in what they call the "kitchen-side of life." They say that it is only by submitting willingly to a strict discipline in such incidentals that we can realize freedom in the more important phases of life. They say that you cannot get music out of an orchestra unless the performers consent to play in time. If the first violin insists on going too fast—well—you can call that liberty if you want to, but the result is not music.

Deep rooted in their philosophical tradition is the great dualism of Kant, the contrast between the heaven of pure reason and the world of matter. In dealing with "things"— in their struggle to dominate and use the material world— they believe in working together. They have learned to march in step. Their actual practice is based on the formula, which we all pretend to believe, that there is strength in unity. In their dealings with the material world they have surpassed us all. Their success in industry and commerce, even in their scientific research, has been due to their habit of playing in time—of team-work. And they assert—and this is the crux of their contention—that because they have learned to subordinate the will of the individual in these material affairs they have won to a greater and nobler freedom in the realm of the spirit.

They are full of pitying contempt for the undisciplined Americans or Frenchmen and Britishers who have not sense enough to keep off the grass, who are forever breaking ranks and getting in each other's way, forever working at cross purposes, and who—following a will-o'-the-wisp fantastic conception of individual liberty—have become the slaves of disorder.

It is, of course, a bootless quarrel over terms. But there is no gain in pitying the Germans because of the lack of liberty in their political *régime*. They like it, and think they enjoy more freedom than the rest of us.

This ideal of the Deutschtum—that every German who was doing good work where it was demanded in the scheme, in the fields and workshops, in the army or laboratory, in political life or the public school, was working for a great and worthy cause, the "making of this nation, the regenerator and restorer of the world"—has given to the German peoples national unity, which, with reason, they value highly. It has given them a material prosperity, which all the world can estimate—and envy. It has given them a political *régime* which is powerful and imposing and which they consider a satisfactory substitute for what we call liberty.

But there has been a reverse to the medal. The effort of Fichte and his friends to awaken an invigorating pride in his people has resulted in a great deal which is merely vulgar conceit. The effort of the German historians to find warrant in the past for their great hopes for the future has led them to falsify the records. Even their science has been debauched in order to find fuel for their flame of "holy pride."

In order to justify the claim of their philosophers that the Germans were a peculiar race with a special mission, it was necessary to invent a false theory of ethnology. There is no fact more firmly established about development of humanity than that there is no such thing as a pure race. Man has developed by an immensely long process of hybridization. From the biological point of view the Germans are no different from the English. The "kitchen middens"—the refuse heaps of prehistoric communities—along the shores of the Baltic show beyond dispute the presence of the Alpine and Mediterranean brunettes side by side with the northern blondes. Modern science—outside of Germany—is unanimous on this point. But in Germany the myth of a pure race is still taught.

Professor Dewey, in the book referred to above, quotes a remarkable passage from a treatise on philology. This learned professor, to bolster up the decidedly rickety race-theory, points out that the German language is the most wonderful invented by man, because the accent always falls on the root syllable. His premise is doubtful, but his deductions from it are amazing.—"Hence the faith of the German in his mission among the nations as a bringer of truth, as a reorganizer of the real value of things as against the hollow shell of beautiful form, as the doer of right deeds for their own sake and not for any reward beyond the natural outcome of the deed itself." It is a decidedly sweeping generalization from the fact of a not very important peculiarity in speech. But such pseudo-erudition inspires a dynamic sort of pride.

The race idea has become little short of an obsession with the Germans. Much comment and indignation has been caused in Europe by some of the maps used in the school geographies of Germany. Neighboring independent countries have been given a color very nearly the same as that of the German Empire. But the men who drew these maps, far from intending to insult the people they represented as almost German, undoubtedly thought they were complimenting them.

The same naïve conceit is evidenced in the work of Professor Woltmann. To add to the glory of Leonardo da Vinci he tried—not very convincingly—to prove that his family was an illegitimate offspring from some German prince, who passed a night in their village on his way to Rome. Quite a polemic sprang up between the German and Italian newspapers on the subject of this alleged historic discovery. It is evident that the Germans, who took up their pens in defence of Professor Woltmann, simply could not comprehend why the Italians resented the idea that their great painter was not pure Italian. It seemed to them that it was obviously finer to have some German blood.

Little has happened of late in the intellectual world as amazing—and as significant of this psychological condition—as Chamberlain's book, "The Foundations of the Nineteenth Century."

Despite his Scotch name, Professor Chamberlain is a fanatic apostle of the religion of the Deutschtum—*plus royaliste que le Roi!* His thesis is simple. Everything of virtue in the nineteenth century is of German origin, everything unsavory came from other sources.

The amazing thing about the book is its gravity. Spread-eagle books—in cheap and popular style—have been written in every language to prove that one nation or another is the salt of the earth. But this book pretends to erudition. He begins with minute and formidable definitions—which always gives an impression of scientific methods—and then uses the words so carefully defined in a dozen different senses in as many pages. He impressively cites as established facts of history things which no historian believes.

As one instance out of his immense tome, he casually states that the Paris Commune—the revolution of 1871—was the work of the Jews. It has long been a project of mine to write a history of this period. I have read everything I could lay hands upon on the subject. I have never encountered that statement anywhere else.

And from this "fact"—which no one else believes—Professor Chamberlain deduces the turpitude of the Jewish race. With the same inexorable logic he eliminates all other non-Germanic people from the treasure-house of the spirit. Anyone in the nineteenth century who performed a work of culture, carved a beautiful statue, sang a beautiful song, discovered some new truth, or won a victory over nature, must—whether he knew it or not—have been a German.

More amazing than the book itself is the fact that it was cordially received in the intellectual circles of Germany.

An equally interesting book—in the matter of appreciating the psychological background of the international politics of Europe—is that of Rudolf Götte, "Deutscher Volkgeist," —the "soul of the German people." He writes: "Respect for personality and for one's own rights, the sentiment of what one owes to oneself and to others, is our special virtue." . . . "But," he continues, "this is not in contradiction to our expansion, for that is our law of life. To live and expand at the expense of other, less meritorious (minderwertig) peoples finds its justification in the conviction that we are of all people, the most noble and the most pure, destined (bestimmt) before others to work for the highest development of humanity."

There is no gain in laughing at Mr. Chamberlain and Herr Götte. It is necessary to realize the extent to which the Germans felt themselves "called" to play a stupendous rôle of reformation in the world—or all their recent foreign policy is inexplicable.

Undoubtedly these writers, from whom I have quoted, von Bernhardi and others, whose works have suddenly been called to the attention of Anglo-Saxon readers, are extravagant exaggerations of the German pride. But, cutting off these manifestly crack-brained excrescences, there remains the great mass of the nation, who although they did not join the pan-Germanic societies—did not protest against this sophisticated history and super-heated pride. The ideal of the Deutschtum did not seem to them a sinister plot of world domination but—with all its implications of orderly progress, advanced methods of general education, social amelioration and the harnessing of modern science to the needs of man—it appealed to them as a holy mission.

That the realm of the Deutschtum was destined to transcend the existing frontiers of the Deutschland, that German ideas would rule over all the world, seemed to Bismarck and his followers part of God's plan. Those who opposed this progress either failed to understand the benefits which would come to them with new light, or they were wicked ones who loved darkness.

Bismarck and the Germans of his day had an immense respect for their army. Individual Germans had here and there made names for themselves in pacific pursuits, but Germany was a creation of *Eisen und Blut*. The great Chancellor certainly believed in keeping the sword sharp and the powder dry. But he was a follower of Von Clausewitz, he accepted the theory that "war is only a continuation of state policy by other means." In the carrying out of the divine mission to which they were called war was only one—and not necessarily the most important means.

The apostles of the Deutschtum have relied greatly on intellectual and economic propaganda. The policy of the present Kaiser towards the United States in recent years has been typical. There is scant reason to think that he has seriously considered attacking us, but he has undoubtedly tried to convert us. By his gifts to our universities, his encouragement of exchange professorships, by his courtesies to American commissions who have gone to Germany to study their institutions, and so forth, he has tried to show us the inestimable blessings of the Deutschtum, tried to educate us to the point of appreciating how unfortunate we are to live in a haphazard republic, instead of in his progressive and orderly domain.

If a Paris audience applauded a German opera; if the king of a cannibal island decided that a breech cloth of German manufacture was preferable to one "made in England," if a German professor invented a new drug to cure the ills of humanity; if German shipyards could get the contract—underbid all the world—for the giant dredges with which we dug the Panama Canal, these were triumphs for the Deutschtum quite as important as a mere battle won.

There have always been Cassandra-like prophets in Germany who preached the virtue, the necessity, the inevitability of war. Few countries have escaped such plagues. But the great mass of the German people and—for more than a generation—the responsible rulers of the empire have given a deaf ear to such promptings. There is no reason to believe that their faith in their divine mission weakened or that they had allowed their swords to rust. But they hoped to win without fighting. War was the supreme weapon, the last resort. They were resolved not to unchain it lightly—not till other means had been exhausted.

If it is necessary—as I believe—to try to reach a real understanding of the German attitude, to appreciate the sincere and deep devotion they have given to their ideal, to reckon up its real values, its positive achievements, as well as to point out its fantastic perversions, it is equally necessary to sound the thoughts of non-German peoples and to understand what the rest of Europe thought about the Deutschtum.

In a matter like this it is relatively unimportant what any one of us individually thinks about the rights and wrongs of the controversy. The fact—writ large in the newspapers of France and England, in most Russian and Italian, and Scandinavian and Dutch and Spanish publications, more discreetly but just as emphatically in almost every diplomatic despatch—was that the rest of Europe did not want to be Germanized. The other peoples of Europe resented the German pretension of superiority. They preferred their accustomed institutions and did not want to have them forcibly reformed after the German model.

Most European history of the last thirty years could be compressed into two statements:

The non-Germanic peoples felt that it was not only their right, but their most sacred duty to resist the encroachments of the Deutschtum.

The Germans could not conceive how any but idiots and perverts could resist the realization of their beneficent and reforming mission.

CHAPTER IV

THE RESURRECTION OF FRANCE

The rebirth of France after "the terrible year" of 1870 is one of the romances of history. And France will cease to be France before she reaches that happy condition of a nation which has no history. Almost alone of all people in this drab commercial age, the French have managed to fill the record of their daily life with color, tense suspense—and thrills.

The Third Republic was born out of the blood and travail of war and revolution. Peace had scarcely been signed with Germany when the working class of Paris took up arms in a desperate insurrection against the threat of a monarchical restoration.

The new government inherited most of the vices of the bas empire of Napoleon III. Its first and most imperative duty was to pay off the staggering war indemnity—five milliard francs—which Bismarck had imposed. The German army still occupied a great part of France, and according to Bismarck's terms they would only retire as the instalments of the indemnity were paid.

A generation ago a thousand million dollars was an unheard of sum. But very pluckily the French set to work to pay it off.

The necessity of great internal loans—credit operations on an unprecedented scale—resulted in granting immense power to the financiers. They rose to the occasion and freed France of the German occupation within three years. But when the immediate crisis was safely passed the French financiers were quite as reluctant in giving up their privileges as some of our railroad magnates have been slow to relinquish their grip on the western territories they had helped to develop.

As a result of its pressing financial need in the first stage of its history the French Republic has been more closely and openly allied with Big Business—more often smirched by its scandals—than the countries of Europe which have had a more placid history. Also the French—like us—have the habit of fighting corruption with publicity. So, many things which would be carefully covered up in England or Germany are openly discussed in their newspapers.

The Royalists died hard. If the various anti-republican forces—Bourbonistes, Orléanistes, Bonapartistes—had united in the first decades of the Republic they could have restored the monarchy. The Republic survived because there were three rival pretenders for the throne. It was not until the third president, Grévy, was inaugurated—January, 1879—that the nation had a chief executive who was a republican. And this event, while a definite victory for progress, by no means ended the danger of reaction.

The eighties and nineties were two decades when a vast amount of unspectacular work was done in organizing the internal life of the Republic. Encouraged by the amazing success of the credit operations by which they had paid off the war indemnity, the government, under the technical leadership of de Freycinet, the financial advice of M. Léon Say, launched on gigantic expenses for the improvement of harbors and canals and roads, the buying of existing private railroads and the building of new ones. Large sums were spent on improving agricultural conditions. And above all, money was poured out on strengthening the system of public schools.

The parliamentary history of these years is largely a record of debates on finance. The Republic was accused by its enemies of wanton extravagance, of leading the country to bankruptcy. Certainly no government had ever been so lavish in borrowing money to capitalize the community. The pessimists foretold ruin. But de Freycinet and Say and the other Republicans had faith in the future of France. In the light of the present results it is easy to criticize some of this expenditure in detail. There was a normal amount of log-rolling and stupidity—but the general policy has certainly been justified by the event. Most of this borrowed money was invested in increasing the earning capacity of the nation. The present extraordinary wealth of France is largely due to the financial daring of the eighties and nineties.

This is especially true in regard to the expenses on public education. There is a statue of Danton in Paris and on its base is carved a sentence from one of his speeches: "*Après le pain, l'éducation est le premier besoin du peuple.*" (After bread, education is the first need of the people.) This has been the most revered motto of the French Republic.

But this immensely important foundation work furnishes dreary reading. The "dash" which is so typical of French history is furnished by "colonial enterprises." Tunisia was conquered in 1881—thereby incurring the bitter enmity of the Italians. Soon the French began their advance in Indo-China, so gaining frontiers which marched with those of the British Empire and gave rise to new quarrels. It was the same in Madagascar, Zanzibar, Egypt, and Morocco. Everywhere that the French and English colonial interests touched there was friction.

These over-seas adventures had the hearty indorsement of Bismarck. He was primarily a Continentalist; it was only reluctantly that he turned to colonial enterprises. The more the French squandered their resources in "foreign parts" the better he was pleased—especially as it kept them at loggerheads with their other neighbors.

But in one thing Bismarck's theory was wrong. He thought that colonial adventures would make the French forget Alsace-Lorraine. It is one of the picturesque incidents of history that when, shortly after the fall of Bismarck, a French column, after an exceedingly hard march through bitter jungles and over desperate desert trails, entered Timbuctoo (12th February, 1894) they renamed the main street of that African town, the Boulevard Alsace-Lorraine. One of the blockhouses they built they christened Fort Metz, another Fort Strassbourg. The chief of this expedition was a relatively unknown young "commandant" named Joffre. It was his first notable achievement and he was given the Legion of Honor and the rank of lieutenant colonel.

Colonial adventure did not make the French forget Alsace-Lorraine, and it gave a rugged, hardening training to a great many French officers.

Ten years after the Congress of Berlin Wilhelm II. ascended the throne. Two years later—20th March, 1890—Prince Otto von Bismarck retired to private life. And almost at once a striking change was evident in European politics.

What were the real causes of the rupture between the young Kaiser and the old Chancellor are obscure—they were probably multiple. But one thing is well established. They differed as to the proper policy towards Russia. Bismarck was in favor of tightening the bonds with Russia. The Kaiser, preferring the Austrian alliance, did not renew the *Dreikaisersbund*, and it lapsed immediately.

On the 27th August, 1891, a diplomatic understanding was reached at Paris, between France and Russia. Its purpose was announced to be the maintenance of peace and of the balance of power in Europe. A year later—August, 1892—a Russo-French "military convention" was signed, and in March, 1894, the Franco-Russian alliance—or "Duplice"—was definitely concluded. All of these texts and the exact date of the last two have been kept secret. But on the 23rd August, 1897, the Tsar Nicolas II. and President Félix Faure met and exchanged toasts in which the existence of the alliance—which had been an open secret for a long time—was publicly and officially proclaimed.

From one point of view, the Franco-Russian alliance seems incredible. Tsars are not expected to be friends with decidedly red republics. And it is indeed an anomaly that the France of the great revolution should seek an alliance with the most stubborn defender of the *ancien régime*.

But the text of the German-Austrian alliance had become known and clearly showed to Russia the uncertain value of Bismarck's friendship. Besides the Tsar needed money. The young Republic, whose citizens were a saving people with hoards to lend, needed a friend—any friend at any price.

There is much difference of opinion among the historians of our times as to the extent to which French policy has been influenced by the idea of "*revanche*," revenge for the defeat of 1870. That the French profoundly mourn the loss of Alsace-Lorraine is beyond dispute. And a certain noisy clique have taken "The Revenge" for a watchword. The so-called "nationalist party"—the remnants of the old monarchial groups—have monopolized most of the jingoism in France of recent years. It is noticeable that their writings are an attack on the Republicans for having forgotten *la revanche*, and on the Republic for being a form of government which is hopelessly pacific and could never lead the French back to the Rhine.

But after all, the question of revenge is relatively unimportant. There can be no doubt that the fear of a new attack from Germany has been the constant preoccupation of almost every French ministry. 1875, 1887, 1891, 1906, 1911 are some of the years when the tension was especially sharp. The Germans have never allowed the French to forget their Terrible Year.

The Germans say that this fear of a new aggression was unfounded; that they never dreamed of re-attacking France—except once or twice when they did not like the way the Republic was behaving. Very probably this fear has been exaggerated. Sometimes, perhaps, the French thought the Germans were preparing a new war, when they were only indulging their vanity in a meaningless display of force. This seems to have been the case more than once.

But whether the fear of a new aggression was justified or not, it was very real and of profound influence in French policy. If it had not been for the constant rattling of the German sword, much of the bitterness might have evaporated from the memory of 1870.

The comparison with the aftermath of our own Civil War is inevitable. Happily for us, most of the rancor of that struggle has died out. To a very large extent the new generation has forgotten it. The new generation in France was not allowed to forget.

And France, threatened—or believing herself threatened—by Germany, certainly on bad terms with her neighbors, Italy and England, needed a friend. Republican scruples against an alliance with the bloody Tsar went by the board. With so powerful an ally, the French began to dare to breathe freely once more.

This dual alliance was primarily significant because it indicated to all the world that the epoch of Bismarck was over. Something had happened in Europe without the consent of the Germans, something which Bismarck had taught them to believe was undesirable.

The French and Russian statesmen, although they refused to publish the text of these agreements, insisted that they were purely defensive; that their sole object was to safeguard the peace of Europe. But the Germans could not consider it simply defensive—it was so manifestly a blow at the prestige of the Deutschtum. And here we are very close to the subtle psychological misunderstanding which has had a great deal to do with the present conflict.

The French attitude towards this alliance was very clear. Their action seemed to them above reproach. To be sure, a few enthusiasts of the *revanche* hoped that there would be a war and a chance to wipe out old scores. But everyone who was well informed about Russia knew better. The Tsar tried to bring about a *rapprochement* between France and Germany, an attempt which met the approval of the French foreign minister, Hanotaux. In 1895—at the suggestion of Russia—the French sent some of their war-ships to participate in the fêtes at the opening of the Kiel Canal. It was the first instance of official cordiality between the victims and victors of 1870. In 1898 Nicolas II. sent out his invitation to the peace conference at the Hague. There was very little in the Russian alliance to encourage the bellicose element in France.

To thinking Frenchmen the alliance meant an end to their dangerous isolation. It meant a counter-balance to the German "Triplice." It meant that the chances of a successful defence in case of a new attack were greatly increased. And so—of course—it meant that there was less chance of their being attacked. They did not consider that the Germans had any moral right to dictatorship in Europe. They did not want to succumb to the Deutschtum. And with Russia for an ally they could feel themselves more at their ease. They could not see how any right thinking people could object to their desire for independence.

But while the dual alliance was not in a geographical sense aggressive, while it did not threaten to take an inch of soil from the Deutschland, it was—from the German point of view—a very definite assault on what they held most sacred—the prestige of the Deutschtum. If you announced to a Second Adventist that you and your neighbor had formed a defensive alliance to resist the second coming, you would hardly shock him more than the typical German mind is shocked if you announce that you do not want to enjoy the manifold blessings of order and disciplined comfort and happiness which thrive under German kultur. He cannot conceive how any right thinking people would combine to resist the expansion of this beneficent *régime*.

As long as Bismarck had been chancellor he had thumped on the table whenever this alliance had been suggested and by keeping alive his flimsy counter-assurance with Russia he had managed to prevent its consummation. But it is doubtful if he could have postponed it much longer. If there is any one proposition in regard to European history which has been proved so often that it can be made the basis of a "law," it is that the continent cannot be ruled from any one capital. All attempts at a European empire, whether they have started from Rome, Madrid, or Paris, have eventually been met by a hostile coalition and at last defeated. So the fall of Bismarck was not so much the cause as the signal. The announcement of the Franco-Russian alliance was the tangible indication that resistance to the Deutschtum was crystalizing.

Would Germany passively accept this diminution of its prestige; this open revolt from its thrall?

The young Kaiser and his new chancellor, Caprivi, can hardly be thought to have refrained from war through fear. To be sure, the Russian army was supposed to be formidable, the military power of the Duplice was not to be despised, but still it was weak as compared to the Triplice. The Germans could have gone to war at that time with every chance of success.

Wilhelm II., far from having less reverence for the Deutschtum than Bismarck, had an even more ardent devotion to the mystic idea of the mission of his people. Nothing but a sincere love of peace on the part of the rulers of Germany in this period can explain their acceptance of the dual alliance—in spite of the chagrin and vexation it caused the nation—without going to war. The Germans, who speak of the Kaiser as a pacifist, have very good arguments to support their statement. The German jingoes have always attacked him for weakly preferring peace to his duty as the standard bearer of the Deutschtum.

This new Kaiser had no intention of abandoning the ideals of his house nor of his people. But for a quarter of a century he ruled without drawing the sword. He was apparently proud to receive the Nobel peace prize.

Wilhelm II. is inexplicable in the hypothesis that he is a crude hypocrite, always, in spite of his peace talk, desiring war. But if one considers him as a man of mystic temperament, who took his kingly position seriously, who was profoundly convinced that he was "called" of God to the high mission of extending his rule on earth, then his speeches and acts fall into line. Of all the apostles of the Deutschtum, he was the most convinced, the most devout. Only he differed from his more military *entourage* in believing that it was best to argue first. The sword seemed to him not sinful, but too holy to be drawn lightly. He hoped to convince his barbarian, degenerated, and miserly neighbors of the righteousness of his cause. That it was a difficult task only went to prove that these vile names were deserved.

While he has never neglected his army, has given especial attention to his navy—has always felt that in this world of sinful humanity it might be necessary to use force in the cause of righteousness—his real interest has been elsewhere. In a blundering, tactless, German way he has tried to live on as good terms with his less meritorious neighbors as might be possible for an apostle of *unserer guten, alten, Deutschen Gott*. He has relied principally on economic and intellectual arguments to win converts to his German creed. At least, he did not declare war at the first symptoms of rebellion.

The French seem to have worried very little about what the Germans would think of their alliance. As a general proposition, as is almost always true in a republic, they are very much more interested in internal affairs than in their international relations. And a matter came to their attention of such passionate and absorbing interest that they always speak of it as "the affair."

Several French writers have pointed out that *"l'affaire Dreyfus"* was the struggle of the new generation, who had grown up since the Terrible Year, to break forever with the tradition of defeat. And to a large extent, it was a revolt of forward-looking youth against backward-looking age.

An unimportant Jewish officer—Captain Dreyfus—was accused and convicted in a military court of selling state secrets to the enemy. The question of his guilt or innocence had little importance. Some of those who fought hardest for him believed he was guilty. But—guilty or innocent—he had been unjustly convicted. He had not had a fair trial. Certain officers—perhaps believing that he was a traitor and that it was a patriotic act to insure his punishment with the least possible scandal—had forged the documents on which his conviction was based.

To a large extent the matter was taken out of the courts and tried in the newspapers before public opinion. *Esprit de corps*, and a desire to stop an exposure which would discredit the army, led some of the officers of the Etat Major to try to deny the forgery and cover the culprits. Never was there a more glowing example of the tangled web we weave when first we practise to deceive.

The conflict became bitter to the verge of civil war. On one side was all the idealism of the young Republicans who said:—Let justice be done though the heavens fall. On the other side were a number of gray haired old gentlemen who wanted to keep the heavens in their place at any price; who were willing to perjure themselves to maintain the honor of the army; who held that it is expedient for one man to suffer for the people—especially as he happened to be a Jew. Perhaps it was only a chance coincidence, but most of the anti-Dreyfus party were good catholics.

To the everlasting glory of France the Dreyfusards kept up the fight for ten long years and at last won. But the personality of the man over whom the ruction arose had been lost sight of in the more fundamental quarrel which grew out of his case. Most of those who began rioting in the streets of Paris—and even in the outlying villages of France—to the cry "*Vive Dreyfus*" soon found themselves shouting "*Vive la République*" "*A bas l'Armée.*" And the mobs who had gathered to the slogan "*A bas le Juif*" began to shout "*A bas la République*" and "*Vive le roi.*"

There was much which was incoherent in "*l'Affaire.*"

Sometimes anti-Semiticism seemed the dominant element. Again, it appeared to be a struggle between the army and the civilian population, between court martials and "due process of law." And at times it seemed that the cause of all the trouble was a royalist or Bonapartist conspiracy. The anti-republican forces of France have always maintained—and perhaps believed—that *"l'Affaire"* was caused by "foreign gold," that England or Germany was trying to stir up civil strife to weaken France. But out of all the turmoil came the clear cut issue which was to dominate the internal life of the Republic on the threshold of the new century,—the conflict between Church and State.

Rightly or wrongly, all the sinister elements of French life which were trying to undermine and discredit the Republic became typified in the priest. Neither side kept their temper in this fight. Neither side was always just and reasonable. But out of the conflict the Republic emerged solidified and at last firmly established.

By 1910 it was no longer a question of whether or not the king should come again to France. But—was the French Republic to be a solid and respectable form of government like ours, severe on "agitators" and strikers, and kindly disposed to people of wealth, or should it push forward along the paths of democracy and strive to win the affection and loyalty of all its citizens?

As a result of their alliance with Russia the French worried less over the probability of a new attack from Germany, but their relations with England grew steadily worse. The English also disapproved of an alliance between their two "hereditary" enemies.

"Allant" young officers like *le commandant Joffre*, were exploring and conquering vast territories in Africa. Every day the young Republic was becoming more of a rival to Britain in the colonial world. And French officials—M. Gabriel Hanotaux was minister of foreign affairs—were forever telling about their "rights" in Egypt. And those Englishmen who were well informed in the matter knew that the French "rights" in Egypt—as "rights" go in colonial enterprises—were better than their own. So such discussion was annoying. When the British landed troops in Egypt in 1882 they had solemnly covenanted that it was only a temporary "police" measure to reëstablish order. One British minister after another had formally promised to evacuate Egypt. 1888 had been set as a final date for the occupation. And when one is determined to repudiate a promise it is unpleasant to be reminded of it.

An old but quite explicit treaty gave the French the right to maintain fisheries along the "French coast" of Newfoundland. The British government did not exactly tear up this scrap of paper—they gave the colony of Newfoundland a self-governing charter. And the colonial assembly promptly passed laws in violation of the French rights. The situation was not unlike that which the Californians have caused for us by their anti-Japanese laws. When M. Hanotaux protested on behalf of the Breton fishers, the British government said that they could not coerce a self-governing colony. This reply, however, did not satisfy M. Hanotaux—he kept on protesting. The English decided that he was a troublesome person—a gentleman, they felt, would not be so querulous.

This long series of disputes—and I have only mentioned two—came to a head over the Fashoda affair. A French expedition under Colonel Marchand started up the Congo from the Atlantic to cross Africa to the Upper Nile. The English "rights" in lower Egypt were sketchy in the extreme, they were too small in the Soudan to be visible to the naked eye. But someone started the fool story that the French intended to ruin Anglo-Egypt by damming the Upper Nile and diverting its waters into the Sahara— or perhaps into the Canals of Mars. A great hue and cry arose at once and the British government annexed the Soudan while Colonel Marchand was still struggling in the heart of the jungle. When at last he struck the Nile at the little mud village of Fashoda, he had a memorable interview with a British officer, named Kitchener. For several days the issue of war and peace hung in the balance. But at last France gave in.

This Fashoda incident demonstrated a fact of diplomacy worth noting. It is dangerous to allow the Department of Foreign Affairs to operate singlehanded. International relations should be the business of all the ministers in common. More than any other phase of government it requires teamwork.

There is this overwhelming criticism to be brought against the policy of M. Hanotaux. He worked alone—and it caused his downfall. He was a high-minded patriot. He was above the cheap chicanery which has often disgraced diplomacy. His actions were based on a fine conception of international law. He was engaged in insisting on the recognized "rights" of France. But the nation which was threatening these "rights" was the greatest naval power in the world. And the French fleet of that time was a joke. If war had been declared, France could not have sent one of her soldiers overseas to protect her far away colonies. M. Hanotaux had led his country to a crisis from which there were only two exits—war or humiliation. And France was not prepared for war.

If M. Hanotaux did not foresee the crisis he was a very shortsighted diplomat. If he foresaw the crisis and did not consult with his colleague, the minister of marine, he was a rather lightminded statesman.

He has been variously criticised by his compatriots. My own impression is that he was somewhat *naïf*. He seems to have been convinced that his cause would triumph because it was just: but the English refused to argue. Their navy was overwhelming. So Colonel Marchand ignominiously marched out of Fashoda and M. Hanotaux resigned—following the example of many other men who have been too good for this world.

M. Hanotaux was followed at the Quai d'Orsay—the French foreign office—by M. Théophile Delcassé. He is one of the most outstanding personalities in recent European history—and in this present crisis. A rather insignificant man to look at, he is of that dynamic kind, whose every relation is fierce. His friendships and enmities—both at home and abroad—are intense. Quite as many, and as diverse estimates have been written of him as of the Kaiser. But in one point at least—and it is to his credit—he differs profoundly from his great antagonist. He has never claimed to be inspired by God.

His enemies—in France as well as in Germany—accuse him of a sinister, persistent, and fanatic will to war. Seeing the results of his policy—or rather the course European politics have taken during his years of prominence—they jump at the conclusion that from the cradle up he foresaw his destiny; that his every act has been inspired by a venomous plot to prepare the cataclysm we now witness. There is a legend that his father administered to him an oath of hate against Germany, even as Hannibal was sworn to overthrow Rome. But this interpretation of his character tends towards the miraculous. History does not record any other case of a statesman who enjoyed so marvellous a prevision, such a remarkable consistency of purpose. Until there is overwhelming evidence to the contrary, it is well to assume that M. Delcassé is a man quite like the rest of us.

When he became minister of foreign affairs there was very little difference of opinion among intelligent Frenchmen as to the principal point of danger. The most serious menace came from Germany. The Dreyfusards, who had come into power, were pacific. They had no idea—in spite of the Nationalist noise about *"la revanche"*—of starting a war to regain Alsace-Lorraine. But there was a chance of a new German aggression. The humiliation of the Fashoda incident had been indeed painful, but after all the gage involved had been small,—at most they stood to win or lose a distant colony. It had been an affair of *amour propre*. But in a war with Germany, the very existence of France would be at stake.

At least twice, the French government had tried hard to heal the breach with Germany. One such movement towards *rapprochement* had been attempted by Gambetta. Another had been tried more recently, after the signing of the Russian alliance, under the auspices of the Tsar. They had both failed. The Germans could not or would not treat on any base of equality. If the Republic had been willing to admit its inferiority—numerically, in military power, morally—if it had asked for "protection," the Germans might have been willing to be friends.

Undoubtedly M. Delcassé disliked the Germans. Most Frenchmen did. It is very rare for anyone to like people who are openly disdainful. The Nicaraguans—for instance—do not like us.

There were only three solutions.

(1) A change of heart on the part of the Germans, a willingness to treat their neighbors as equals and to accept sincerely their collaboration in the common work of civilization.

(2) A French acceptance of defeat without fighting.

(3) War.

How clearly M. Delcassé saw this situation we do not know. There are many indications of hesitancy and indecision on his part. At times he seems to have felt out the ground as to the possibility of an accord with Germany. In the early days of his administration he certainly did not foresee the entente with England. But in spite of such waverings most of his acts group about a central and consistent theory.

France, in the face of the threat from across the Rhine, was in an unnecessarily weak position. Her energies were being dissipated by endless, scattered, and relatively petty quarrels all over the world. This Fashoda incident had been typical. France had had nothing to gain compared to what she might have lost. Nothing would have more pleased the Germans of the Bismarckian school than an Anglo-French war. M. Delcassé realized—as did most thoughtful Frenchmen—that these subsidiary quarrels were playing into the hands of the Germans.

M. Delcassé's theory was to liquidate these secondary quarrels and to conserve the force of France for the threatening life and death struggle.

Ever since France had snatched Tunisia and Italy had entered the Germanic alliance, these two Latin sisters had been accusing each other of treason to the proposition that blood is thicker than water. A tariff war had been started in which each country was biting off its own nose to spite the other's chin. It did neither any good and the net result was to throw the Italian market open to German enterprise and to fan the bitterness between the two peoples.

M. Delcassé began his career by smoothing out the Italian quarrel. With rare diplomatic skill he succeeded, first in reducing the quarrel to its simplest being and then in persuading the statesmen of Rome that the matter was not worth losing one's temper over. By the middle of 1902—neither the exact date nor the text of the document have been published—he was able to sign with Italy the first of his "*ententes*." It was not a formal treaty, it was "a gentleman's agreement"—a frank statement of a desire to live on cordial neighborly terms.

The German chancellor spoke of this affair—whereby the ally, Italy, showed a disposition to make friends out of the family—as a harmless flirtation—*un tour de valse*. But this witticism did not content the more ardent adepts of the Deutschtum. There was a great outcry in Germany. Italy, they had thought was completely converted to their ideal. Her pretension of independence was an even more serious matter than the Franco-Russian alliance. The force of the ungodly was growing.

Simply *un tour de valse?* In this matter the German patriots saw more clearly than their chancellor. It was more than a harmless flirtation. In one of his rare statements of policy before the French Chamber—for M. Delcassé believes in secret diplomacy and has never erred on the side of taking his people too much into his confidence— he was able to say (3rd July, 1902): *"en aucun cas et sous aucune forme l'Italie ne peut devenir ni l'auxiliaire ni l'instrument d'une agression contre notre pays."* (In no case and under no form will Italy become the accomplice nor the instrument of an aggression against our country). In the same year, the Triple Alliance was renewed, but Signor Prinelli, the Italian minister of foreign affairs, announced to his Parliament that the treaty contained no clause of aggression against France. The real sense of this *entente* became apparent in the early days of August, 1914, when Italy refused to march with her allies against France.

Did M. Delcassé foresee the harvest of war which would spring from the seeds he planted? There are many who think he did, who say that the Italian Entente was only the first link in the chain he was forging for the binding of Germany; who scoff at every word he said about peace, and see in his every act the inspiration of a vindictive hatred against the victors of 1870.

It may be true, but it is not a necessary assumption in order to explain his activity. In fact, there are several indications which point in the opposite direction. While he was working on the Italian *rapprochement* he was carrying on negotiations with Spain in view of an eventual partition of Morocco. Very little light has been thrown on this matter by French publications, but some Spanish "indiscretions" indicate certainly that M. Delcassé had not at this time definitely thrown in his lot with Great Britain, for these first Spanish negotiations seem to have had an anti-British tone. The Spaniards at least were afraid that the deal proposed by the French would offend the English. There are other indications—less certain to be sure, but worth consideration—that M. Delcassé was also carrying on anti-English negotiations with Germany at this time.

In 1901 he made a trip to Saint Petersburg. Its object seems to have been to persuade the Russians to withdraw their opposition to the German plans for railroad development in Asia Minor. But more of this Bagdad railroad venture in the next chapter. The point I wish to establish is that in the early years of his ministry, M. Delcassé seems to have explored the political wilderness in all directions. He does not seem to have been committed to a venomous anti-German policy. In fact, more than once in this period he was accused by the English—and by the French "nationalists"—of having sold out to the Germans.

It is now evident that two conflicting—apparently unreconcilable—ideals were abroad in Europe. A determination on the part of the Germans to spread their religion of the Deutschtum. A determination on the part of almost everybody else to resist Teuton domination. Even in the early days of the century there were those who said that war was inevitable, but it is quite likely that M. Delcassé hoped that the catastrophe might be avoided. It is not only possible, but more than probable, that he did not possess any mystic clairvoyance.

Why should he think that the smoothing out of a quarrel with Italy was a cause of war? They were sovereign, independent nations. They certainly had a right to be friendly if they cared to.

As soon as M. Delcassé had arranged matters to his satisfaction with Italy, he turned his attention to England. The difficulties here were much greater. His first task on entering the Foreign Office had been to get out from under the Fashoda crisis, which his predecessor had bequeathed to him. By very large surrenders of the "legitimate aspirations" of the French in the Nile valley—by sweeping concessions to the "British point of view"—he paved the way to a better understanding. And various other events had been playing into his hands.

CHAPTER V

THE ANGLO-GERMAN FRIENDSHIP COOLS

In the years which immediately followed the Congress of Berlin there was no friction between the empires of Germany and Great Britain. It is rather amusing now to read the honeyed words they exchanged not so very long ago.

The roots of the discord which was soon to separate these "friends" run far back. The Germans were much quicker than the English to foresee the coming conflict. At a time when the relations between Downing Street and Wilhelmstrasse—the two foreign offices—were most cordial Treitscke had begun to teach that war with Great Britain was inevitable.

But the English were slow to read the signs of the times, they were preoccupied with their colonial rivalries with France and Russia. In the eighties and nineties almost any Englishman would have said that the Tsar was the great enemy. Every advance of Russia into central Asia towards the borders of India was a new menace. And the French were considered to be riotous, unreliable, dangerous people.

The circumstances which gradually developed ill-feeling between Germany and England are too complex to allow any single date to be set for the change. But roughly it coincided with the advent of Wilhelm II. and the fall of Bismarck.

The great man theory is no longer popular among historians, and it is ungracious in these days of democracy to attribute a high rôle to a king. And while it is manifestly foolish to give the Kaiser credit for all the marvellous advance of Germany since his accession, it is true that his influence was great. He knew how to group about him and to encourage everywhere the artisans of this stupendous progress.

Mr. O'Farrell in his very careful study in political economy, "The Franco-Prussian War Indemnity and its Economic Results," argues that the foundations of the amazing prosperity of modern Germany were laid, not by the present Kaiser, not by the War of 1870 and its immense indemnity, but ten years farther back by the organization of the "Zollverein" or the tariff federation of the disunited German states and principalities. Professor Veblen, in his "Imperial Germany and the Industrial Revolution," also contends that the Kaiser had little to do with the remarkable growth of German economic strength.

But ever since Wilhelm II. came to the throne there have been in his *entourage* apostles of war. And the leaders of the German war party were men whose devotion to the ideal of the Deutschtum the Kaiser could not doubt. It was also his most cherished ideal. But all through the first quarter of a century of his reign he turned from them and chose for his ministers men who believed that the way to spread the influence of the German idea was by the peaceful means of economic organization. And, on the surface, his wisdom seemed to be proved by results.

It would be easy to mass statistics on the amazing growth of German industry and commerce. I choose only a few which were current at the time the relations between Britain and Germany began to cool. The *Revue de Statistique* of 21st October, 1900, gives some tables on the number and capital of new industrial and financial stock companies in Germany. In 1894, 92 companies were chartered with a capital of 88,000,000 marks. In 1899, five years later, 364 new companies with a capital of 544,000,000 marks, were formed. From 1876 to 1895 the weight of merchandise carried on the rivers of Germany increased 159 per cent. The freight traffic on the railroads in this same period went up 143 per cent. In 1895 the number of ships which entered the harbor of Hamburg was 9,443. In 1900, the number of ships was 13,103 and the tonnage was over 8,000,000, more than the record of Liverpool for the same year. In the total movement of commerce—importation and exportation—Germany climbed up between 1871 and 1900 from fourth place to second.

Inevitably much of this progress was at the expense of England. But this commercial competition might possibly have continued without producing war. There were many other currents flowing in the direction of trouble. Towards the end of Bismarck's career the merchants of the German seaports organized a colonial society and began a vigorous campaign in this sense. Rather reluctantly Bismarck gave in to their urgings and launched the empire on a colonial policy. But he was half-hearted about it and anxious to avoid a quarrel with England. He confided to them that Germany had developed ambitions in Africa.

The two largest sections of Africa which were then unclaimed by any European power, were the districts which are now called German East Africa and German South West Africa. The British government at once strengthened its grip on Zanzibar, the island off the coast of East Africa, which is the natural economic gate to the territory which the Germans wanted and also "occupied" Walfish Bay and the important islands off the coast of South West Africa. Then they made no serious objection to the German occupation of the hinterland.

The colonists—the individual citizens of the two countries—came into the sharpest kind of conflict. The story of the efforts of these pioneers of Britain and Germany to over-reach each other reads like a romance. Some chapters are as blood-curdling as the best of Nick Carter, full of murder and intrigues, the fomenting of native rebellions, the smuggling of arms. Some chapters are like a story from the Arabian Nights. The Germans—if not the central government, at least the local consul—encouraged a handsome young German boy to climb over the harem

wall and elope with the Princess Salme, the sister of the
Sultan of Zanzibar. And some of the chapters are side-
splittingly funny. Little has happened in the record of
Weltpolitik more amusing than Stanley's rescue of Emin
Pasha—who did not want to be rescued and at last had
to pretend to be sick and jump out of a hospital window
in order to escape his rescuer. But as the relations between the two foreign offices did not become strained over
these matters, they hardly enter the realm of European
politics.

But as the years passed, the Germans, when they set
to work to develop their colonies, found that they had been
tricked and outplayed at every point. Walfish Bay is
typical of the entire situation. The West Coast of Africa
suffers from lack of natural harbors. Walfish Bay is the
only one on the long coast line of the territory Germany
wished to colonize. They quite naturally lost their temper
when they discovered that the English had forestalled
them. It was a crude case of the dog in the manger. The
British have never used Walfish Bay in any way. Time and
again the Germans have tried to buy it, but the English
would not sell. Apparently they did not care to have their
new neighbors become prosperous. By stubbornly holding on to this natural harbor they have forced the Germans to spend millions in developing an artificial port.
The situation is very similar in Zanzibar.

Such incidents began to cause friction at home. But
the young Kaiser, after he had dropped Bismarck, tried to
reëstablish cordial relations. By the treaty of 14th June,
1890, he received from the English the Island of Heligoland
off the mouth of the Elbe, which from the point of view
of naval strategy was of immense value—but at that time
the English did not regard the Germans as dangerous
naval rivals. And in exchange he paid four million marks
for a strip of East African coast (which was as much his
as it was England's); gave up all claim to Zanzibar (in
spite of the money which had been spent on the trousseau

of the Princess Salme); ceded to England the rich country of Uganda and agreed to a northern frontier to the East African colony which entirely suited the English. When Stanley, who knew these African countries intimately, read the treaty, he threw up his hands in amazement and said that the Germans had been cheated. Of course the German colonists on the spot and the Colonial Society at home raged.

The explanation of these sweeping concessions to England is to be found in the fact that the young Kaiser, having dropped his pilot, was worried by the trend of European politics. In the face of *rapprochement* between France and Russia, he was willing to make sacrifices overseas to maintain the English friendship. And in such matters the British statesmen have always shown themselves shrewd bargainers.

But towards 1893 the German colonial policy became aggressive again and new frictions arose. The Kaiser's famous telegram to President Kruger at the time of the Jameson raid in South Africa was a symptom of the rivalry. From that time on the colonial conflict between the two nations intensified.

But even more important than this colonial and commercial competition was the fact that the Kaiser was a passionate yachtsman. He loved the sea. It was not only the navy which interested him. He was even more interested in the merchant marine. He broke over all the traditions of caste and religion to make a personal friend of the civilian Jew, Herr Ballin, who has engineered the stupendous growth of the Hamburg-Amerika Line. "Our future," he told his people, "lies on the seas." And committed to pushing, aggressive colonial enterprises, fascinated by oversea expansion, he needed a fleet of war.

The Deutschtum—when it ceased to be merely continental and entered Weltpolitik—required a navy as much as it did an army. The beneficent work of German kultur was being limited in South West Africa—to take only one point of the globe—because the English held Walfish Bay. The Kaiser would have preferred to buy it. The English would not sell. A fleet was necessary.

The English were slow to realize the significance of this steadily growing friction with Germany. Deep sunk in their mind was the tradition that their hereditary enemies were France and Russia. Her navies supreme in the seven seas, Britain had no fear of invasion. Her worries were with her armies on the far-away frontiers of her colonies. The two foreign offices—Downing Street and Wilhelmstrasse—continued to exchange honied words.

The quarrels of traders and colonists might be compromised, but this naval competition was quite a different question. The English attitude towards their navy was very well expressed by a member of Parliament, Mr. Urquhart, in 1862:—

"Beware. The sea threatens, while it serves you; it bears you, but it environs you. The position of this island is such that there is no *via media* for her between being all powerful and being nothing at all. This is why she was always conquered until, having subjugated the sea, she became mistress of the world. England will be the sea's victim on the day she ceases to be its queen."

Sir Walter Raleigh expressed the same sentiments long before, and one can find them re-stated in the latest speech in Parliament on the naval situation.

The growth of Germany's sea power was early noted by English observers. And naval supremacy is to the British mind very like the conception of the Deutschtum to the Germans. It is sacro-sanct. It is something one does not dispute. Several years ago one of the German comic papers had a picture of a worried looking John Bull, busily turning over the pages of his Bible and asking his wife, Britannia, "Where is that verse, where God told the English to rule the waves?" If there is no such injunction in the Bible a great many Englishmen think it is due to a careless oversight on the part of one of God's stenographers.

He certainly must have said it. To dispute the manifest justice of England's sea-rule is to show an evil and impious heart.

Here are the disturbing facts. The naval budgets of Germany grew by leaps. These are the approximate figures in dollars by five year periods.

In 1883 the naval budget was 9.0 millions;
" 1888 " " " " 12.0 "
" 1893 " " " " 19.8 "
" 1898 " " " " 30.4 "

And here is the Kaiser's comment. "As my grandfather worked for the reconstruction of the army, I will work, without letting myself be checked, to reconstitute this navy, so that it will be comparable to our land army."

It took the English a long time to realize that they could not make their old friends, the Germans, understand and appreciate their reasons for ruling the sea. There is no doubt that the English made a sincere effort to open the German eyes in this matter. There is a large literature on the subject, leading articles in *The Times*, profound discussions in the reviews, not a few books and endless speeches by cabinet ministers and leaders of the opposition, by landlubbers and sea-lords.

The British Isles are not self-supporting. They do not produce sufficient food. If any hostile power closed the sea-routes the English would starve. Anyone can see that. The English need naval supremacy.

The British empire is not like Germany, a compact geographical unit. In the farthest corners of the world the English have taken up the white man's burden. And some of the "native" races are so unintelligent that they pretend to a right to carry their own burdens. The only way the British empire can go on with its duty of carrying burdens that are not its own (and there *is* something in the Bible about other people's burdens) is to be able to send troops to the ends of the earth to impress—and if needs be to kill—these unruly natives. It is as evident as the nose on your face that England needs the most powerful navy in the world.

And besides Britannia always has ruled the waves.

These arguments did not impress the Germans any more than their arguments in favor of the Deutschtum impressed the English. One of the most authoritative expressions of the German attitude in the matter is given by the ex-chancellor von Bülow in his book—"Imperial Germany." He makes a careful analysis of the history of British foreign policy. Since the days of the great Elizabeth, the English have fought every nation which has tried to rival them on the sea. She made and broke a kaleidoscopic series of treaties and always with the object of smashing some sea power. The Dutch fleet followed the Spanish armada to the bottom of the sea. She fought protestant nations just as blithely as catholic—if they dared to build ships. This is von Bülow's interpretation of our War of 1812. The French fleets of Louis XIV. and Napoleon followed those of the Dutch.

Now Germany was building ships. Von Bülow makes it clear that he expects whatever sound and vital elements there are in English life to seek an excuse to smash the German fleet before it would reach a threatening size. Nevertheless he is an optimist about it. He believes that Germany will succeed in wresting the rule of the waves from Britannia. Although he does not say so in so many words he evidently thinks that there is very little in modern English life which is virile and sound. He thought the English would be afraid to fight.

As it became evident that the Germans, instead of listening to these arguments were going ahead building warships, the English naval men began to grow suspicious of the cordial and genial messages exchanged by the two foreign offices. Plainly it was impossible to be friends with people who were evil minded enough to dispute England's right to supremacy in the sea-world.

Side by side with the growing suspicion that Germany's

intentions on the sea were not honorable there grew the certainty that British trade and industry were in danger.

For a long time—too long a time for their own good—the English had enjoyed a practical monopoly in over-seas trade. They not only reaped the profits of manufacturing the goods and selling them, but also they had the carrying business in their hands. This favored position in the world's industry had not been won by force of arms. Even their own historians admit that to a large extent it happened to them.

In the early days winds and currents favored the English shipping and after the invention of steam engines England had a great advantage in her easily accessible supply of coal. And besides other people had been too busy with wars and revolutions and internal developments to worry about international trade. Our case is typical. Our Civil War distracted our attention from "foreign markets" and besides we had the nearer and much more profitable work of winning the West.

This monopoly bred its inevitable results. British trade methods grew slack. In some markets—I happen to have seen the statistics of the Moroccan port of Mogador—the English trade had begun to fall off before any rivals appeared.

Suddenly the world was overrun with pushing, hardworking, keen young German salesmen. They had very little trouble in demonstrating that they were better business men than their easy going British competitors. Of course this seemed to the Germans a new proof of their racial superiority and of the divine mission of the Deutschtum. And just as the English navalists felt that it was not right for other people to compete with them in warships, so the merchants of England felt that it was not right for other people to successfully undersell them.

It is worth while analyzing this commercial rivalry a little deeper. The unsatisfactory condition of British industry became evident as far back as 1879, when Parliament appointed a commission to study the subject. Another "commission on the depression of trade" sat from August, 1885, to December, 1886, collected an immense number of consular reports and statistics and unanimously decided that the trouble was German competition. Another parliamentary commission reached the same results in 1896.

When the British merchants first felt the pressure of this new rivalry, they began to cry "unfair competition." The claim was general that the German goods were "shoddy." There was some truth in this charge at first, goods "made in Germany" often fell below "the good, old English standard." But very soon it became evident that the English business men had to do with a phenomenon much more serious than such "unfair" competition. The German products became as good—or better than—the English and everywhere cheaper.

The new industrial Germany had no traditions. It did not stop work for afternoon tea, it did not care for cricket nor football, it did not close the factory on Derby Day. It did not pay such heavy ground rents to foxhunting gentry, nor hand over such a large share of its profits to unproductive heirs. It did not sit down in dignity and wait for business to come to it. It sent out "hustling" salesmen—no Yankees have more thoroughly deserved this adjective—who felt that it was their first duty to learn the native languages.

And these salesmen were much better educated than their English rivals. "Education" in England is to a large extent intended to produce "gentlemen." In Germany it is much more practical. "Technical" instruction both in the production and sale of material is among the principal causes of German superiority in industry. In industrial rivalry there can be no doubt that "a two-power naval standard" is not as efficient as a progressive system of public instruction. And in educational matters Great Britain is notably retrograde.

But probably of greater importance was the fact that

British industry was seriously handicapped by having an immense amount of capital invested in antiquated plants. A reluctance to "scrap" obsolete equipment is a cumulative impediment. The older the industrial life of a community, the larger is the proportion of capital tied up in out-of-date machinery. In this matter England is inevitably worse off than her upstart rival. The German factories from which this threatening competition came were new, they had been planned on the lines of modern efficiency. In general—aside from the question of wages and the price of raw material—the cost of production because of up-to-date methods and machinery is less in Germany than in England. It is not necessary to believe in any mystic superiority of the Teuton race to understand why they beat the moss-grown, custom-ridden English in every department.

Perhaps in no other point has the superiority of the German methods been more evident than in the special pride of the English—the sea-trade. The Hamburg-Amerika Line has built just as pretentious "show-boats" for the North Atlantic route as the Cunard or White Star, but it is in the freight trade that they have completely outdistanced the English. The German merchant marine—in the Pacific trade; through Suez or around the Horn—has been better equipped in almost every detail than that of their rivals.

For a great many years the trade along the west coast of South America was a practical monopoly for the Pacific Steam Navigation Company. They had no rivals and no need to be obliging. A few of their ships were less than twenty years old and those which came around the Horn to England had to live up to the British board of trade rules. But when their ships became too old and battered to pass the home inspection they were kept on the west coast. Recently a German line, the "Kosmos," decided to cut in on this trade. They built a fleet of great modern freighters and their agents and captains were told to be polite and obliging—not to call the natives "niggers."

The loss of trade to the P. S. N. C., was a mathematical certainty. In desperation they sold out to the Royal Mail Steam Packet Company and the new management intended (before the War) to build some ships which would have a chance in the competition. Now that the War has driven their rivals to cover they may decide that this expense is unnecessary.

It is typical that while all these modern German ships were handling their cargo by hydraulic derricks, most of the English merchant marine still relied on the antiquated steam "donkey engine." And of course this means higher operating expenses. If the War had not come, the English—in order to compete with the Germans on equal terms—would have had to "scrap" the largest part of their older merchant fleet.

The connection between this commercial rivalry and colonial disputes is very close. The two questions are continually interlocking. Future historians of this period will give a good deal of attention to the German project—"*Die Bagdadbahn.*" No phase of the Near Eastern problem has called forth more bitterly passionate discussion than this German attempt to build a railroad through Asia Minor to Bagdad. The heat of the argument has been so great that it is difficult to reach a cool judgment on the dispute.

The German point of view is this. The market most suited for their wares is the Turkish empire. The great valleys of Mesopotamia, which once supported dense population, are now deserts which can be reclaimed by irrigation. It is a no man's land (of course the "natives do not count"). Their colonial enterprises in other directions have been thwarted and limited by other powers who had preëmpted the best territories. Asia Minor is a part of the world where no one else has a prior claim, which is ideally suited to their needs. It is a climate where Germans can live, a reservoir into which they can pour their surplus population and their surplus production. They hoped to make the desert blossom like the rose and give to all the world a new and impressive demonstration of the beneficence of the Deutschtum.

The dominant English point of view was that all this fine talk of economic development was merely a blind to a sinister political project of wresting from them Egypt and India. From a military point of view the weakness of the British empire lies in its immense extent. The sun never sets on the Union Jack and this means that the British system of protection must extend to the ends of the earth. Of all the imperial possessions India and Egypt are at once the most vulnerable and the most valuable. The memory of the Sepoy Rebellion is in the minds of all colonial administrators. And the English have looked with hostility on any efforts of another power to establish itself near the borders of these not over loyal colonies.

The German projects in Turkey and Mesopotamia were grandiose. Their cleverest diplomat since Bismarck, Marschall von Bieberstein, at Constantinople had wrung very sweeping concessions from the Sultan. The Kaiser himself had honored the Sick Man with a personal visit. The enterprise came to be called "the Bagdad railroad," although the rights to construct the line from the coast to Bagdad was the smallest part of the concessions. The German promoters had the privilege to extend the rails in almost any direction. They were granted vague, all-embracing "development" concessions, for irrigating, land purchase, mining, trading, and forest rights. To any one familiar with the district it was evident that to be really profitable the railroad must be extended to the Persian Gulf. It needed an Eastern port for a terminus.

The Transiberian railroad had proved how such a commercial enterprise could be used for political and military purposes. The concessions also granted the right to the Germans to take the necessary measures to protect their property from the Bedawi bandits which infest the desert. This clause might readily serve as an excuse for the establishment of a military outpost on the confines of India. A port on the Persian Gulf might be a base for German spies to encourage the chronic sedition in India. The railroad would allow the Germans to throw two or three army corps into the colony in support of a rebellion. The same class of Englishmen who a few years earlier had been "mervous" over the Russian advance, and had thought that Colonel Marchand was going to divert the waters of the Nile into the Sahara, took alarm over the fell designs of Germany.

An equally numerous and influential section of the English public—those whose wealth depended on the Indian trade—also took fright.

But it is true that a smaller and less influential section of the English welcomed this German "outlet." Sir Harry Johnson, in his book "Commonsense and Foreign Policy," argues that Germany should be encouraged in this venture. He believed that there was enough work in Asia Minor to absorb the excess of German energy for a century or more. But it was not till too late that the British government began to listen to the advice of this liberal section of their nation.

The announcements of the Bagdad railroad concessions attracted the attention of all diplomats—not only the English. The non-German critics of the project said that it was "crooked." The Turkish government not only gave away very valuable rights, but it guaranteed the railroad builders an annual income of so much for every mile they put in operation. In the opinion of most unbiassed observers there was no chance of the railroad earning anything like the amount of this guarantee for a great many years. This meant a heavy drain on the already bankrupt Turkish treasury. In other words, the Turks accepted a heavy debt towards the Germans.

England gained her present position in Egypt from the fact that the Khedive owes her money he cannot pay. France was preparing to absorb Morocco by lending money to the unbusinesslike Sultan—money he could never hope to pay. It is the traditional method. Everybody felt that the Bagdad railroad concession was a first step towards a German protectorate over Turkey.

To Russia this meant the end of her dream of getting to Constantinople. It threatened French "interests" in Syria. But the main opposition came from England. I do not think a single British politician would deny that their government did all it could to block this German advance. They could not—without immediate war—stop the building of the road to Bagdad, but they put every obstacle they could contrive in the way of its extension towards the Persian Gulf. They revived a shadowy protectorate over Koweit—a little principality which contained the logical harbor for a gulf terminus. And later they made peace with Russia and divided Persia with their old enemy, so as to erect a barrier between India and the new enemy.

Whether or not the English opposition to the Bagdad railroad was justified (and in the spring of 1914 they seemed to have changed their mind and rallied to the advice of Sir Harry Johnson) their action in the matter created immense bitterness in Germany. The Kaiser may have had a secret and sinister plan of political aggression against India, but the great majority of his people considered the Bagdad development plan as a legitimate business undertaking which the English had ruined out of pure spite. The Bagdad railroad took a place beside Walfish Bay as an example of the British policy of trying to smother Germany—of denying it a place in the sun. A great many of the anti-English jingo books and pamphlets of the Navy League and the pan-German societies took the Bagdad railroad as a text in their sermon of hate.

The Germans were much quicker to notice the clouds of the coming storm than the English. It was not in fact until the Boer War that the British suddenly woke up to the fact they they did not like the Germans. The awakening was so abrupt that they could hardly remember that they had ever liked the Germans.

CHAPTER VI

L'ENTENTE CORDIALE

THE war in South Africa had a profound effect on British life.

The issues involved in that conflict are within the memory of all of us. It is idle to discuss the rights of the case but it is well to remember that all through the war there was a strong opposition in England who loudly denounced the policy of the government. Rarely have the issues between imperialism and liberalism been more sharply drawn in British politics. According to the accepted standards of imperialism, it was a righteous war. According to the slowly formulating ideals of liberalism, it was unrighteous.

It was the work of the British imperialists. The Tory government, who represented this element, mismanaged the war in a most humiliating manner. But more distressing than the early military reverses, than the army furnishing scandals, than the ugly rumors of inhuman treatment of the wives and children of the Boer in the concentration camps, was the sudden realization that Great Britain did not have a friend in the world.

I do not suppose that a single Englishman ever doubted that sooner or later the empire could crush the Boer resistance. But there were many anxious months when every one in touch with the diplomats knew that a hostile continental coalition to save the South African republics was a possibility. With one despatch after another bringing news of another defeat, Britain was in no position to resist new attacks. Europe almost unanimously took the side of the Boers. The comic papers of the continent were full of virulent caricatures of the Boer David and the English

Goliath. Protest meetings against British atrocities were held right and left. This anti-English campaign reached its climax in Germany. A mob smashed the windows of a British consulate.

The Kaiser, in a bizarre interview which he gave to the London *Telegraph* some years later, professed to have been England's friend throughout this crisis. He even claimed to have helped them by his advice when their own strategy was going wrong. But the general impression in England was that the Germans—of all the European nations—had been the most unfriendly.

The watchword of British foreign policy was "splendid isolation." They had developed an unfounded legend that this had always been their policy. In the years which had followed the vast adventure of Napoleon, Great Britain—the richest and industrially the most advanced country in Europe and the only one which had not been ravaged by the wars—found it relatively easy to maintain a land and sea force amply strong enough to protect her frontiers and now and then to conquer a few thousand more miles of new territory. But this did not prevent her from frequently entering into the various and constantly changing combinations of continental policies. The Crimean War was only the most notable of her departures from splendid isolation.

But in the last half of the nineteenth century the nations of Europe, recovering from the devastation of the Napoleonic wars, grew strong. The Boer War demonstrated to the English the danger of their position. If they were to be able to meet single-handed any combination of their rivals, they would need an army not only much bigger, but also very much better than they had been able to muster against the Boers. The logical defenders of the old imperialist policy—like the late Lord Roberts—began to agitate for universal military service. "Isolation" in the face of a hostile Europe was evidently going to be either immensely expensive or anything but "splendid." The only escape from this distressing dilemna was a policy of making friends.

So when M. Delcassé, having arranged a reconciliation with Italy, turned his attention to Great Britain, he found that events had been working in his favor. And in M. Paul Cambon, his ambassador to the Court of St. James, he found a most able lieutenant.

The *rapprochement* with France began where the friction with Germany had been keenest and most widely felt—in business. The Associated Chambers of Commerce of London passed a resolution—14th September, 1901—in favor of an arbitration treaty with France and based their proposal on the argument that better and more cordial trade relations would result. Similar resolutions were passed by various French societies. In 1903 some deputies from the French Chambre made a courtesy visit to the British Parliament. Sir Edward Sassoon in a speech of welcome said: "Our aim should be to arrive at the one entente which is really stable—that based on material interests." The chambers of commerce of both countries endorsed the idea. In the same year King Edward VII. visited Paris. Two months later President Loubet and M. Delcassé returned the visit. The fêtes and official toasts were most friendly. The hereditary enmity was being decently buried.

On 8th April, 1904, "l'Entente Cordiale"—the cordial understanding—was signed.

The rôle which King Edward played in this reconciliation is the subject of much heated dispute. The polemics which have raged over his character and motives have been as vehement as—and very similar to—those which have been waged over the personalities of M. Delcassé and the Kaiser.

To the Germans, the late king was a close rival to the legendary devil, the very embodiment of this Satanic revolt against the Deutschtum. It is pretty well established that he was not fond of his nephew, the Kaiser, and—according to the German tradition—his whole life was spent in giving vent to this jealous and personal spite. The epoch which saw the gradual grouping of Europe against them, they call the Edwardian period. He was the arch conspirator in the plot to encircle and smother Germany. With malignant and mealy-mouthed hypocrisy he talked of peace, while all the time he was deliberately planning to drench the world in blood.

A man is rarely as bad—or as clever—as his enemies think him. There is even less reason to believe that King Edward was mystically clairvoyant and foresaw all the results of his diplomacy than in the case of M. Delcassé. At least the French foreign minister has very definite responsibilities. But with a constitutional king it is impossible to distinguish what he does from what he is told to do. The British sovereign has no more responsibility for the foreign policy of his nation than he has for the bad pictures painted by his subjects. The German emperor accepts responsibility in both matters.

After all, it is relatively uninteresting to speculate over the degree of the royal initiative. Perhaps King Edward imposed his will on his ministers—first Tories, then Liberals. Perhaps he was a docile tool in their hands. The important thing is that the foreign office, under Lord Lansdowne and Sir Edward Grey, and Buckingham Palace, inhabited first by King Edward and then by his son George, have worked in complete accord.

That King Edward's dislike for his nephew was not the sole foundation of the British foreign policy is evidenced by the numerous, if not altogether intelligent, efforts by which the British diplomats strove from time to time to reach an amiable agreement with Germany.

L'Entente Cordiale—and whether its author was M. Delcassé or King Edward is a small matter—was an agreement in regard to the colonial world. In the published texts Europe was not mentioned. Like the Franco-Italian entente it was a compromise. The two contracting parties, desirous of stopping their quarrels, took up one point of friction after another and split their differences.

Now for England and France to stop quarrelling over colonial affairs was contrary to the theory of international relations which Bismarck had taught his people. The bare fact of their shaking hands disturbed the "balance of power." It decreased the relative strength of the Germans. And they believed that it was part of God's and nature's plan that their power and prestige should increase. But Britain and France can hardly be called bellicose because they refused to accept this viewpoint, because they refused to continue to snarl at each other for the greater glory of the Deutschtum.

From this point of view the Entente was above reproach, it was a definite step towards a more peaceful condition in Europe. For the contracting parties the only alternative to this policy of friendship was one of intensified armament. France gained certain advantages in Indo-China, the Newfoundland fishery dispute was amicably settled and there were some frontier "rectifications" in equatorial Africa to the benefit of the English.

But the crucial—and also the questionable—part of the understanding dealt with the opposite corners of North Africa—Egypt and Morocco. As the importance of this document can hardly be overestimated—the importance of its wording as well as of its subject matter—I will quote from the official text the parts dealing with these two points:

Art. I. His Britannic Majesty's Government declare that they have no intention of altering the political status of Eygpt.

The Government of the French Republic, for their part, declare that they will not obstruct the action of Great Britain in that country by asking that a limit of time be fixed for the British occupation or in any other manner. . . .

Art. II. The Government of the French Republic declare that they have no intention of altering the political status of Morocco.

His Britannic Majesty's Government, for their part recognize that it appertains to France, more particularly as a Power whose dominions are conterminous for a great distance with those of Morocco, to preserve order in that country, and to provide assistance for the purpose of all administrative, economic, financial and military reforms which it may require.

They declare that they will not obstruct the action taken by France for this purpose, provided that such action shall leave intact the rights which Great Britain, in virtue of Treaties, Conventions and usage, enjoys in Morocco. . . .

Art. III. His Britannic Majesty's Government, for their part, will respect the rights which France, in virtue of Treaties, Conventions and usage, enjoys in Egypt.

Art. IV. The two governments, being equally attached to the principle of commercial liberty both in Egypt and Morocco, declare that they will not, in these countries, countenance any inequality either in the impositions of customs duties or other taxes, or of railroad transport charges.

Art. IX. The two governments agree to afford to one another their diplomatic support in order to obtain the execution of the clauses of the present declaration regarding Egypt and Morocco.

Since Napoleon's battle of the Pyramids France had had what are called "interests" in Egypt. The digging of the Suez Canal had been their work and French engineers had built the "barrage," the first step in the irrigation "reclamation" scheme of which the British dam at Assouan is the latest. The French had also done a great deal of "cultural" work. They had taken the lead in the study of archæology and their language was current among the educated. They also—as well as the English—were heavy creditors of the Khedival government and for some years the two governments exercised a joint financial control over Egypt. In 1881, a native rebellion broke out under Arabi Pasha against this foreign interference, to the cry of "Egypt to the Egyptians." The British fleet bombarded the open city of Alexandria (Mr. Winston Churchill had not at that time invented the phrase "baby-killing" to describe such naval operations) and in the next year a British expeditionary force smashed the native army at Tel-el-Kebir. This was done as "police work," nominally on behalf of the lawful sovereign, the Sultan of Turkey. As the Sultan was not exactly enthusiastic over this unasked for help and the other European powers were a bit sceptical of the disinterestedness of the English, the British foreign office assured everyone that the occupation was temporary. But their grip tightened and tightened. In 1884 in the face of a very general protest the British government renewed its promise to evacuate as soon as order was established and set 1888 as an extreme limit of their occupation. But circumstances over which they had no control. . . .

By the entente the French promised not to remind the English of these antiquated pledges nor to "obstruct" her action in Egypt . . . "in any other manner."

The French situation in Morocco was not so well established. By a long series of costly wars, France had conquered Algeria and Tunisia, she had annexed the Sahara, and had pushed her way up from the South to Timbuctoo and Lake Tchad. With the exception of Morocco all of North West Africa was under French rule. And Morocco was potentially the richest colony of them all.

The Sultan was an independent sovereign. He did not rule his realm very well from the French point of view. He did not rule it very well from the point of view of his own subjects. There was widespread discontent, chronic rebellion, and continual disorder.

As so often happens in similar cases much of this unrest was financed by foreign interests. And—also as often happens in similar cases—the seriousness of the situation was methodically exaggerated by these same foreign interests.

In the years which have passed since, a great many Moors have given their lives to prove that they preferred the misrule of their own Sultan to the superior civilization of the French.

The great mass of French people were as little interested in Morocco as the average American is in Nicaragua. But even a republican form of government does not purge a nation of imperialists. And the Colonial Party believed that it was "the manifest destiny" of France to absorb Morocco.

By the entente Great Britain promised not to thwart French action in Morocco.

But more important than these promises to get out of each other's way in Egypt and Morocco is Article IX., in which the two governments pledged themselves "to afford to one another their diplomatic support in order to obtain the execution of the clauses of the present declaration regarding Egypt and Morocco."

It is difficult to avoid the conclusion that the wording of this document is intentionally obscure. France's pledge not to remind England of her broken promises is clear enough. But what is meant by preserving "order" in an independent country? We, *vis-à-vis* to Mexico, see what differences of opinion such a phrase allows. England had done the job in Egypt in a straightforward strong-arm way. Was similar action in Morocco intended by the signers of this declaration? And who was to decide when Morocco needed tranquilizing? France? England? The Moors? Or somebody else? All these vague phrases give rise to wide possibilities of interpretation.

But the clause about giving each other diplomatic help is most worthy of note. If I pledge my honor not to dun you for money you owe me, I do not need your diplomatic help to live up to that promise. The only possible meaning of this Article IX. is that if any third party tried to interfere with them in the execution of the clauses of this present declaration, they would bear each other help. If Honduras protested against the continued occupation of Egypt by British troops, French diplomats would assist the English in explaining why the promise to evacuate could not be kept. If Persia or Siam objected to French "action" in Morocco, British diplomats would intervene.

This criticism of mere words may seem trivial. But the fate of Europe has depended on the interpretation of this phrase. What did the signers of the entente mean by "diplomatic support?" To what extent was England bound to back up France when Germany interfered with her Moroccan policy? "Diplomatic support" the text says. At one stage in the long tension—during the Agadir crisis—the British home fleet, cleared for action, was sent cruising in the North Sea. Was such action implied in the word "diplomatic?"

The very vagueness of the terms employed in this document as published, indicated a more far-reaching, unpublished accord. It was hard to believe that the representatives of the two governments who prepared and signed this declaration had any doubts as to the meaning of the words they used. When two governments decide to remove all causes of friction between them they are not likely to be content with half measures. The entente, as published, was a half measure, eminently fitted as a starting point for new disputes.

No European statesman read the document without asking himself what were the probable contents of the secret clauses. I do not think that any experienced diplomats doubted their existence. Both the French and British governments protested that this published text was all there was to the entente. But public treaties with secret riders are a commonplace of diplomatic history. But it was not until November, 1911—seven years later—that the existence and nature of any of the secret clauses was known to the public. All that could be assumed with any certainty at the time was that undoubtedly the two Foreign Offices had talked over and agreed upon many of these disputable points.

Why was there any necessity of secrecy about it? The

British and French governments seem to have been inspired by a very realistic sense of politics. They knew that the published text would be passionately discussed in the newspapers and parliaments of their respective countries. To have written in anything which the public opinion of France and England would not accept, would have ruined the whole enterprise. The men who signed the entente certainly foresaw the probability of German opposition. But the pacific democracies of the two countries would undoubtedly have rejected any sort of a military alliance which seemed an affront to Germany. It was so in regard to other points. The diplomats could only publish what they knew their people would approve of. The rest had to be kept secret. The entente was the first step—the proverbially difficult first step. It was intentionally modest. It could be developed.

In fact the very day it was signed, it was amended in detail by the method of interpretation. In the clause about the Newfoundland fisheries there was a phrase of uncertain meaning. And M. Cambon wrote a letter to Lord Lansdowne:—

M. PAUL CAMBON,
Ambassador of the French Republic at London.

To the MARQUIS OF LANSDOWNE, *Secretary of State to the Office of Foreign Affairs.*

8 April, 1904.

In the second article of to-day's Convention in regard to Newfoundland it is said in the third paragraph that the French fishers should abstain from using "stake-pots" and "fixed engines" without the permission of the local authorities.

I will be obliged to your Lordship if you will kindly let me know what should be understood by "stake-pots" and "fixed engines." . . .

To this Lord Lansdowne replied:

Foreign Office, 8 April, 1904.

I have the honor to acknowledge receipt of the note which you have addressed to me requesting to be informed what signification is to be attached to the words "stake-pots" and "fixed engines" used in the Third paragraph of Article II. of the Convention we have just signed respecting Newfoundland.

I have the honour to inform your Excellency in reply that according to various acts of Parliament relating to salmon fishery these words include all nets and other implements for taking fish which are fixed to the soil or made stationary in any other way so that they may be left unattended by the owner.

This is the signification attached to the words by His Majesty's Government.

LANSDOWNE.

This correspondence is published in the same collection (Documents Diplomatiques. Accords conclus, le 8 Avril, 1904, entre la France et l'Angleterre. No. 7 & 8) which contains the official text of the entente. It was a sort of cipher language. To the layman it seemed innocent enough. "Stake-pots" and "fixed engines," have a harmless bucolic sound. To the initiated it indicated the method by which the published text could be expanded without limit. Were there similar letters exchanged to precise the meaning which His Majesty's government attached to the words "diplomatic support?"

That such suspicions were justified was proved by the event.

A secret naval agreement—the text of which has not yet been published—was reached, whereby the British entrusted their interests in the Mediterranean to the French navy and so were able to concentrate their war-ships in the North Sea. In 1911, *Le Temps of Paris* published what purported to be the text of the secret annex to the entente. And at the outbreak of this War Sir Edward Grey read in the House of Commons some correspondence in regard to military coöperation, which had been exchanged in 1912.

It is probable that some day the opening of the archives will show that this interpretive correspondence in regard to the entente has been voluminous.

But at the time—1904—all this was only a matter of guess work. To be sure, practically all continental statesmen felt that they had a "moral certainty" that the entente went much further than the published text. Only a few of the English liberals were naïf enough to believe that what Sir Edward Grey told them was true.

On the whole the news of this accord was well received in England and France. Public opinion had been "prepared." But the praise was not unanimous. There was a small but bitter opposition in both countries. Those Frenchmen who had "special interests" in Egypt wailed that they had been deserted by their government. The English in Morocco raised a similar complaint. In fact it had been a *quid pro quo*. Each government, in order to gain greater advantages elsewhere, had ruthlessly sacrificed the interests of some of their citizens. French "interests" in Egypt were already compromised. In order to preserve them they would have had to fight the first sea-power of Europe. In Morocco there were only half-civilized, disorganized tribes to fight. And the English interests in Morocco were only possibilities for the future, Egypt and Suez were actualities. The entente was popular in both countries.

It is rather hard for an American to grasp the European attitude towards colonial adventure. First of all, we are not an exporting nation. Of all the wealth we produce less than ten per cent goes abroad. Our colonial markets are an insignificant part in the prosperity of our small foreign trade. Since we grabbed Texas and California we have not extended our frontiers to any extent. The few colonies which happened to us as a result of the Spanish War are not popular. We have neither the need for colonies nor the tradition. We would probably fight if anyone assaulted our "national dignity" by trying to steal the

Philippines, but if those islands should gently fade off the map, the few of us who would notice the difference, would feel relieved. But it is hardly an exaggeration to say that no one in Europe understands why we did not keep Cuba, nor why we have not annexed Mexico.

It is one of those differences in the social mind which divide one nation from another—like that which separates the English and the Germans over the respective merits of militarism and navalism. Few Frenchmen could have told why they were interested in Morocco, but many of them felt like cheering when it was announced that Great Britain had recognized "the manifest destiny" of their country to "tranquilize Morocco."

There were however, groups in France—they were not sufficiently united to deserve the name of a Colonial Party—who saw very definite, concrete advantages to be gained by this new colonial enterprise. The army is important in a country of universal conscription. The officers—professional soldiers—inevitably develop an *esprit de corps* which is a factor in politics. And promotions are dolefully slow unless something is doing. The French colonial policy has not been that of the open door, they have sometimes been constrained to render lip-service to this idea, but they have done so reluctantly and wherever possible they have arranged tariffs to favor their own trade. The French manufacturers who make a "protected" profit in their exports to Tonkin and Tunis are in favor of colonial expansion. And France has a highly developed bureaucracy. There are all sorts of "civil servants," men on the government pay roll, postmen, police, railroad employees, forest guards, the "*ponts et chaussées*"—a corps of civil engineers for public works. When a new colony is organized the administrative personnel is taken from this bureaucracy, which means advancement all along the line. Almost every French "*fonctionnaire*" is an ardent advocate of colonial expansion. But perhaps of greatest importance are the financiers. Besides all the opportunities for profitable investment in a new colony, there are sure to be great credit operations. All of these varied forces were organized in "*Le Comité Marocain.*" For Morocco was manifestly the next step.

There was, however, bitter and organized and continuous opposition to the "Moroccan adventure" on the part of the Socialists. Their motives were complicated. The working class whom they represented would have to pay the piper, in taxes and blood, and would have a very small share in the plunder. As humanitarians they objected to the inevitable slaughter of the "natives." As Republicans they were instinctively opposed to imperialism. Some of them felt that a Moor had quite as much right to political independence as a Frenchman. And of course the whole theory of colonization is in direct conflict with the idea of the rights of man. The Socialists of more penetrating vision—men like Jaures—clearly foresaw that colonial adventures tended—if they did not fatally lead—to European war. In fact a party as profoundly opposed to war and militarism as the French Socialists were in inevitable conflict with M. Delcassé and his policy of colonial expansion.

But the most dangerous opposition to "l'Entente Cordiale" came—as was to be expected—from Germany.

The Germans had little interest of any kind in either Egypt or Morocco. The published text of the entente was explicitly pacific. Nevertheless, it would have been difficult to contrive anything which would have seemed to the Germans a more definite affront. The document was communicated to the foreign offices of the Sultan and the Pope as soon as to Wilhelmstrasse. If it had no hostile intent, why was it prepared so secretly? Once upon a time nothing had happened in Europe without the consent of Bismarck. Evidently the times had changed. More and more Europe was escaping from the thrall of the Deutschtum.

The Kaiser's pacific method of Germanizing the world by arguments was not working well. A policy which tended to dispute German predominance in Europe was becoming more and more manifest. The Franco-Russian alliance. The Franco-Italian entente. And now this Anglo-French arrangement! It was necessary to rap for order, it was necessary to remind Europe of the stern realities of life. If they would not listen to argument it was necessary to make a display of grim force—to rattle the sword.

The issue was joined in the sharpest possible manner.

The non-German nations were grouping themselves with no avowed intent of attacking Germany, but with an open determination to resist the development of the Deutschtum.

It is necessary to recall the interpretation I have tried to give (Chapter III) of the nature of this mystic ideal—the Deutschtum.

"Two great German movements were born from the German intellectual life, on which, henceforth, all the intellectual and moral progress of mankind must rest:— The Reformation and the critical philosophy (Kant). . . . The German nation not only laid the foundation of this great struggle for a harmonious development of humanity, but took the lead in it. We are thus incurring an obligation for the future from which we cannot shrink. . . . It is this quality which especially fits us for leadership in the intellectual domain and imposes upon us the obligation to maintain that leadership."

It is not a mere coincidence that a cavalry officer—von Bernhardi—should use such philosophical terminology to express the mystic mission of the German race. Phrased in simple language, it would sound absurd. But such pseudo-philosophic ideas are commonplaces in Germany; they are taught to the nation from kindergarten to the universities, and especially in the barracks.

And it is evident that people who felt so about the mission they were called to perform, could not help considering that this effort to resist it—typified by the entente—was a serious affront.

CHAPTER VII

THE ALGECIRAS CRISIS

THE European question raised by *l'Entente Cordiale*—this colonial agreement between England and France—was: Will the Germans give up their pretensions to overlordship without a struggle?

Anyone who thought they would was singularly ill-informed on the temper of the German people. If it was not for the exaggerations of their claims—as witnessed by the quotations in Chapter III,—it would be hard to deny that this agreement gave them cause for complaints. After all, why should anything happen in Europe without the Germans being consulted? Whether one likes or dislikes their ideals, there are eighty millions of them and Austria besides. They are not a negligible quantity. They naturally resent being ignored.

Their claim that they are the only people of true culture in Europe is puerile, but no one, unless the heat of the War has warped all the accustomed meanings of words, can deny that their contribution to the common work of civilization has been immense. Their claim to dictatorship cannot be admitted by any nation which loves freedom, but their right to at least an equal vote in the councils of Europe cannot be denied with any show of justice. They were not consulted over the fate of Egypt and Morocco.

Everyone who followed European politics was greatly relieved—and not a little surprised—at the attitude which official Germany took in the matter. At a session of the Reichstag—April 12, 1904—four days after the entente was published, the chancellor Herr von Bülow, speaking of this event, said: "We have, from the point of view of German interests, nothing to object to it. In this which concerns Morocco . . . we have there above all else commercial interests. We ought to protect them and we will. We have no reason to fear that they will be ignored nor troubled."

The chancellor's speech was literally true. The material interests of Germany were not openly threatened. But he dodged the real issue—that of prestige. The German newspapers pointed out this fact and the War Party—it is a poor term for a heterogeneous group of interests, like "Colonial Party" in France—made a good deal of noise. The 20th April the Pangermanic Society of Wurtemburg in its congress at Esslingen protested and a few days later the Union of Pangermanic Societies held their annual meeting at Lubeck and adopted a long resolution on the subject. The clause of greatest interest said they were profoundly wounded by the humiliation to Germany in not being consulted in so important a matter. In private conversations it was a commonplace to say that Bismarck would not have accepted the affront, and that the Kaiser's love of peace was a treason to the German idea.

Very few people were optimistic enough to believe that the incident was closed.

It had become the custom in the diplomatic world to take the Kaiser's speeches as a sort of barometer of the political weather. And they certainly indicated a coming storm. At Karlsruhe (28th April), at Mayence (1st May) at Saarbrück (14th May) it sounded as if he was trying to reassure those of his subjects who charged him with being enslaved by peace. It was necessary to bury internal difference in order to be united in case Germany should be forced to intervene in world politics. The bridge which he inaugurated at Mayence was a work of peace but it was well to remember that it might have been a use in war. He bombastically recalled the victories of 1870. Germans were not looking for a quarrel, but woe to anyone who sought trouble with them, etc.

On the 31st March, 1905—almost exactly a year after

the publication of the Anglo-French entente—the Kaiser's yacht *Hohenzollern* dropped anchor in the harbor of Tangier. He went ashore and made a speech to the representative of the Sultan—which like the famous shot at Lexington was heard around the world.

"It is to the Sultan, in his quality of an independent sovereign, that I make my visit today. I hope that under the sovereignty of the Sultan an independent Morocco will remain open to the peaceful competition of all nations, without monopoly, or annexation, on a footing of absolute equality. My visit to Tangier has had for its object to make known that I am decided to do my utmost to safeguard efficaciously the interests of Germany in Morocco. Since I consider the Sultan as an absolutely independent sovereign, it is with him that I wish to reach an understanding on the necessary means to protect these interests. As to the reforms which the Sultan is considering, it seems to me advisable to proceed with great caution, taking into consideration the religious sentiments of the population to the end that public order may not be disturbed."

There were three outstanding points in this short speech. (I) The Kaiser addressed the Sultan as an independent sovereign. A defiance to the French projects of a protectorate. (II) He said he intended to protect German interests in Morocco. The French by the ententes had freed themselves from Italian, English and Spanish rivalry, but not that of Germany. (III) He advised the Sultan to go slow in introducing reforms in his realm. The French had submitted a long program of "reforms" which—none too gently—they were urging the Sultan to accept. The whole speech was an indirect but definite promise from the German government to back up the Sultan in resistance to French "action in Morocco."

When the report of this incident was printed, a few hours later, in the newspapers of Europe, everyone knew that the fat was in the fire. Germany was not going to submit to what seemed to her an affront. The struggle had commenced. It was the first of the series of European crises which have disturbed the world these recent years.

Why had it taken Germany a year to make up her mind to throw down the gauntlet? For the French the answer is simple and their explanation is plausible. In September, 1904, the Japanese gained their first big victory at Liao-Yang. In March, 1904, the Russians were definitely crushed at Mukden. For a good many years the French had felt that the only thing which protected them from a new German aggression had been their alliance with Russia. The last day of the month which saw the military power of the Tsar crushed, the Kaiser exploded his bomb at Tangier.

There is another—German—explanation of the abrupt change in the chancellor's attitude since he had assured the Reichstag that there was nothing for them to object to in the Anglo-French understanding. It is alleged that by means of an international "indiscretion" on the part of some members of the Spanish diplomatic corps the complete text of the secret agreements between France and England and Spain reached the German foreign office. There has always been a pro-German and therefore anti-French and English element among the ruling class of Spain, so this explanation also is plausible.

Although it was not until 1911 that any of the secret documents were published it is well to have them in mind at this time. In the "secret annex" to the Anglo-French entente the two governments, while reiterating their desire to maintain the status quo in Morocco, envisaged the possibility of a partition of the country. Great Britain did not ask for any share of the spoils, but insisted that her position of dominance over the Straits of Gibraltar should not be menaced in any way. She did not want to have a strong nation established on the African side of this important waterway, so she stipulated that when the Sultan of Morocco could no longer protect his country from foreign domination, all the northern part of his realm, the Mediterranean coast, should go to Spain, and that Spain should be pledged not to erect any fortifications which would threaten the British supremacy in the Straits. It was agreed that France should at once begin negotiations with Spain to get her to become a party to this accord.

M. Delcassé—3d October, 1904—published a statement that an entente had been reached with Spain. The text of the agreement was published by *Le Matin* in 1911 a few days before *Le Temps* published the secret annex to the Anglo-French entente. This Spanish treaty restated—a little more in detail—the arrangement on which Britain had insisted.

If Germany knew of these secret agreements for the partition of Morocco—at a time when the three contracting parties were solemnly proclaiming their desire to maintain the integrity of the Sultan's realm—it certainly gave the Germans a legitimate reason for intervening.

The probabilities are that both these matters influenced the German government. Knowledge of these secret treaties had almost surely reached them. This gave them a reason to act. The Russian defeat offered a favorable occasion. But the French and British public did not know of these secret treaties and of course felt that the German action was unjustified.

The Germans, having decided on action, did not content themselves with a mere speech of defiance. Their newspapers, evidently acting on an official tip, summed up the situation in this fashion: "We are a peace loving people. We do not want to go to war with France. But this M. Delcassé has misled the French people into a policy which displeases us. It is their move. They can choose between our friendship or the friendship of M. Delcassé. If they do not act reasonably their blood will be upon their own head."

To make sure that the French understood how they felt about it, they carried the newspaper war into the enemy's country. An ambiguous character, the Prince Haenkel von Donnersmarck, had lived in Paris for many years. He held no official position but was supposed to be on a "mission" comparable to that which brought Dr. Dernburg to the United States. Early in June he gave out interviews to the Paris papers, from one of which I give some characteristic quotations. "Is this policy (the entente) that of France, or must we consider it as being merely personal to Monsieur Delcassé? . . . We are not concerned with M. Delcassé's person; but his policy is a threat to Germany; and you may rest assured that we shall not wait for it to be realized" . . . "In a war against Germany, you may possibly be victorious, since in her most tragic crises France has always found extraordinary resources in herself; but, if you are vanquished—and my first hypothesis deprives my second of all offensive character—if you are vanquished, as you probably will be, it is in Paris that the peace will be signed." . . . "Believe the word of a German, who has always had great sympathy for you. Give up this minister, whose only aspiration is to trouble the peace of Europe; and adopt with regard to Germany a loyal and open policy."

It would have been hard to be more explicit. Germany was resolved on war or M. Delcassé's scalp.

When at last the archives of the various foreign offices are opened, the documents in regard to this affair will be of immense interest. What attitude did Great Britain take in this crisis? How did they interpret the phrase "diplomatic support?" Two serious French writers on international politics—André Tardieu and Ernest Lémonon—believe that the British government urged the Republic to stand firm—and this meant war. This is one of the crucial points of modern diplomatic history and it is veiled in secrecy.

At all events France decided not to fight. Her army was in a pitiful state. The Dreyfus affair had discredited the high command. The Dreyfusards, several of whom had had their heads broken for rioting to the cry of "*A bas l'armée*," had become ministers. Those in power were preoccupied with internal affairs—the great fight against clericalism. The various ministers of war had not dared to ask the Chambre for large military credits. The eastern fortifications had been neglected. Munitions, equipment, everything was lacking. And, as usual, the Germans were ready.

On the 6th of June, M. Delcassé's resignation was accepted. Nothing in modern history can be compared to this humiliation—one government forcing another under threat of war to sacrifice a minister.

The new generation, which had come into power in the Republic, had been rapidly forgetting 1870 and the idea of "revanche." France—not only the Socialists, but a comfortable majority of the voters, the existing ministry—was anti-militarist. But this Delcassé affair embittered the nation profoundly. A great many people who had hoped that, with the passage of time, the relations with Germany would ameliorate, gave up the hope and regretfully decided that France would have to fight or abdicate!

Delcassé, in a remarkably similar way, had repeated the blunders of Hanotaux. He had tried to run the foreign policy of his country single-handed. He had not consulted his colleagues in the ministry, nor had he taken them into his confidence. He had not even laid his secret treaty with Spain before the cabinet. He had been very reserved—in fact rather contemptuous—in his relations to the deputies of the nation in the Chambre. It is hardly an exaggeration to say that no one—not even the president of the Republic nor the premier—knew what he was doing.

And in this manner he had steered the ship of state to a place from which there were but two exits:—war or humiliation. If he had not foreseen this he was rather stupid. If he had foreseen it and had not taken the trouble to see if France was prepared for war—he deserved humiliation. But the humiliation fell on all the nation.

The Germans were not content with this reassertion of their prestige. The Kaiser gave von Bülow the title of

Prince as a reward for his successful tilt with Delcassé, but success tempted them to new proofs of their power. They decided to give France a public spanking. They demanded a European conference to discuss the affairs of Morocco.

There was nothing the French Colonial Party wanted less. They did not want public attention, even in their own country, called to their manner of work in Morocco. They did not want to admit that this was a matter of European interest. They wanted to "localize" their dispute with Morocco—just as in 1878 Russia had wanted to treat single-handed with Turkey and as in 1914 Austria was to insist on "localizing" her affair with Servia.

By ententes with Italy, England, and Spain, France had been able to arrange things quietly. German interests in Morocco were admittedly small, but if the Kaiser insisted on making a noise about them it was much better to discuss the matter *à deux*.

The French made it clear that they would grant any reasonable demands which Germany would formulate in regard to Morocco in order to avoid a conference. But concessions in Morocco were only a part of what Germany wanted. We have the words of Prince von Bülow himself. An interview with the chancellor—which he had had the opportunity to correct—was published in *Le Temps* of Paris (5th Oct., 1905).

"There are," he said, "in the incidents of the last six months, which have given rise to the Moroccan affair, two distinct things to consider. Morocco is the first and general politics (the international relations of Europe) are the second. In Morocco we have important commercial interests. We had and we have a duty to protect them. In regard to general politics we have been obliged to reply to a policy which tended to isolate us, and which, with this avowed intention, took on towards us a clearly hostile character. The Moroccan affair was the most recent and most characteristic manifestation of this policy; it was for us the necessary occasion to strike back."

The German government felt that this matter of *amour propre*—of prestige—had not been satisfied by the ignominious resignation of Delcassé. All the nations of Europe—and the United States—should be called together to witness the application of public punishment. The Kaiser rattled his sword. The conference or war.

The French government had had to give in in regard to Delcassé, it had to give in again and accept the conference. But under these repeated threats the attitude of the governing Radicals had changed completely. The Minister of War, instead of being ashamed to show himself in the Chambre, became a personage. The Deputies were ready to give him all the money he wanted. For the first time since 1870 France began seriously to prepare for war. It was not like the spread-eagle jingoism of the Boulanger episode. It was a quiet—grim—adult period in French politics. In the interval between the fall of Delcassé and the opening of the European conference in the little Spanish town of Algeciras immense military credits had been voted and spent.

If Germany had been seriously pre-occupied over her "interests" in Morocco she would not have insisted on the conference. To avoid this public discussion, France had been willing to cede to Germany much more of the spoils than Germany could claim any "right" to—much more than she could hope to get from a European conference which would have, in principle, to treat all equally.

Whoever tries to write history must have an especial gratitude towards the Germans—they are so amazingly frank. The interview from von Bülow, quoted above, shows that in his mind the Moroccan affair was primarily a matter of Weltpolitik. The concrete commercial "interests" at stake were secondary. And other German utterances—too numerous to quote—show clearly that they had two more important but indirect objects in insisting on this conference. (I) The public humiliation of France and (II) the testing—and if possible the breaking of the entente cordiale. And . . . "Pride goeth before destruction and a haughty spirit before a fall." They were signally defeated. The Germans themselves admit that they are poor diplomats and almost every time, since the passing of Bismarck, when they have risked their prestige on the diplomatic "terrain" it has been diminished.

During the months which had preceded the conference French diplomats had been exceedingly and successfully busy in preparing their case and in enlisting the sympathy of the other nations. The Germans accused the French of planning to annex or at least to declare a protectorate over Morocco which meant quite the opposite from the open door. Judged by the French methods in Tunisia these suspicions were justified. (And the events which have passed since give further justifications.) But the French denied any such intentions.

In the very first session of the conference (February, 1906) M. Regnault, the chief of the French delegation, took the fire out of the German guns by proposing that the basis of the discussion should be the reaffirmation of the sovereignty of the Sultan, the integrity of his realm, and the policy of the open door. It was clever, even if insincere diplomacy. Besides, the French delegates were courteous and they knew their subject. The German delegates were offensively brusque and—as the affairs of Morocco were for them of only secondary interest—they were ignorant of the highly technical questions which came up.

The first vote—it was only a detail, a question of procedure—was the test. Of the thirteen nations represented, nine voted with the French and only Austria and Morocco voted with Germany. All the little states, instead of obediently doing as the Kaiser told them, showed signs of an heretical independence. Even the ally, Italy, voted against Germany. The jury of Europe instead of condemning France for her independent attitude, by a vote of 10 to 3 blamed Germany. Evidently Bismarck was dead.

Germany also hoped by this conference to break the

accord between England and France. Before the delegates had begun work (3d Feb., 1906) the Count von Tattenbach, one of the German delegates, approached Sir Arthur Nicholson, the chief of the British mission, and urged him to abandon France and join the Germans in "saving" Morocco. His argument took this form: The bare fact that a European conference has assembled to regulate the fate of Morocco wiped off the slate all merely private agreements between two Powers; England had already reaped all the gain she could expect from the entente, France had withdrawn from Egypt; Germany was ready to recognize English rights there; the conference gave a technical excuse to declare the entente dead. If the British deserted France at this moment they and the Germans could divide up North Africa at their leisure. But to the great chagrin of the German diplomats, Albion refused to be perfidious.

Sir Arthur Nicholson's instructions were very simple. At the opening of the conference and whenever the German newspapers spread the rumor that England was about to desert France—it happened more than once—the government at London let it be known that the only instruction given to their mission at Algeciras was to act in accord with the French delegates under every condition and in all circumstances.

In so far as the Germans insisted on the conference in order to test the strength and meaning of *l'entente cordiale*, they secured the information they sought. This Anglo-French agreement was more than a simple colonial deal, it was more than a compact the one to the other, it also united them in European politics against Germany. Whether or not they were pledged to give each other military help was still unknown, but England was evidently prepared to live up literally and loyally to the phrase "diplomatic support."

All that Germany had gained was the personal overthrow of M. Delcassé. His *policy*—the ententes with Italy, England and Spain—was greatly strengthened by the Conference of Algeciras.

Those who were opposed to the domination of the

Deutschtum were greatly heartened. There had been successful, open resistance. The prestige of Germany, especially in the secondary states, was lessened. It is probable that the trend of Belgium away from Germany and towards friendship with France and England dated from that vote of 10 to 3 at Algeciras.

But a more tangible symptom of the new state of things in Europe was given—by the international comedy of the Spanish marriage. For a long time European princes had been in the habit of marrying German princesses. Young Alphonso had been fêted from one end of the Empire to the other, he had passed in review the Royal Gretchens of all the courts of the Deutschland. And when he returned to Madrid and wrote his bread-and-butter letters of thanks for all their lavish hospitality he announced his engagement to a niece of King Edward. A Prince of the House of Hapsburg preferred an English girl! German women are among the things listed as *"über alles"* in the famous song. Not long afterwards a Norwegian prince followed the example of Alphonso and chose an English bride. German prestige was falling.

The Conference of Algeciras—although everyone politely said that "no one was victor, no one vanquished"—was a very real diplomatic defeat for Germany. France had not been condemned by Europe. The entente was stronger than ever. And for almost the first time in history, English and Russian diplomats had worked together in a European assembly.

Official Germany made the best of a bad job, and claimed victory. It had been demonstrated that England and France could not divide up the map without consulting Germany. The conference was the German reply to their effort to ignore her and run the world to suit themselves. They had not wanted the conference but had had to accept it. And Germany had forced from France a pledge to respect the independence of the Sultan and the principle of economic equality—the open door.

The first claim was true. France had come reluctantly to Algeciras. But it could hardly be called a *diplomatic* victory. France had accepted the conference under the direct menace of war. In this department Germany was undoubtedly strong.

But the second of these official claims was pure falsification. France had promised repeatedly before to respect the sovereignty of the Sultan and the equal rights of all commerce. It was not necessary to set all Europe upside down to get that pledge repeated. The Germans—with considerable justification—had doubted the sincerity of this promise. Its renewal at Algeciras under threat of war was not any better. The German diplomats did not get anything in the way of commercial concession in Morocco at the conference which they could not have secured by direct negotiation *à deux*. There is every probability that they would have received much more by the less noisy method.

In spite of the chants of victory from the government very few Germans were fooled. Forcing France to sacrifice her Minister of Foreign Affairs, dragging her against her will to the conference had been good. But something had gone wrong at Algeciras. The result had been bitterness and humiliation.

The conference had been a victory for France. Her gains were great and manifest. The Republic had not held so favorable a position in Europe since the Terrible Year of 1870. After endless humiliations, she had been able to enter the arena against her old conqueror and win. Powerful friends had rallied beside her loyally. The little countries of Europe had lost their awe of Germany. Every Frenchman was proud of the result.

But it was not an undiluted victory. There was a fly in the ointment. For all this new feeling of dignity—of being once more one of the Great Powers—France had to pay by pledging her word to Europe. And these promises, if they did not seem onerous to the mass of the nation, who—

I repeat—cared as little about Morocco as we do about Nicaragua, were decidedly distasteful to the various elements of France who may roughly be called "the Colonial Party."

The question of whether or not France was sincere in signing *l'acte d'Algesiras* can not be answered simply. Some of the French were sincere about it, some were not. M. Tardieu in his book "La Conférence d'Algesiras" (the best on the subject) takes the attitude that France had never intended to "Tunisify" Morocco, really hoped to maintain the sovereignty of the Sultan, did not seek any special commercial nor financial advantage. And while he—and many other people at home—may have been surprised by "the course of events" which later led to the establishment of the protectorate, a great many Frenchmen—especially those on the scene in Algeria and Morocco—were not surprised.

They believed that France had a "manifest destiny" in Morocco, that a promise made under duress was not binding. They treated with open scorn this "scrap of paper" and went on blithely, as they had been doing in the past, undermining the authority of the Sultan, fostering the kind of disturbance which would give a pretext for armed intervention and by all sorts of discreditable tricks trying to drive out their commercial rivals. And the "Colonial Party" at home, grouped about *le Comité Marocain*, encouraged them by maintaining a powerful "lobby" in the corridors of the Chamber of Deputies, and by carrying on a very clever and thorough-going campaign of misrepresentation in all the "venal" press.

The central government at least tolerated the conspiracy by which it was being forced to "tear up" its solemn promises. I have chanced to read some of the reports of our consular force in Morocco. It is hardly conceivable that our government did not bring these complaints to the attention of the French government. Certainly the Germans knew what was going on—their commerce fared worse than ours—and it is impossible to the point of absurdity to believe that they did not protest: the French government knew that it was not loyally observing its promises.

The history of colonial enterprise is seldom fit reading for children. Christendom has spread its civilization to the four corners of the world by devious and shameful means. We are not proud of the way we despoiled and killed off the Indians. Very few European nations can find much to be proud of in their colonial records. And France certainly has weakened her claim to be the Apostle of Light, the Defender of the Rights of Man by her record in Morocco. Murder, rapine, broken promises, the fanning of old vices among the natives, the introducing of new ones, intrigue and bribery were among the means used to overthrow the independence of Morocco. Women—poor wrecks of the Paris gutters—have been taken to Morocco and "married" to native chiefs to act as spies. It is a sorry story and all one can say in the way of extenuation is that there are so many others every bit as bad or worse.

It is necessary to stop the narrative a moment and philosophize a bit on the nature—the as yet imperfected nature—of democratic political institutions. Nothing is more clearly established than the fact that the French nation as politically organized, took the promises of Algeciras seriously and wanted to live up to them. At least once a year the Moroccan question came up for attention before the French Parliament. Every time a large majority of the Deputies rallied to a resolution in which the government was specifically instructed to keep its agreement. In 1908 such a resolution was passed at least four times— 24th January, 28th January, 19th June and 23d December. During all these years any minister who had even hinted to the Chamber that the Algeciras treaty should be torn up would at once have been hissed out of office. The people of France did not have their heart in the Moroccan adventure.

That was just the trouble—they were too much interested

in internal problems to really worry over what was being done in their name in Africa.

This is the crux of the problem—as yet unsolved—of how to develop a democratic diplomacy. The tradition of secrecy is bad. It breeds suspicion and encourages aggression. It is essentially aristocratic. But the real difficulty lies deeper. It is that the democracy tends to be self-centered, absorbed in domestic problems, indifferent to foreign affairs.

The Algeciras crisis gave a striking example of how this general truth of politics applies to us in the United States. We are accustomed to congratulate ourselves on our freedom from the evils of "secret diplomacy." None of us knew at the time how important a rôle our government was playing in this crisis. But some of the diplomatic conferences which went on in the White House—and on the tennis court behind it—were quite as important as those held in the little town hall of Algeciras, or in the porches of the Hotel Reina Cristina.

Our government has not even published a special "White Paper" on the subject: but it was the most important departure made from our "traditional policy" of non-intervention in European politics which has happened in recent years. And it is idle to turn to the publications of our government to discover what part we played. In the *Congressional Record* there is nothing about the Algeciras crisis beyond a bare account of Senator Bacon's vain attempt to get information on the subject laid before the Senate. In the State Department's publication on foreign relations there is very little more. It is necessary to turn to a French book—André Tardieu's "La Conférence d'Algesiras"—to get an inkling of what our diplomacy was about. In his index there are more references under Mr. Roosevelt's name than under Sir Edward Grey's—almost as many as under Delcassé. Our delegate, Mr. White, in every instance, voted on the French side.

One result of the conference was to greatly strengthen

the War Party in Germany. Those who really believed in the sacred mission of their race, those who put the ideal of the Deutschtum above mere peace, felt and loudly said that a grave mistake had been made in allowing the contest to take place in the field of diplomacy, where they were manifestly weak. There is little doubt that future German historians will blame the Kaiser for not having drawn the sword at this time.

If, for a moment, we grant the official German doctrine that they are called of God to spread the reign of the Deutschtum—this beneficent ideal of freedom in the realm of the spirit, and discipline and duty in the world of matter, this "system" of ordered and organized progress—it was a fatal mistake to keep the peace at the epoch of Algeciras.

The Kaiser, again and again, had professed this doctrine. At many times—although he apparently preferred to succeed in his mission by peaceful means—he had clearly told his people that they must be ready for war. Here was his chance.

Russia—France's one ally—was practically eliminated as a military power. The revolution was paralyzing what the Japanese had left of her army! And Russian public opinion had not then turned against Germany. The entente between France and England was still new. Whatever the diplomats thought about it, the people of the two nations were not ready for military coöperation. The idea of going to war to help France over a Morocco squabble would have been most unpopular in England. Great Britain might have—probably would have—come in, if Germany had attacked France. But there had been none of the moral preparation which lent great strength to their united action in 1914.

And in 1906 the breach between Italy and Austria had not become acute. The Franco-Italian entente had not developed the strength it has shown since. Even if she had not joined in an attack on France—as she was pledged not to do—she would probably have remained neutral.

régime. And some Englishmen read the writings of Homer Lea and von Bernhardi and were convinced that Germany was planning to annihilate them. They did not want war either, they wanted an army and navy so strong that Germany would be afraid to attack them. The great mass of the people did not worry much about foreign relations or imperial risks. Some few of the Liberals took such matters seriously and worked hard to lay the foundations of peace. Nobody wanted war. The British statesmen also wanted peace. As long as quarrels could be kept on the field of diplomacy, victory was so much surer and cheaper.

They all wanted something to which they quite sincerely believed they had a right. But it was highly improbable that the adversary would acknowledge that "right" without a fight. And on all sides there was a good deal of faith in bluffing. There were a good many threats of war by statesmen who did not really want to fight. Not everyone of them put certain considerations above peace. There were very few Tolstoists in the diplomatic service.

International politics have not furnished a very lofty picture of late—but no more have internal politics. There are not many Tolstoians in private life. Perhaps some future historian of a mathematical turn of mind will deduce for us a formula by which we can determine the ratio between the ethics which govern the actions of individuals and the moral standards which regulate the conduct of the nations to which they belong. We cannot reasonably expect diplomats to observe a higher standard of morality than members of Parliament and business men.

"Competition" is still the rule of life in the internal affairs of christendom. "Mutual aid" is as yet only a pious ideal. In industry everywhere we see this bitter spirit of conflict. One group of "oil-interests," to take one example—and it is just the same with the trade in milk or corsets—tries by hook or crook to get an advantage over its rivals, to gain supremacy in its particular world. We

They were able to point out with entire truth that the Powers of the Entente had extended their realms and their influence ten times as much in the last ten years as had the Powers of the Triple Alliance. Quite naturally the Germans refused to take the English sermons about the status quo with any seriousness.

And each side felt that the balance of power was iniquitous unless it fell more and more in their favor. France and England coöperated actively in reëstablishing the military and naval power of Russia. They worked hard—and the event has proved successfully—to weaken the Germanic group by seducing Italy from her alliance. Russian and Austrian diplomats were exceedingly busy in the Balkans trying to turn the balance of power down there in their favor. German diplomacy everywhere was trying to break up the unity of the Entente.

And everyone talked of peace. The Kaiser—unless he was absolutely and superhumanly insincere—meant that he wanted victory for the Deutschtum without having to fight for it. The Tsar also wanted peace—if the power of Slavdom could go on increasing without war. France wanted to escape definitely from the humiliatingly subordinate position in which Germany tried to keep her. Her colonial enthusiasts wanted to carry out their ambitions in Morocco without fighting anyone but the natives. And Great Britain—of course it is only figurative to speak of any of the nations as units. Many men have many minds.

Some Englishmen wanted to see Germany submit without fighting to their theory that they had a right to dominate the seas. Some Englishmen were more affected by the bitter trade rivalry and wanted their government to do something to reëstablish their former easy-going supremacy in the world's markets. They did not want war—certainly not if their profits could be protected by some peaceful means. Many of them believed that they could overcome the superior efficiency of German industry by a high tariff

CHAPTER VIII

EIGHT YEARS OF TENSION, 1906–1914. A. MOROCCO—BOSNIA.

The period which followed the Algeciras Conference was one of diplomatic insincerity. There were eight years of ever increasing tension. The storm-center swept back and forth from Morocco to the Balkans, but the issues were always fundamentally the same. Everyone talked of maintaining the status quo and conspired to alter it. Everyone gave lip-service to the balance of power and tried to upset it. Everyone preached peace and coveted the spoils of war.

Great Britain was the most outspoken defender of the status quo. But in these heated days it is a rare rule which works both ways. With Russia she sweepingly upset the status quo in Persia. She made no protest at changes in the map which benefited her other friend, France. But whenever Germany showed dissatisfaction with the existing frontiers, British statesmen were deeply shocked. "What we have, we hold," became a sort of watchword for a large class of Englishmen. It gave them a comfortable feeling of being real lovers of peace, who only kept their guns loaded out of fear of a German aggression. The Germans—rather fantastically—compared this attitude to that of a highway robber who refuses to give up his ill-gotten gains. It is hard for an outsider to reach a conclusion as to the validity of the British title to some of their possessions. They have always refused to discuss the matter. "Possession," according to their legal maxim, "is nine points of the law." And their fleet—their power to hold—was the other tenth. But the German case against Great Britain went much deeper than the attack on the validity of her title to all the seas and much of the earth.

And Turkey, then, as now, under German influence, had not been weakened by revolution and the defeats of the Balkan War.

Never again would there arise so favorable an opportunity for the German crusade. The Kaiser missed it.

see manufacturers uniting in powerful fighting ententes to resist in common the aspirations of their employees. We see the working men everywhere binding together in offensive and defensive alliances to fight for what they consider their "rights." With such rivalry and bitter conflict between neighbors it is hardly surprising that there has been little which could be called "peace" in the relations between nations.

The whole tangle of recent diplomacy has been immensely complicated by secrecy. Very few of the men, who are now fighting so desperately throughout the length and breadth of Europe realized during these years of tension how little they knew of what their governments—and often inner circles of their governments—were doing in their name. In each Foreign Office of Europe there was a man of mystery! To some degree at least, all of them were supposed to be responsible to the people, but none ever rendered a frank report of his activity.

Most—if not all—of the foreign ministers were honorable gentlemen, who would not steal a penny from a blind beggar, nor be cruel to a dog. And none of them wanted war. But all, without exception, had a very definite idea of the "manifest destiny" and "legitimate ambitions" of their country—all had "patriotic" ideals which seemed to them more sacred than peace.

So well-established was the tradition of secrecy in these matters that very few outsiders protested. Other honorable patriotic gentlemen assumed ministerial responsibility without thinking it necessary to inquire about what their colleague in the Foreign Office was doing. And when at last war broke out, three members of the British Cabinet resigned—committed political suicide in the face of a popular war—because they were horrified and *surprised* to discover where Sir Edward Grey and the inner circle of the ministry had brought the nation. And if Cabinet members did not know what the Secretary of State for Foreign Affairs was doing, it is evident that the people at large were led—perhaps wisely, but certainly blindly—like sheep to the slaughter.

Nothing which can be written about the diplomacy of our generation can claim the dignity of history. Almost every event of international politics is susceptible to diverse interpretations and is the subject of violent and bitter controversy. Many points will remain hopelessly uncertain until the archives are opened to future students.

During the last two years quite a number of secret treaties in regard to the intricate Balkan situation have been published, and no one knows how many have been signed during the course of this War. Any moment one government or another may publish a new collection of documents, or some minister out of office may write "indiscreet *mémoires*" which will force a new interpretation of events.

No one outside the Holy of Holies of the French and British Foreign Offices could pretend to define the nature of the agreements between these two governments, which have influenced their action during the last ten years. Was there a "second annex" to the Anglo-Russian accord similar to that known to have been added to the Entente Cordiale?

But in spite of these unknown quantities it is possible to trace through this period between the Conference of Algeciras and the Great War a certain rhythm of events, a swinging back and forth of the pendulum of power, a tendency towards more daring bluffs—an increasing tension.

Nothing succeeds like success and the diplomatic victory at Algeciras encouraged the anti-German forces to new efforts. There was the Spanish marriage and a general strengthening of the Mediterranean understandings, between France, Italy, Britain and Spain. And this grouping was soon strengthened by the Anglo-Russian Entente.

This document (signed 31st August, 1907) was in its form and substance similar to that between France and England. It was a colonial arrangement, eminently pacific in its phraseology. The two contracting parties liquidated their quarrels in Asia, where for so many years they had been bitter rivals. They came to terms over their disputes in Thibet and Afghanistan and they divided Persia into "spheres of influence." But of course even the partition of Persia was a side issue. The main object of the agreement was to avoid useless and dissipating friction over incidentals so that the two governments could work in harmony in the great European conflict, which was not mentioned.

If there was a secret annex to this convention it probably dealt—among other things—with the Balkans, and perhaps with the fate of Constantinople and the Straits.

A new crisis suddenly arose over an insignificant and vulgar brawl between some French officers and the German vice-consul in the Moorish port of Casablanca. On the 25th September, 1908, Herr Just tried to help six deserters from the French Foreign Legion to escape to a German ship in the harbor. The deserters were recognized by a policeman and in the row which followed their arrest, Herr Just's cane was broken. For a month Europe was *en crise* over this petty affair and for a week it looked as if war was inevitable.

The French government was so sure that it had right on its side that it wanted to arbitrate! The Germans said that if France would apologize for the vice-consul's broken cane they were willing to arbitrate on the amount of "damages." Great Britain and Russia "demonstrated" diplomatically. France stood firm on her original offer to arbitrate the whole incident. For several days the crisis was acute. Abruptly—as abruptly as she had precipitated the crisis—Germany gave in. (The Hague Tribunal did its duty gracefully, rendered a conciliating, Scotch verdict and sentenced both nations to apologize mutually for the undue zeal of their subordinate officers.)

Once more—according to the German explanation—the affair had been indirect. The Kaiser and his chancellor had not been especially interested in the fate of these deserters nor of the cane of Herr Just. France, they said, was not loyally observing the treaty of Algeciras and this incident served as a pretext to rap on the table and recall France to order.

But France was no longer so weak as when she had sacrificed M. Delcassé. The cohesion among the non-German states of Europe had grown stronger. The French army was more nearly prepared. The Algeciras Conference had given them confidence in England's loyalty: France was not going to throw over another foreign minister just because the Germans happened to dislike him.

And once more French diplomats had put their case with cleverness. It was an exceptionally good incident for arbitration. It would have been rank aggression for Germany to have insisted on war. The Kaiser had to give in. Another diplomatic defeat! There were wild denunciations of his peace-policy in the more rabid pan-Germanic newspapers.

There followed a period of diplomatic comings and goings which is hopelessly obscure. This Casablanca crisis had had a sobering effect. The matter at issue had been so trivial and war had been very near. No one except a few military lunatics wanted war. There were attempts at conciliations from all sides. All through these years of tension there were in each country fairly well organized groups who were working for peace. Momentarily at least they seem to have been told to go ahead and see what they could do.

King Edward visited the Kaiser and hopeful, friendly toasts were exchanged. There were "conversations" between Downing Street and Wilhelmstrasse. We do not know what went on in all these private conferences. But nothing definite was accomplished. The negotiations seem to have come to grief over the naval question. The Germans would not consent to recognize the validity of the British claims to sea-rule. And unless Germany would be good and stop building warships, it was not to be expected that the English would be friendly.

The "conversations" between France and Germany

had a more tangible result. A Moroccan agreement was reached.

" 9th February, 1909.

"The Government of the French Republic and the Imperial Government of Germany, animated by a mutual desire to facilitate the execution of the Act of Algeciras, have agreed to define the meaning which they give to its clauses, in order to avoid all cause of misunderstanding between them in the future.

"In consequence

"the Government of the French Republic, entirely attached to the maintenance of the integrity and independence of the Moorish Empire, is resolved to safeguard in Morocco economic equality, and therefore not to hinder the commercial or industrial interests of the Germans there;

"and the Imperial Government of Germany, pursuing only economic interests in Morocco; and on the other hand recognizing that the particular political interests of France there are closely connected with the consolidation of order and internal peace, is decided not to hinder these interests:

"They therefore declare that they will not continue nor undertake any measure of a nature to create in their favor or in the favor of any other power an economic privilege; and that they will endeavor to associate their citizens in the business for which they may obtain concessions."

The news of this accord was a great relief to the French. They did not want to go to war with Germany over Morocco, they wanted to give their undivided attention to their internal problems. And it looked as if this quarrel was over. But the matter was not so simple. This public declaration of good will was supplemented by some financial agreements, which were to give to German bankers a share in the exploitation of Morocco. The most important points were in regard to the railroads.

The French colonial authorities had planned a railroad which, connecting with their already developed system in Algeria, would enter Morocco across this eastern frontier and reach the inland capitals of Fez and Morocco City. Such a line would have for them two great advantages:

(I) Strategic. The French regularly maintained large garrisons in Algeria. Such a system would permit them at any time to throw their troops into the heart of Morocco.

(II) Economic. According to the *Acte d'Algesiras*, all nations were to have trade equality in the Moroccan ports. By establishing economic routes from central Morocco to Algeria all this rich commerce would be diverted to the Algerian ports where the regular French tariffs were in force.

The Germans, from economic reasons, and also no doubt to hinder the French strategic plans, wanted the railroad to have a terminus in a Moorish port where the rule of the open door applied. In this mood of conciliation which followed the affair of the Casablanca deserters the French conceded this point, and promised not to build any other railroads in Morocco until the line from Fez to Tangier was opened.

Perhaps, when the diplomatic archives of this period are opened, we will find that somewhere, somebody was making a sincere effort to lay the foundations of peace. From the scanty information now available it seems that everyone was saying: "If you let me have what I want I am willing to be your friend."

These half-hearted efforts towards conciliation might possibly have borne fruit in time, but suddenly all the foreign offices of Europe were thrown into confusion by the emergence of the Near Eastern question. Here again the most interesting point is obscure. Who financed the Young Turk Revolution?

An oriental despot cannot reign without making enemies among his own people and as Abdul Hamid had reigned a long time his enemies were legion. They fell into three groups. The most numerous were his personal enemies; typical "Old Turks," who felt that they had been mistreated. They were the "outs" who looked enviously at the crooked profits which were being made by those who were "in" on the remunerative business of government. There was a second group of army officers who had been trained in western military schools, mostly in Germany. They were young men, intensely Nationalists and bitterly opposed to the Sultan's policy of "selling Turkey to the foreigners." And there was a third group,—the real Young Turks—who were sincerely stirred by the ideas of the French Revolution and believed in the rights of men. But none of these groups had enough money to accomplish anything.

Suddenly these various elements centered about the Committee of Union and Progress in Salonika which had somehow gotten hold of the sinews of war. No one, who knows where this money came from, has told. Some people claim that it was in rubles, others that it was in twenty-mark pieces or francs, or pounds sterling. At all events it came from "the outside."

The Committee of Union and Progress was able to buy the allegiance of a couple of army corps by paying their back wages. They marched on Constantinople and the rotten old *régime* of Abdul Hamid fell to pieces. The idealistic element seems to have been in control at first. They made a large number of impressive speeches about brotherhood. They issued a number of resounding proclamations about liberty. But before they had time to begin to realize their high promises foreign aggression played into the hands of the military clique. Turkey was "attacked" by Austria and Bulgaria. Reforms had to be postponed in the face of danger. The hopeful element was shoved into the background and the revolution fell into the control of the army officers,—of whom Envers Bey has proved himself strongest.

The money which financed the first step in the movement probably was not in marks. The Germans had no interest in starting trouble, they were on the best possible terms with the old Sultan. They had their best diplomat, the

Baron Marschall von Bieberstein, at Constantinople. He had succeeded in displacing the British ambassador in the favor of Abdul Hamid. Under his management, the Kaiser had made his pilgrimage to Jerusalem, at Damascus had proclaimed his protection over the Mohammedans, at Constantinople had disfigured the old race-course of the emperors with an *art nouveau* fountain, and had secured the concessions for the famous Bagdad Bahn. The most hopeful future for the advance of German industry was in Turkey. Abdul Hamid had given them all the concessions they wanted. Germans were building railroads and harbors, opening mines and furnishing the army; everywhere their commerce was entering new Ottoman markets and pushing out all competitors. They had no reason to upset the old *régime*.

The Young Turks, in the first enthusiasm of their victory, were hostile to all the Sultan's friends and so were anti-German. Naturally the Germans were convinced that this unexpected set-back was caused by English gold. But von Bieberstein stuck to his post and soon won the Young Turks away from the influence of the Entente Powers, as he had previously won Abdul Hamid.

It was clever diplomacy on his part but most of the trumps were in his hand. If there is such a thing as "logical enmity" the Turks must inevitably hate the Russians. The English claim to have been "true friends" of Turkey, and they have in fact protected her from Russia in the past, but the price they put on their friendship—Cyprus and Egypt—was too high to encourage gratitude among the Turks. And all patriotic Moslems naturally tend toward friendship with the Germans. They do not know the Germans as well as they do the British and French, and Russians. These three Powers—the Entente—are those the Mohammedans think of when the conversation turns to "alien domination." The Germans have never had a chance to oppress the Moslems.

But the most important element of the recent politics

of the Near East is that no one any longer thinks that England will protect them from Russia. When Great Britain signed the Entente with the Tsar in 1907 she lost all individuality in the affairs of Persia and the Balkans. We, of the United States, are likely to think of Britain and France—as their own citizens do—as the principal element in the Entente group. But the people of the Near East always think of Russia first when the Entente is mentioned. The Roumanians, for instance, would not hesitate a moment if they had to choose between France and Austria. Perhaps the Bulgars would put more reliance in the pledge of England than in that of Germany. But as England and France are "disinterested" in the Balkans and have recognized the peninsula as a "zone of Russian influence," they have lost the benefit of the respect which went to them as individuals. They have become satellites of the Tsar. It is exceedingly improbable that any Turkish government—old or young—will live on good terms with the Russians, who so openly covet their capital. Von Bieberstein did not have a difficult time in persuading the Turkish revolutionists that their national interests were in accord with those of Germany.

The most formidable reverberation of the Turkish Revolution was the affair of Bosnia and Herzegovina.

Before starting her campaign against Turkey in 1877 it had been necessary for Russia to assure herself against attack from the flank. By an "agreement" signed at Reichstadt she secured from Austria a pledge of neutrality. The text of this treaty has not been published. But the terms of the deal are known. Russia promised to confine her activities to the eastern half of the Balkan Peninsula, and recognized the preponderant interest of Austria in the western half. It is probable, although this is not definitely known, that the two provinces of Bosnia and Herzegovina were specifically mentioned as coming within the Austrian sphere of influence.

At the Congress of Berlin, the next year, all the other

Powers were trying to minimize Russia's gain in the Balkans. As the Bulgars were a Slavic people, and had been "liberated" by the Tsar, it was generally thought that they would be a docile protectorate of Russia. So the Powers cut Bulgaria to pieces and gave more than two-thirds of it back to Turkey. And to further offset this diminished Russian gain, her rival, Austria, was given special rights in Bosnia and Herzegovina. They were left under nominal Turkish sovereignty, but the rights granted to Austria were not unlike those we hold on the Canal zone. Our treaty with the republic of Panama says that we are to enjoy the same privileges and responsibilities on this strip of land as if we were the real sovereign. The Congress of Berlin established a very similar *régime* in this case. It was veiled annexation and no one doubted that in due time the veil would be removed.

The Young Turks had the disastrous daring to act on the letter and not the spirit of the Berlin treaty. They tried to treat Bosnia and Herzegovina as if they were really part of the Turkish empire. The statesmen at Vienna had become so used to ruling this territory that they had almost forgotten the technical flaw in the deed. They were startled by the news that this new government at Constantinople was asking these two provinces to elect deputies to the Turkish parliament. To put a stop to such foolishness, Franz Josef announced the formal annexation of Bosnia and Herzegovina which he had been governing for thirty years.

This action was technically a violation of international law—a treaty signed by the Great Powers of Europe was slightly altered by one of them without the consent of the others. But the Austrians were probably sincerely surprised by the ruction this little misdeed caused. The Berlin treaty was already old and decrepit. In diplomatic history such a document becomes of age in ten years, at twenty it has passed its prime and begun its decline. Everyone who had cared to, had already broken the treaty, some of its clauses had never been enforced. Austria had watched most of her neighbors take greater liberties with "international law" without protesting.

But Bosnia and Herzegovina were inhabited by Slavs of the Serb branch. No one had thought that mattered in 1878. But the "theory of nationality" had been growing popular of late. The Serbs, having "removed" a king of Austrian sympathies, had given the throne to the present dynasty, which is pro-Russian. They had projects of incorporating Bosnia-Herzegovina in a Greater Serbia. And while they could have reasonable hopes of sometime conquering this territory from the Turks, nobody in 1909 dreamed that Serbia could fight a successful war with Austria. So the Serbs appealed to Russia to prevent this transfer which stood in the way of the pan-Serb dream.

The Tsar does not sit any too firmly on his throne. He needs the support of every reactionary element in his realm, he cannot with impunity offend any of them. And the pan-Slavs—or Slavophiles, as they call themselves—are one of the important elements in his internal policy. During the revolutionary movement of 1905-1907 the Society of the True Russian People had been one of the pillars of loyalism. These reactionary organizations were insistent that the Tsar should protect the orthodox Slavs of the Balkans against the catholics of Austria. So the Russian Foreign Office protested against the Austrian action and precipitated a new crisis.

Once more the affair was complicated by secret diplomacy. There is strong reason to believe that before starting out for the Japanese War, Russia had again—as before her war with Turkey—taken action to insure Austrian neutrality. She had probably renewed the treaty of Reichstadt and again acknowledged Austria's "rights" in Bosnia and Herzegovina. So, being in a weak position to protest against the annexation, Russia took the attitude that the entire Near Eastern question needed attention and demanded a new congress of the six Great Powers to revise the treaty of Berlin.

In such a congress, Russia was sure of the support of Great Britain and France. At Algeciras Italy had voted against her allies. And Italy was especially afraid of Austrian advance in Albania where she had "legitimate ambitions" of her own. She was nearly sure to vote with the Entente Powers in a Balkan dispute. Naturally Germany and Austria did not want to go to a congress of six Powers, where they were sure to find three hostile votes and probably a fourth.

The Tsar, to satisfy his pan-Slav supporters, insisted. The Kaiser "donned his shining armor." In the speech in which he used this famous phrase he made it clear that he was ready to fight beside his ally rather than consent to the congress.

The situation was strikingly similar to that which arose in the summer of 1914—only in 1909 the Tsar was bluffed out. If it came to war France was prepared to stand by her alliance and back Russia to the utmost, but she was not enthusiastic about going to war over the Balkans. And as far as she could, without seeming to try to escape from the obligation of her treaty, she urged Russia to make concessions.

But the most important aspect of this crisis was that England was evidently reluctant to fight on behalf of Serbia. The Balkans were not mentioned in any of her Ententes. The British Foreign Office worked feverishly for peace.

There were very cogent arguments which her friends could bring to bear on Russia. She was in no condition for a great war. She was in the midst of a vast military reorganization—necessitated by her Japanese defeat. Under English advice—as France was helping her with her army— she was laying the plans for a new fleet. She would not begin to feel the advantage of this great effort till 1912 or 1913, it would not be completed till 1916 or 1917. If it was necessary to fight Germany—as most people hoped it was not, but feared it might be—it was manifestly wise to postpone the clash. Every year was a great gain in strength of German construction. Their traders had, by bona-fide commerce, established themselves in the various ports. Some of their enterprises, however—like the mining ventures of the Mannesmann Brothers—were highly speculative. These German merchants did not get on well with the French officials. They claimed—a claim borne out by all other non-French merchants—that the promise of economic equality was being violated.

And France had not lived up to her railroad agreement. "Circumstances over which she had no control" had forced her to commence other lines before work was begun on the Fez-Tangier system. All Europeans in Morocco believed that France was preparing to tear up the Algeciras treaty and proclaim a protectorate. And this, in spite of the fact that the French Parliament, at every opportunity, was solemnly voting to observe the treaty.

The matter came to a head in April, 1911. The European telegraphic news agencies began to tell of disorders—or threatened disorders—in Fez. The Germans in this city reported that no trouble was visible to the naked eye. But a certain section of the Parisian newspapers—those especially favored by the Comité Marocain—began to clamor for a military expedition to protect the lives of the European residents in Fez. The stage was being set for the last act of the comedy. ("Comedy" of course applies only to the European aspect of the case. It was pure "tragedy" for the Moors who loved their independence.)

The curtain was rung up on this last act by a note sent out from the Quai d'Orsay to the various Foreign Offices announcing that—with heartfelt regrets—it had been decided to despatch an army into the interior to protect the lives of Europeans. "Circumstances over which . . ." etc.

The expedition to Fez was the "last straw" as far as German patience was concerned. However, the German government did not act abruptly. The chancellor told the French minister at Berlin that he could not regard this expedition with indifference: he was, however, willing to give the French the benefit of the doubt. If the military expedition to Fez performed the mission promptly and returned to the coast without infringing on the sovereignty of the Sultan and the independence of Morocco, he would still consider the *Acte d'Algesiras* in force. If, however—his warning was formal—the French army established itself in the interior or went beyond its avowed intention of protecting European lives, he would consider that France had torn up the treaty, and that Germany would act as though no treaty had existed, according to her own interests.

The responsibility of the French people in this shabby affair is not very clear. The case illustrates one of the unsolved problems of democracy. How many of us, Americans, are sure of the ethical justification of our own "action" in Nicaragua? We read in the papers one morning that our marines had been landed and that there was some fighting. Most of us were busy that morning, we know that we did not know what it was all about—so we forgot it. What happened? Are our marines still there? So it was in France. The great mass of the people did not know what was happening in Morocco. Few had read the text of the railroad agreement. They did not have the facts at hand to know that this military expedition was only the most flagrant of a long series of violations of the pledged word of the republic. They had entrusted—just as we have—their foreign relations to a department of the government, which worked in secret.

It is in just such matters that the French form of government is weakest. Between the signing of the Algeciras Treaty and this expedition to Fez, dozens of different ministers of foreign affairs had been established at the Quai d'Orsay. Some of them had held office several months, some a few days. Some of them were bitterly anti-German, some of them were in favor of a *rapprochement* with their old enemies. Some of them were the tools of entirely unpatriotic financial interests. The result was a hodgepodge. Abruptly a minister who blew hot was followed by a minister who blew cold. The methodical Germans could hardly be expected to understand this merry-go-round. The change in the point of view of the French Foreign Office was often quite as sharp as the changes in our policy towards Latin-America,—Root,—Knox,—Bryan.

The military expedition settled down in Fez and pushed out in all directions. The German government decided to "act." And here again we have—parenthetically—a point of especial interest to Americans: Did Germany ask our government to join her in a protest against the violation of this Algeciras Treaty, which we had signed five years before? There are many indications that they did—but our government has not taken us into its confidence. At all events, Mr. Taft, remembering our "traditional policy" of non-intervention in the affairs of Europe—which Mr. Roosevelt had momentarily forgotten when he sent delegates to Algeciras—made no protest.

The average Frenchman did not know any more about the diplomacy of this country than the average American knows about ours.

So they were sincerely surprised and deeply outraged when they read in their newspapers that the German warship "Panther" had cast anchor (1st July, 1911) in the Moroccan port of Agadir—by way of protest. As they did not know why the Germans were protesting, this action looked like an unwarranted aggression.

But the German position was very clear. It is doubtful if they ever had a sounder ethical basis for pounding the table. "If," they said, "you are going to conquer Morocco, in violation of your repeated promises, we want our share. It is you who are upsetting the status quo, not we."

But if Germany—noticing the reluctance of Great Britain to being drawn into the quarrel over Bosnia and Herzegovina—had concluded that the Entente was weakening, she was sadly mistaken. Mr. Lloyd George, in a speech in the Mansion House in London, "donned his shining armor." The British home fleet cleared for action. The Germans discovered that when they touched any of the interests mentioned in the Ententes, the three Powers—England, Russia and France—were shoulder to shoulder. The crisis lasted several months, all through a very hot summer, and at last Germany gave in. On 4th November, 1911, a new Franco-German agreement was signed by which the Kaiser recognized the French protectorate over Morocco and received as "compensation" a large but unhealthy slice of Congo swamp.

It was the most serious blow the Deutschtum had yet received. The bitterness in Germany was great; it was much worse than the Algeciras fiasco. The Kaiser's government certainly ought not to have made its rude and aggressive protest unless it was prepared to follow it through. This time they had been bluffed out. But their troubles were not over.

From this time on events followed each other so rapidly that it is hard to distinguish one crisis from another. Tension became chronic.

Before the Agadir affair had been concluded, Italy declared war on Turkey (September, 1911).

By the Delcassé entente, Italy had recognized France's "rights" in Morocco and France had recognized Italian "rights" in the Tripolitan. (The text of this agreement has not been published, but there is little doubt that this deal was included.) And Italy grasped the opportunity—afforded by the fact that everyone's attention was centered on the Franco-German quarrel—to realize this section of her "legitimate ambitions."

Her move was decidedly distasteful to the Germans. First, because the Kaiser was posing as the friend of Turkey and the protector of Islam. He was not only unable to protect the Mohammedans of Morocco from his enemy, the French—but he could not even keep his ally from declaring war on Turkey. It very seriously threatened to compromise the work of the Deutschtum in the Near

East. And secondly—of more importance in the general politics of Europe—this independent act of Italy showed that the bonds of the Triple Alliance were weakening. Italy's harmless flirtation with France, which von Bülow had called *un tour de valse*, was becoming serious. Italy had dared to work, not only without the consent of Germany, but contrary to the interests of the Germans. Decidedly the prestige of the Deutschtum was in a decline.

CHAPTER IX

EIGHT YEARS OF TENSION. B. THE BALKANS

WHILE Turkey was signing away to Italy her last province in Africa—October, 1912—the Balkan alliance declared war on the Sultan and raised a new crisis—the last which passed without a general European war.

It is almost hopeless to try to untangle the immensely intricate and obscure problems which have given to the Balkan Peninsula so tragic a rôle in the affairs of Europe. There are the age-old conflicts between the christian victims and their Turkish oppressors. There are the more recent but equally bitter conflicts between the christian nationalities themselves. There is the intense struggle between the two groups of Great Powers. And to confound confusion there is the fact, often ignored, that the members of each group—both the Alliance and the Entente—have conflicting interests in the Balkans. The ambitions of Italy and Austria in Albania are exactly opposite. Great Britain and France have had to sacrifice their own interests as well of those of civilization in general in order to give the Tsar a "free hand" in this zone of influence.

However, the importance of the Balkans in the cause and course of this War has been so great that it is necessary to try to compress some of the main elements of the problem into a special chapter.

One fact stands out firm from all the confused and conflicting legends of the past. The Balkan Peninsula is the threshold of Europe. The narrow waters of the Dardanelles, the mountains of Albania, have watched the passage of almost every invasion which has come out of Asia. Very likely in the shadowy days of pre-history, ape-like men with broad foreheads broke their stone axes on the longer skulls of other ape-like men they called barbarians. It is probable that Hittite adventurers invaded the land. The Persian army passed that way towards its defeats in Greece. History begins with the coming of the Roman soldiers who conquered the country. They stayed long enough to leave a marked strain of their blood and the memory of their language to their half-breed descendants.

The Slavs first appeared in the Balkans near the beginning of the second century. Some tribes came by the shores of the Black Sea, others came down from the north by the passes of the Carpathians. They grew in number and in military power. In 512 the Basileus Anastasius had to build a wall twenty feet high around Constantinople to keep them out. They had raided even into the suburbs of the Imperial City.

Most that we know about them comes from the old Byzantine chronicles, which refer to them parenthetically, between more detailed accounts of ecclesiastical disputes. These Greek historians were not ethnologists. Sometimes they called the raiders Huns, sometimes Gepides, or Serbs or Bulgars or Avars. They were more likely to describe the clothes of these barbarians or their method of fighting, than the shape of their skulls or the peculiarities of their dialects.

Apparently they all came from the steppes—and no history was written in those days in the country which is now Russia. As far as there was any real difference between these invaders, it may have been that some, coming by the Black Sea coast, had the habits of lowlanders, and some having come down from the mountains wore more fur. This is one of the highly speculative hypotheses put forward with a great show of erudition to explain the differences between the modern Bulgars and Serbs. It is quite as plausible as the rival theories. At all events, out of all the successive tribes which came by the coastal route and naturally settled more to the east—the Bulgars imposed their name on the rest. And gradually the tribes which came down from the north and settled in the more mountainous country of the western Balkans and along the littoral of the Adriatic, acquired the habit of calling themselves Serbs and Croats.

During the centuries before the coming of the Turks, there was a constant flux and flow. Sometimes a strong man, like Justinian, ruled at Constantinople and reduced the Slavs to allegiance even beyond the Danube. Sometimes a western chief, who called himself a Serb, conquered his neighbors and founded a short-lived dynasty. And a few years—or decades—later the great chief of the Slavs called himself a Bulgar.

Every shred of evidence we have supports the common-sense supposition that the mixing of races was intense.

The fastnesses of the mountains were centers of a sort of brigand cosmopolitanism. It is a fact well known to ethnologists that the more inaccessible the mountain districts, the more mixed is the breed. In the face of each new invasion of the low countries, the irreconcilables flee to the mountains and there, in new and hard conditions, they strive to maintain the old customs and the familiar tongue. So we find Gaelic still spoken in the Highlands of Scotland, Basque in the Pyrenees, Berber in the Atlas. And before the Slav inundation some of the old language of the Cæsars was preserved in the mountains of Albania and Transylvania. But although the dialect is preserved in such circumstances, the purity of the blood is soon lost. To the mountains flee all the excommunicated of the lowlands, those who dislike civilization and those whom civilization dislikes. And the men of the mountains, when they raid down into the plain, take back with them such women as they chance to lay hands upon.

In the fourteenth century the Turks crossed the Dardanelles into Europe. In 1361, Murad I. captured Adrianople and made it his capital. Dissensions among their victims made conquest easy for the Turks. Sofia was taken in 1382. The battle of Kossovo, which overthrew the western Slavs, was in 1389. And Constantinople fell on the 29th of May, 1453.

Until the beginning of the last century the christian population led a life of passive submission. But by the middle of the century the Greeks, the Serbs, and the Roumanians (who had come down from the mountains of Transylvania and had occupied the lower valley of the Danube) had established semi-independent principalities on the fringes of the Ottoman empire. The Serbs of the small mountain top of Montenegro had never entirely lost their independence. But none of these races had been able to extend their national organization to more than a small percentage of the people who spoke their language.

In 1877 there came the Russo-Turkish War, followed by the Congress of Berlin. The independence which these little states had already gained was formally admitted by the great Powers, a fraction of Bulgaria was added to their number and the concert of Europe solemnly announced that the status quo so created, should never be changed. But of course all these little incompleted states at once set to work to accomplish their national unity and bring in the "unredeemed." No one who applauds the movement for national unity in Italy or Germany can blame them in the least.

These little states were not strong enough to hope to liberate their oppressed brothers single-handed. They had to look for help to the great Powers and so "foreign intrigue"—the curse of the Balkans—was introduced.

The first political grouping of the great Powers grew out of the treaty of Reichstadt, mentioned above, whereby Russia claimed predominating interests in the eastern half of the Balkans and recognized Austria's similar claim in the west. So at first the Tsar had no interest in Serbia and centered his attentions on Bulgaria. England and Austria—at the Congress of Berlin—had been very hostile to the Bulgars, who, as they thought, would form a Russian advance post. They had insisted on giving most of the Bulgars back to the Sultan.

When Bulgaria made her first step towards the realization of national unity by absorbing eastern Roumelia, which the Congress of Berlin had made a Turkish province, Austria—and in those days the English were hand in glove with the Hapsburgs—persuaded Serbia to declare war (September, 1885). But Austria has always proved a bad guesser in the Balkans. She backed the wrong horse. The Bulgars defeated the Serbs at Slivnitza—18 November, 1885.

But the Bulgars had suffered so much from servitude, had fought so hard for liberty, that these words had taken deep root in their consciousness. It took them some time to realize that the Tsar liberator was only a new oppressor, that the big Slav sister could be just as tyrannical as the Turk. But once they made up their mind to it, they acted promptly. Under the leadership of an uneducated but enterprising patriot named Stamboulov, they ousted the Russians and the figure-head king who had been imposed on them.

Through an interregnum Stamboulov reigned as dictator. His methods were not unlike those of Diaz in Mexico. He was ruthless, but above all determined that Bulgaria should not become a Russian province. Of course in this attitude he was cordially supported by England and Austria. In those days any enemy of Russia was sure of encouragement from London. Under the leadership of Stamboulov and of their new sovereign Ferdinand of Saxe Coburg-Gotha (on his mother's side a grandson of Louis Philippe of France), who ascended the throne in 1887, the work of making a nation out of the newly liberated Bulgar peasants went on with progressive success.

Constitutionally Bulgaria, with its single legislative chamber, is the most democratic monarchy in Europe. Almost entirely agricultural, it is free from the curse of landlordism. Most of the population is composed of peasant proprietors who are very generally prosperous. And—as is inevitably true in a democratic community—they are greatly attached to public education. There were practically no schools when the Turks were driven out in 1877. Today almost all the young recruits in the army can read and write. In their primary schools forty-five per cent of the children are girls. And female education is practically unknown in the other countries of southeastern Europe.

Aside from these problems of internal organization, the one thing which passionately interests the Bulgars is the liberation of their brothers in Macedonia. Roughly fifty per cent of the leaders of Bulgaria—cabinet ministers, army officers, school teachers, and clergy, are of Macedonian origin. I happened to be in Sofia one day which was the anniversary of some special Macedonian massacre. It was the custom for all those who came from Macedonia or had relatives there, to hang out a flag bound in crape. There was hardly a house in all the capital which did not display the symbol of mourning—and of hope.

The Serbian problem has had a different character. In the first days of her "independence" she was a sort of feudal appanage of Austria. The Tsar was "disinterested" in her fate. While much of her traditions tended to draw her towards Macedonia, where some of the heroes of her legends had ruled, her aspirations turned inevitably towards the north. As the national spirit which was fomenting all over Europe awoke in Serbia, her patriots discovered that it was the house of Hapsburg which stood in the way of their "legitimate ambitions." The language spoken by the peasants of the Austrian provinces of Dalmatia, Herzegovina, Bosnia, Slavonia, Croatia, and Istria, was the same as—or very near to—their own. As their savants dug up the forgotten traditions of the past they discovered that all this mass of southern Slavs had come down into the Balkans from the north by the same passes over the Carpathians that had been the road of their own ancestry. Some of these tribes had at one time or another given allegiance to their mediæval kings. Here to the north lay their "manifest destiny."

It was a dream no more presumptuous than that of

Garibaldi or Fichte. Its realization was rendered the more possible by two factors,—(1) the Hapsburg misrule—(2) the growing Slavophile movement in Russia. The Slav population of the Dual Monarchy had ample reasons for discontent. And the Russian government was only too glad to encourage private societies—and unofficially their consuls—who carried on an agitation so embarrassing to their traditional enemy, the Austrians.

However, Serbia was very small and Austria-Hungary very large and quite as unscrupulous as large. The house of Hapsburg, warned by the rise of their rivals of Savoy, smarting under the loss of their fair Italian provinces, did not intend to tolerate more of such nonsense on a new frontier. They had two classic methods of statescraft— bribing and bullying. They bought up the Obrenovitch dynasty, which then reigned at Belgrade, and also a controlling interest in the "court." Whenever the Sobranje showed signs of discontent at the arrangement, Austrian troops were mobilized across the frontier or recourse was had to the less spectacular but more efficient "pig-disease diplomacy." Serbia had no outlet to the sea. Her principal export was live-stock, driven across the frontier to the Austrian markets. Whenever the foreign office in Vienna disapproved of Serbian politics, the health authorities discovered cholera among the Serbian pigs and commerce was interrupted until the Serbs became docile again. Long acquaintance with such economic strangulation has given the Serbs a subsidiary aspiration. They wish, not only to unite all their race under one flag, but also to have a commercial outlet on the Adriatic.

Russia, having lost the game in Bulgaria, turned to Serbia. And at last with the connivance if not the actual coöperation of the Russian legation at Belgrade, a band of Serbian officers broke into the palace and killed the Obrenovitch king and queen. (The more one studies the lives of this kinglet and his consort, the less reason one finds to regret their sudden death.) The rival dynasty, Karageorovitch, was called to the throne. Peter, the present king, understood which side of his bread was buttered, and has been consistently pro-Russian in his politics.

So there was a complete turn in the political whirlgig. Russia, in a pet against Bulgaria, became the protector of the Serbs. Austria and England, outraged over the Belgrade regicide, became backers of Bulgaria. Few, if any, of the Balkan people, were so naïf as not to see the small value of such vacillating friendships. The great Powers only cared for them as pawns in the all absorbing game of balancing power. General disregard for the wishes or welfare of these people struggling up from Turkish oppression towards civilization had been clear enough at the Congress of Berlin. And scarcely a year has passed since, when some new lesson on this point has not been given them.

Few things have been more grotesque than the way some of the great Powers have—in the course of this War—appealed to the "gratitude" of the Balkan people in an effort to get them to fight their battles for them. If there is one thing about this War to make the great gods grin it must be the idea of a British minister at Sofia asking the Bulgars to drive the Turks out of Constantinople in gratitude for the English friendship. It was Disraeli at the Congress of Berlin who threw back to the Unspeakable Turk two-thirds of the Bulgar people. To be sure, the English encouraged Stamboulov in his struggle against the Tsar, but that burst of friendship only lasted until 1907 when, by her entente with Russia, Great Britain withdrew from the Balkans and left her "friends" to their fate. The Bulgar memories of their Russian liberators are equally painful. They have about as much reason to be grateful to the Entente Powers as the United States of Colombia has to be grateful to us.

The other states of the Balkans have as little reason to put faith in the fair promises of the great Powers.

Roumania stands quite apart from the other Balkan

nations. She was Latinized by the Roman conquest. They came by their language in much the same way that the Goths of Gaul developed the present French speech. It is doubtful if there ever were 50,000 Roman citizens in Gaul, but none the less France was Latinized. And so, although there is probably very little Italian blood in the Roumanian veins, they are Latin in speech.

The historical development of this country has not been parallel to that of her neighbors. In the first place, being on the outskirts of the Ottoman empire, she was never thoroughly brought into the Turkish system. The Sultans ruled her indirectly by tribute-paying governors, generally christians of Greek origin. Most of the mediæval aristocracy was of this alien stock and a feudal system of land tenure was developed.

Roumania was freed from Turkey more by diplomatic intervention than by insurrection. The gentry was naturally interested in the Greek struggle, but the Roumanian peasants never learned those lessons in national consciousness which come from fighting for liberty. The liberal ideas of '48 had their reverberation in Roumania and a group of young radicals, momentarily in power, arranged a parlor revolution. The titles of nobility were abolished and the word "serf" removed from the law books. But the mass of the people did not know what was going on and nothing happened to show them that the words were changed. Roumania remains today the most feudal country in Europe.

Its people are exceedingly rich or dolefully poor. The alluvial wheat lands are divided up into great estates. For generations the landlords have reaped large and easy profits from the soil. Some years ago oil began to bubble up through the wheat fields, and Roumania has become one of the great oil producers of the world. This facile wealth has built palatial manor houses throughout the country-side, it has made Bucharest one of the gayest and gaudiest capitals in Europe. The habitual stakes in "bridge" at the casino of Constanza are said—it is a frequent boast—to be the highest in the world.

The mass of the people are the poorest and most illiterate in Europe.

Political life centers in Bucharest. It is the picturesque politics of personalities. Each of the parties has a high sounding name—National Conservative, Constitutional Liberal, or the like—but they are generally called by the name of their leader. There are no popular political organizations, no public opinion outside of the capital. In a broad way the half dozen parliamentary groups fall in "the party of the pure and simple wheat-growers" and "the party of wheat-growers who also own oil wells."

It is hardly possible to find a sharper contrast in Europe than to cross the Danube from the mediævalism of Roumania to the very modern democracy of Bulgaria, with its universal education, up-to-date sanitary laws, its small farmers and coöperative societies.

In 1877 when Russia attacked Turkey, it was necessary to march through Roumania as, in 1914, Germany found it necessary to march through Belgium. Roumania did not resist and so did not get hacked through. But not content with this "benevolent neutrality" Russia, after her first defeat at Plevna, demanded active help. Their country occupied by the Russians, the Roumanians could not refuse. Their army reached Plevna in time for the unsuccessful general attack of 11th September. The affair settled down to a siege. Osman Pasha had 60,000 men and 77 cannons. The christian allies mustered 150,000 men and 600 cannons. But it was not till the 10th of December that they starved the Turks out.

At the Congress of Berlin the hostile European coalition forced Russia to disgorge most of her Turkish spoils. In revenge she annexed the Roumanian province of Bessarabia. Naturally the Roumanians do not feel any traditional gratitude towards Russia nor to the other Great Powers who permitted this brutal spoliation.

Roumania has—or theoretically ought to have—an aspiration towards "national unity." The Austro-Hungarian provinces of Transylvania and Bukovina are largely inhabited by peasants of the Roumanian tongue. There is also the "lost province" of Bessarabia. But the mass of the Roumanians are too illiterate to have any public opinion on such a subject. Most of the peasants never heard of these unredeemed brethren. And even if they had national aspirations, the landlord politicians of Bucharest would pay no attention to them, unless they saw some way to utilize "public opinion" to their own profit.

In the first year of this War, it was manifestly to their advantage to stay neutral and sell their grain and oil to the central empires. They did.

The Greek struggle for independence was centered in the decade from 1820 to 1830. To an even greater extent than with the other Balkan nationalities, this movement towards unity was incomplete. A large part of the main land which was indisputably Greek, in language, traditions and sentiments—northern Thessaly, Pinde and Epirus—and most of the Greek isles, were left under Turkish misrule. So little did the Great Powers in the Congress of Berlin care for the Greek nation that Great Britain was allowed to take Cyprus. So far as the Greek aspirations were limited to these territories of undoubted Greek population, they were quite as sound as those of Garibaldi for Venice. Those Greeks who fought for independence have no reason to be grateful to the Great Powers. The story of Crete is typical of the whole disillusioning affair. In spite of the lyric Hellenism of Byron and Shelley, Venezelos and his Cretan comrades know that it was not the Turks they had to fight so much as the concert of Europe.

However, many of the Greek ambitions were inflated beyond measure. Their pretence of being the heirs of and the legitimate successors to the Byzantine empire of Justinian was pure phantasy.

The Greeks are a sea-side people; this is one of the main

determining factors of their history. It must always be borne in mind in considering their problems. And sea-going people—like mountaineers—are always hybrid. In the mainland it is impossible to get a hundred miles from the coast. In the great days of Pericles, it is probable that ninety per cent of the Greeks lived within walking distance of the sea. The majority of those who speak the language have lived in islands. They are a sea-faring, colonizing, trading people. It is typical that Venezelos, their leading politician, is a Cretan.

Alexander of Macedon led the Greeks, whom he had conquered, on an inland adventure. And in the literal sense of the word every Greek you find beyond the smell of salt water is an adventurer. They are an adventurous race. They "leave home" as easily as the English. The analogy could be pushed much farther without exaggeration. In every sea-port in the world you will find Greeks.

In the days of their glory their civilization and language was supreme in all the islands of the eastern Mediterranean. They had colonized southern Italy and the Ionic coast of Asia Minor. Long after their armies had ceased to exist their culture was still winning victories. It was after Athens had fallen under the Roman impact that the Greek school of Alexandria reached its flower. And it was at Constantinople, not at Athens, that the Greek church had its origin.

Their rôle in the Balkans was typical. A Macedonian chieftain, Philip, conquered them; his son Alexander led them to their greatest military glory. The Romans conquered their homeland, but their language overcame Latin in Constantinople. They were able to change the name of the eastern capital to Byzantium. How many native Greeks there were, who accomplished this cultural revolution, is a vexed question. There is little evidence of any great migration, but Greek trading colonies had long been established in all the ports of the Ægean and Black seas. It is not necessarily numbers which win in such conflicts.

Government in those days was largely a matter of administrative bureaucracies. The Greeks were soon the predominating element in the civil service of the eastern empire. And Byzantium became Greek in the same sense that Gaul became Latin. It is interesting to note how English is gradually replacing Turkish in the administration of Egypt.

While the number of Greeks in the capital was probably large, there is no evidence that the inland races of the Balkans were affected by the change in language.

This cultural predominance by a small numerical minority was intensified by the Ottoman conquest. The Turks overthrew all political institutions in the conquered territory but respected the religious organizations. Infidels were, in theory, outlaws; the Turkish government had nothing to do with them as individuals and dealt with them only through the channels of the established church. So the Greek patriarch of Constantinople became the sole protector of the Balkan christians.

Through the long centuries of Turkish domination this arrangement made religious unity the one rallying point of the oppressed natives. In the early days and specially in times of tribulation the Greek prelate often took his position with great seriousness and performed his dangerous functions with nobleness. However, the hierarchy was not entirely composed of saints; some of the patriarchs fell below their duty.

With the last century this religious arrangement became intolerable. The spirit of nationalism was in direct opposition to the catholic and cosmopolitan theory of the church. Serbian or Bulgarian patriotism was considered heresy against christian brotherhood. And all too often the patriarch at Constantinople became the chieftain of Greek nationalism. Ill advised efforts were made to force the flock to become Greek in nationality as well as in religion. The desire for a national church on the part of the Slavs of the Balkans became intense.

According to canon law, only an independent nation

could have an autonomous church organization. As soon as the Greeks and Serbs won their independence, they escaped from the control of Constantinople by establishing patriarchs of their own. The Bulgars, unwilling to stand the continued effort to de-nationalize them, created a schism and organized—1870—an heretical church called the Exarchate. There was no noticeable question of doctrine involved, it was only a nationalist movement. The Turks encouraged it as they did not object to divisions among their subject races. The new arrangement—three churches instead of one—did not lead to more amiable communion among the saints.

This triangular religious conflict, complicated as it was by secular nationalistic rivalries, bore its most bitter fruits in Macedonia. It is a very hard district to define. Roughly it is the central portion of the Balkan Peninsula. It has a large frontage on the Aegean Sea from the Gulf of Salonika to the mouth of the River Struma and extends back into the hinterland until districts are reached where the population is indisputably Serb or Greek. I have never found any two maps of Macedonia which exactly agree in frontiers. But as a general proposition "Macedonia" is the territory stretching from the Struma on the east to Lake Okrida on the west, from the undetermined border of Greek Thessaly on the south to the Serb frontier on the north.

To complete a description of Macedonia it is necessary to add that in all the ports on the Aegean—as is true of the harbor towns throughout the eastern Mediterranean—there are large Greek settlements, which even in those cases where they do not constitute a majority of the population, predominate in influence. Most of the commerce is carried on in the Greek language. But the cases are few where the Greek population has spread back into the interior. In Macedonia as elsewhere, the Greek civilization has kept its essentially sea-side character.

Much of eastern Macedonia, considerably more than half, is indisputably Bulgar. Central and western Macedonia is a "no man's land" or more truly an "everybody's land." The population is hopelessly mixed.

The religious struggle tore this unhappy district to tatters. The more exalted patriots of the three bordering states felt that it was the "manifest destiny" of their flag to fly over all of Macedonia. Bulgar and Greek and Serb bands held revival meetings at the point of the sword in an effort— nominally religious, really nationalistic—to make the Macedonians join their church. Now and then these bands joined hands to fight the Turkish oppressor, but most of the time they fought each other. Not infrequently they sacked the opposition churches and crucified the rival priests.

It is idle to try to partition the responsibility for this hideous condition. It was about as bad as it could be and it would be very much harder to find anyone who was really innocent than to collect any number of people who had some of the blood on their hands.

The capacity for such devastation is undoubtedly great among the native populations, but whenever any of these bands ran out of ammunition they could generally secure the sinews of war from the nearest consulate. Russia of course wanted Serbia to get Macedonia and Austria was backing Bulgaria. Before the Entente of 1907 the British newspapers were horrified at the Russian intrigues in the Balkans. Since that date they have denounced the activity of the Austrians.

It is also idle to try to get at the rights of the case by reading the official "propaganda" literature. The conflicting parties have shown themselves every bit as capable of padding statistics as they have of the cruder kinds of atrocities.

One fact is beyond dispute. There is no such thing as a pure race in these parts. Neither the Serb, nor Greek, nor Bulgar are, in any biological sense "pure." The population of Macedonia is a mixture of these hybrid stocks. Another certainty is that the great preponderance in the mixture is Slavic. Greek culture has greatly outspread the actual number of Greeks in the population. But in spite of the fact that up till 1800 all the schools and churches were Greek, the common tongue of the district is Slavic.

It is much more difficult to distinguish between the claims of the Serbs and Bulgars as the difference between their dialects is not great. However, whatever the ethnological affinities of the Macedonians, it is pretty well established that most of them think of themselves as Bulgars, rather than as Serbs. It is a noticeable fact that the fugitives from the misery of Macedonia go for shelter to Sofia to a much greater extent than to Belgrade. And the treaty of 1912, to which I will refer later, shows that the Serbs recognized this fact.

Although there are sound reasons to think that the great mass of the Macedonians are in their present sympathies pro-Bulgar, it is impossible to maintain that they are all Bulgar. The fringes towards Serbia and Greece become gradually less Bulgar until they are indisputably non-Bulgar. Salonika, the port of Macedonia and necessary to its economic life, is more Greek than Bulgar, more Jewish than either. Here and there, scattered about the country are settlements—often clustered about a fortified Greek or Serbian monastery—which are violently anti-Bulgar.

It is my opinion that the Macedonians themselves and a strong if not always a majority element of the Greeks, Serbs and Bulgars, have for many years recognized this situation and have realized that the annexation of Macedonia by any of the rivals would surely cause war and that any partition of the country would be necessarily artificial, arbitrary, and dangerous. In the last twenty years the best judgment of those outsiders who know the country well has been in favor of an autonomous province of Macedonia under Turkish sovereignty with a guarantee of substantial reforms, or an independent principality.

This solution of the problem would have rallied to its support a larger number of the Balkan peoples than any others. But the Great Powers were too busy with their own jealousies to pay any serious attention. It became more and more evident that if Macedonia was ever to be freed from

Turkish misrule, the people of the Balkans would have to do it themselves.

There is much dispute over who deserves the credit for having originated the negotiations which led to the Balkan alliance of 1912. The situation was not unlike those which led to the signature of the treaties discussed in previous chapters. None of the Balkan statesmen were strong enough to have forced through such an entente, if the ground had not been plowed. "Circumstances" did most of the conspiring. The various prime ministers—Guéchoff in Bulgaria, Pachitch in Serbia, Venezelos in Greece—rode the current.

The Young Turk Revolution had seriously weakened the common enemy. The course of European diplomacy had not been such as to inspire much respect for the Great Powers in the Balkans. Russia had not been strong enough to protect Serbian interests in the Bosnian crisis. Germany, with the Agadir affair on her hands, had not been able to protect the Turks from her Italian ally. A *bon mot* was current in the Near East: "*Les Grands Puissants? Dites plutôt, les impuissants.*"

This *mot* was attributed to Tsar Ferdinand of Bulgaria. Whether or not he was its author, that idea seems to have been the key-note of his policy. The jealousy between the Great Powers was so keen that they were impotent in the Balkans. No one of them could send an army into the peninsula without precipitating a general war. He had plenty of historical evidence to back up this point of view. The concert of Europe had never been able to enforce the treaty of Berlin. How often had they solemnly threatened the Turks if they did not reform! How often had they preached sermons on the status quo! Bulgaria had annexed eastern Roumelia in spite of their fulminations. The king of Montenegro had thumbed his nose more than once at the Great Powers from the fastnesses of his Black Mountain. The Great Powers were impotent. They were too much afraid of each other to do more than protest. It was their only weapon.

If the Balkan states acted together, they had nothing to fear from the concert of Europe. And the moment when Italy was at war with the Turks was a good time to begin.

Some of the secret treaties signed before the War broke out have been published. The most important is that between Bulgaria and Serbia—29th February, 1912. It shows clearly that Bulgaria's principal interest was the liberation of Macedonia and that the main desideratum of Serbia was an access to the Adriatic. All lands won from the Turks were to be held in common until after peace was signed. Northern Albania down to the Adriatic, the Sandjak of Novi Bazaar and "old Serbia" were to go to the Serbs, the Aegean coast to the east of the Struma to Bulgaria. Autonomy was to be given to Macedonia.

If however both parties agreed that it was impracticable to create an independent *régime* in Macedonia, it was to be divided between them. The principles on which the division was to be made—if such division became necessary—were laid down with precision. Serbia conceded that the population to the east of a line running roughly northeast from Lake Okrida was predominantly Bulgar and made no claim beyond that line. The northwestern half of Macedonia, between this line and the Serb frontier, was contested. It was to be divided by the arbitrament of the Tsar of Russia. Neither claimed that all of this contested zone was indisputably theirs, both claimed that a fair arbitration would give them more than half.

An equally vital part of the treaty was the paragraph where they pledged each other to bear aid with "the totality of their forces" in case either was attacked by one or more other nations. This clause had especial reference to the possibility of an Austrian aggression against Serbia.

After this dual alliance had been signed, Greece was brought into the coalition. If there was any secret treaty by which Greece defined her territorial claims, it has not yet been published. It is probable that the necessity for haste, caused by rumors of an approaching peace between Italy and Turkey, prevented the drafting of such a treaty.

In the actual course of the war which broke out in October, 1912, all the members of the alliance were more successful than they had dared hope, much more successful than their allies had anticipated. The Serbs for instance did not expect the Bulgars to succeed in driving the Turks through Thrace to the very walls of Constantinople. The Bulgars did not expect the Serbs to penetrate so far south into Macedonia. And both the Slav allies had very much underestimated what the Greek army would accomplish. They had sought the help of Greece primarily to secure her naval assistance. The Slavs had no fleets and the Greeks were stronger at sea than the Turks. They had expected that the main Greek effort would be the naval campaign to liberate the isles.

All these military provisions went wrong. It was a comedy of errors—of successful errors—too successful. A Bulgar general explained the campaign of the first war in words something like this: "We expected our hard fight at Kirkkilisse. We surprised the Turks and they ran. We sent our cavalry south in pursuit, but the fools retreated east. Our big battle was at Lule Burgos. Before the Serbs, the Turks retreated south instead of west as they should have done. But the Greeks gave us the greatest surprise. Their army was so badly beaten in the last war that we did not expect much of them this time. We thought they might have trouble defending Athens. Their mission was to engage the Turkish army of Epirus and keep it too busy to follow our flank. They jumped the frontier the first days of the war, caught the Turks napping, defeated them. And the crazy Turkish general instead of retreating on his fortified base at Janina, ran to the open town of Salonika."

But more disastrous than the fact that all the allies had won more than they expected, was the fact that the Great Powers were displeased with their victory. The status quo, which the diplomats had sworn to maintain—although they all admitted that it was iniquitous—had been shot to pieces.

Their delicate game of balancing power had been disarranged.

Every true Liberal in Europe, no matter what his nationality, wanted to see this Balkan alliance develop into a strong and stable federation. It was the only hope for the Balkans.

But a Balkan federation between Turkey and Austria stood square in the way of the pan-Germanic *Drang nach Osten*. The temptation for the Austrian Serbs to have joined such a federation would have been irresistible. It threatened the very existence of the Dual Monarchy. And a stable Balkan federation capable of self-defence, stood also square in the way of the Russian ambition to reach the Dardanelles. A Serbian victory was contrary to Austrian policy. A Bulgar victory was contrary to Russian policy. So in each camp of the Great Powers there were currents in favor of wrecking the alliance.

The division of spoils is always a ticklish business. The ancient hostilities—political and religious—were bitter. Each of the Balkan states was inclined to feel that its effort had been greater than that of its allies. Victory rather went to their heads. It is doubtful if—even left to themselves—they could have solved the problem peacefully. But with both groups of the Great Powers—led by Austria and Russia—bent on causing trouble, there was no hope at all.

Austria threw the first bomb. It was her policy to humiliate Serbia, to keep her in economic bondage, to demonstrate to her own Slavs that the Serbs were helpless, so the statesmen of Vienna suddenly developed a passion for the rights of nationalities and proclaimed their intention of protecting the Albanians from Serbian oppression. In other words, Austria refused to allow the Serbs to have their window on the Adriatic and, mobilizing her army, ordered the Serbs to evacuate Durazzo and the other ports which they had occupied. From an ethical point of view this attitude on the part of Austria is quite as hard to justify as her ultimatum to Serbia in 1914. But Italy, having "historic claims" and "legitimate aspirations" on the Adriatic littoral which are hostile to the Servian interests, supported Austria in this matter. Germany in her shining armor, took her stand beside her allies.

The two western members of the Entente have no direct "interests" in the Balkans. From their point of view, it is "a zone of Russian influence." Aside from the intricate combinations of diplomacy, it was manifest that civilization had "interests" in the Balkans, which were contrary to the Austrian contentions. But civilization is not officially represented in the concert of Europe. Neither England nor France wanted to fight over a mere Balkan issue. As during the Bosnian crisis in 1909, France was prepared to fulfil her treaty obligations towards Russia, but was unenthusiastic. Sir Edward Grey worked earnestly for peace—that is to avoid war between the two groups of Great Powers.

The critical point in the affair—so far as the Balkan states themselves are concerned—is still veiled in mystery. By their treaty of February, 1912, Bulgaria was pledged to lend the "totality of her forces" in case Serbia was attacked. Did she live up to this obligation when Austria mobilized along the Danube to browbeat Serbia into withdrawing from the Adriatic? We have nothing but unofficial and conflicting assertions.

Suppose that Serbia had stayed at Durazzo in spite of the Austrian threat. It was the theory of Tsar Ferdinand—before the war—that in such a case the Great Powers would once more prove their impotence. If Austria had attacked Serbia, Russia could not have stayed out. Germany would have stood by her ally. The general war would have begun. And with the two groups of Great Powers at each other's throats. the Balkan people would have had a fair chance to settle their own affairs without interference. It is my opinion—although there is no real proof—it is the most plausible conclusion—that the Bulgars urged the Serbs to refuse to submit. I was in Sofia at this moment and my Bulgar acquaintances were expecting a war with

Austria. It was manifestly to their interests that Servia and Greece should get what they wanted in Albania.

The Serbs retired from the Adriatic. They were certainly urged to do so by Russia, who in turn was being urged by her friends to give in. Somewhat later the Serbs began to claim that the Bulgars had refused to back them up if they stayed. They at once demanded a revision of the treaty of 1912. They asked for as much territory in Macedonia as they had been forced to give up in Albania. They and the Greeks were in actual occupation of Macedonia.

Only a very small fragment of the diplomatic correspondence of this period has been published. Where the perfidy began is hard to tell. The Serbs and Greeks refused to evacuate the territory which by treaty went to Bulgaria. They proposed that the whole matter should be left to Russian arbitration. The Bulgars—rightly or wrongly—felt that they had reason to doubt the disinterestedness of Russia. Some at least of the Russian diplomatic and consular agents in the Balkans were encouraging the Serbo-Greek conspiracy. Austria, wanting above everything the downfall of Serbia, urged Bulgaria to attack.

With so much inflammatory material about, with so many interests anxious to touch it off, the second Balkan war was inevitable. On both sides the high command had issued preparatory orders for the attack on the former allies. What are called "frontier incidents"—small unauthorized skirmishes—had been going on for weeks. But the first definite order for attack came from the Bulgars. Altogether it was a striking case of undemocratic politics, whoever ordered the first shot it was the work of secret diplomatic combinations and relatively irresponsible army officers. On neither side did the representatives of the people, or even the responsible cabinets authorize this second war.

The issue between Serbia and Greece on the one side and Bulgaria on the other hung in the balance, when Roumania, with no plausible pretext, attacked Bulgaria from the north and the Turks coming to life once more, sallied out from Constantinople and reoccupied Adrianople. Caught between four fires, Bulgaria threw up her hands and appealed to the justice of Europe.

But Russia was too much pleased by the downfall of Bulgaria and the discomfiture caused to the Hapsburgs by the Serbian victory to allow the Entente to intervene. There was little Austria could do to help Bulgaria—once more she had backed the wrong horse in the Balkans. So Bulgaria was left to the mercy of her despoilers. They all took a slice from their victim. The treaty of Bucarest—6th August, 1913, which "ended the hostilities" was one of the most iniquitous ever contrived. Austria—from interested motives no doubt—was the only one of the Great Powers to protest.

This peace of Bucarest was a heart-breaking affair to everyone who had hopes of a happier future for the Balkans.

It will perhaps interest historians of a judicial frame of mind to untangle the snarl of evidence—and much of it is not yet available—and to determine who was most to blame for the second Balkan war and, if it was Bulgaria, to decide how much she ought to have been punished. But everyone else—except those who have an unavowable interest in disorder—will be more interested in the problem of restoring peace.

For more than a century the Balkan Peninsula has been the sore spot of Europe. (The infection has now spread to the entire body). There could be no greater problem of statesmanship than the healing of this center of inflammation. In no other department has European diplomacy shown itself more impotent than in dealing with the Near Eastern problem. Never has their impotence been more marked than when they permitted the signing of the treaty of Bucarest. There were no statesmen in Europe who had the qualities necessary to deal with the situation—the imagination to see the danger nor the moral authority to convince anyone that their advice was disinterested.

EIGHT YEARS OF TENSION

The foreign ministers of the Great Powers were so worried over the possibility of a general war, so anxious to count up the score in the diplomatic contest which had been raging at the Conference of London between the Entente and the Alliance, that they were ready to welcome any "settlement" of the Balkan problem—no matter how illogical, no matter how temporary, no matter how unjust.

The Balkan problem will not be solved by ignoring it, nor by postponing it. Sooner or later it will have to be faced. And the men who could not find any solution for it in the calm of peace, were not to be expected to do better in the heat of war. The diplomatic fiasco of the Entente in the Balkans, which among other things has caused the fall of M. Delcassé, was not surprising.

But ignoring (as is the habit of European diplomacy) the interests of the people most nearly involved, the effect of the two Balkan wars on the struggle between the Entente and the Alliance is worth consideration.

During the course of the crisis a diplomatic conference, under the presidency of Sir Edward Grey, sat at London and, while real blood was flowing in the Balkans, they tried to preserve the peace of Europe and keep anyone else from hooking a large fish in these troubled waters. The result was in the nature of a drawn game. Both sides caught some fish.

From a purely diplomatic point of view the honors went to the Alliance. Austria had vetoed Serbia's desire to have a window on the Adriatic. Once more the Slavophiles of Russia called on the Tsar to protect these orthodox christians from catholic oppression. Once more the Kaiser donned his shining armor. Once more Great Britain showed a marked reluctance to fight over a Balkan quarrel. The arguments in favor of peace which her friends had brought to bear on Russia in 1909 were even stronger now. As the Russian military reorganization was nearing completion, there was even more reason to wait. The British attitude at this time, as it had been in the Bosnian crisis, was markedly more pacific than it had been during the tension of 1911 over the Agadir incident. So once more Russia had to sacrifice the interests of her protégé in the Balkans. Once more she had to give in before the German bluff.

It was a new victory for the diplomacy of the rattling sword. But it was solely a victory of *amour propre*—of prestige. From a military point of view the Alliance lost much more than they gained.

The Turkish army, always counted as a German asset, had been crushingly defeated. Austria's hold on her Slav provinces had been seriously weakened. Any growth of the Serbian kingdom threatened her existence. She had hoped to strengthen herself by sowing dissensions in the Balkans, but once more she guessed wrong. Serbia, instead of being crushed by Bulgaria, had come out of the second war with added prestige. The Serb-tum was by so much the more threatening.

Roumania, traditionally hostile to Russia, had always been counted as a satellite of the Triple Alliance. Her king was a Hohenzollern. But in this crisis the politicians of Bucarest found that their interests clashed with those of Vienna. They blithely broke the treaty which bound them and delivered the *coup de grace* to Austria's protégé.

To an even greater extent, the Triple Alliance was weakened by the fact that the ambitions of Italy and Austria in the Balkans had come into sharp conflict. Both of them were nursing "manifest destinies" in Albania. The relations between these two "allies," never cordial, had become more bitter than usual.

When the dust of the Balkan conflicts settled, everyone knew that the fighting power of the Deutschtum had been decreased—the chances for a successful war had diminished. This conclusion was reached—with a wealth of statistics and close argument—in the military magazines of half a dozen countries.

That the Germans realized this was proved by their gigantic army increase law, 30th June, 1913. To this, the

Russian Duma replied by a vote of extraordinary military credits, and the French *Chambre des Députés* by a law—7th August—to increase the term of military service from two to three years.

A year later—August, 1914—all bluffs were called.

CHAPTER X

THE FATAL YEAR

So far I have tried to avoid statements which are not based on ample evidence. But no judgment on the more recent diplomatic events can claim to be real history. What little evidence there is, is conflicting.

The official documents about the crisis are within everyone's reach. It is safe to say that no one interested in the subject has not read them. The various belligerent governments have been so anxious to persuade the neutrals of the justice of their cause that we have had Blue Books and White Papers thrust down our throats. And I have not had access to the secret documents. I can cite no evidence for my beliefs. They are only personal impressions based on a considerable study of the roots—rather than the immediate incidents—of the present crisis.

As I have read into the immensely complicated diplomatic history of Europe since 1878 it seems to me simplified by considering it a conflict between ideals. It is easy, almost too easy, to give it a materialistic interpretation; to show the conflict of economic interests. But that interpretation does not suffice. Business interests, within each country, conflict; for a while competition is bitter; then a "combination" or trust is formed. The whole meaning of the various Ententes is that when two countries set their mind to it and bring a little good will to the task the oldest and most intense economic and colonial disputes can be liquidated. But why did not Great Britain—for instance—reach an understanding in these matters with her old friend Germany instead of with her traditional enemies, France and Russia? Why did not the English divide Asia Minor with the Germans to keep back the

Slavs, instead of reaching a "gentlemen's agreement" with the Tsar to squeeze out the Kaiser? I fail to find economic arguments which apply to one combination and not to the others. It seems to me that the ideal of the Deutschtum frightened the non-German people of Europe more than any mere threat to their economic interest.

Both sides accuse the others of intentional bad faith. There was bad faith on both sides, but misunderstanding seems to me to have been a greater factor in their hostility. To take one example out of thousands, there is a fundamental conflict between the two words *recht* and *le droit*. We translate both by the same English word, "law." But the German when he uses his word has in mind quite a different concept than the Frenchman when he uses his. A German may be acting in complete accord with his idea of "rectitude" and seem most unrighteous to a Frenchman.

I cannot see that this War was in any sense inevitable. It had its origins in the way the people of Europe thought in the stage of evolution they had reached in what we arbitrarily call the Twentieth Century. But it was not inevitable that they should have had such habits of thought. Everyone who hopes that the next generation will be better educated, better equipped for and adapted to the complex environment of our civilization is working on the assumption that human nature does change and can be changed.

The War was not inevitable,—but no more was it surprising. As long as we base our civilization and our habits of thought on the idea of competition among individuals there will be competition between the groups of individuals which form nations. As long as we allow the competition within the nation to work out the manifold injustices which are the commonplaces of our daily life, there will be injustices between nations. The War was "inevitable" only in the sense that it was in accord with the spirit of our time. If that spirit is unchangeable—which is not proved—war is inevitable.

One of the interesting psychological problems of modern times is: Did the Kaiser deserve the Nobel peace prize? Undoubtedly he thought he did. Undoubtedly his people thought he did. No ruler of modern times has been so often and so violently attacked by the patriots of his country on the charge of being too enthralled by the idea of peace. Personally, I do not think that he deserved the prize. Disraeli, after the Congress of Berlin, returned to London announcing that he brought "Peace with honor." He was glad to have peace as long as he could preserve what he was pleased to call "honor." I think the pacivism of the Kaiser was of the same brand. He wanted: "Peace with victory." As long as he felt he was winning he did not want to fight. And victory meant for him the continued growth in power and grandeur of the Deutschtum.

I have intentionally avoided a frequent use of the term "pan-Germanists." Their rôle in the present crisis can be compared to that of our Abolitionists before the Civil War. They certainly had an influence, but it was a limited one. The pan-Germanic societies were only a crude expression of a mystic faith. The Deutschtum was a very much more respectable ideal than mere territorial aggrandizement. To be sure it implied the extension of the Deutschreich beyond the chance frontiers of the moment. And there were always some sincere apostles of the Deutschtum who believed that talk of peace was sentimental nonsense. The German "race" had come into its own by war, only by war could it thrive. But there were some of them—among whom was the Kaiser—who believed that their mission, the spreading of their creed of orderly and beneficent discipline, could be accomplished by peaceful means. During the first years of his reign there could be no doubt that the German idea was growing. As the German merchants conquered ever new markets, the idea of organization which they preached as the foundation of their success, caught in a growing degree the imagination of the world.

But about 1900—an approximate date—a more and more

successful resistance to this peaceful propaganda of the Deutschtum became manifest. It became evident in diplomatic correspondence. It was just as clearly writ in trade statistics. The competitors whom the Germans had caught napping began to wake up. I have told in Chapter V. how the English Royal Mail had begun to build ships to cut in on the easy profits of the Kosmos Line. Great Britain was evidently resolved to resist the spread of the Deutschtum at sea.

By 1910 this resistance had taken concrete shape in the network of ententes. And especially in the realm of diplomacy the prestige of Germany had fallen. It is the weakest spot in the otherwise remarkable organization of the German Empire. The Kaiser, by thumping the table, by rattling his sword, by "donning his shining armor," had constantly increased the anger of his enemies. Sometimes at least he was justified in making a serious diplomatic protest, but his method was bad. He cried "Wolf, wolf," too often. Half a dozen times, notably during the Algeciras crisis of 1906, he might have really drawn his sword with the best of chances. But having scared all the world by drawing it only halfway, he thrust it back with a swagger. His effort to browbeat Europe defeated his purpose. It only increased his reputation for maladroit rudeness, the number and the anger of his enemies. After every crisis—most of which might not have been so bitter except for the crudity of the Kaiser's method—Germany had fewer friends. Anger and fear and hatred are closely associated frames of mind. And the fact that the non-German nations of Europe—whether they were anti-German or not—were drawing together diplomatically, decreased the military power of Germany.

And so, during the early years of this century, more and more Germans of intelligence and peaceful preferences began to realize that the power and prestige of the Deutschtum was not growing but declining. This conviction immensely strengthened the arguments of the military party. And at last—apparently—the Kaiser was converted.

For a moment leave aside the question of whether or not the Germans were insane to believe that they were called of God to regenerate the world, and accept the fact—to which all evidence points—that they did sincerely believe it. What were they to do about this situation—this impious rebellion against the Divine Will?

I translated above some sentences from Rudolph Götte's "Deutscher Volksgeist." "To live and expand at the expense of other, less meritorious peoples finds its justification in the conviction that we are of all the peoples, the most noble and the most pure, destined before others to work for the highest development of humanity." He continues: "and that makes it obligatory for us to be the strongest military power both on land and sea." If one admits the first part of the quotation—the assumption—one cannot quarrel with the deduction. If you are—or believe yourself to be—called of God to build the Temple in Zion, you must make yourself stronger than the Philistines—and of course it is foolish to consider the "rights" or the feelings of the Philistines.

But the assumption of a Divine Mission was just the point the non-German people of Europe did not accept. Most really serious quarrels can be reduced to a disagreement over primary assumptions.

The anti-German forces of Europe had no such cohesive ideal. Against this single concept of the Deutschtum were marshalled half a dozen national aspirations. But they can all be grouped under one sentiment: a reluctance to be reformed against one's will. As far as I can discover any ethical conflict in this War, it is here. Is one race, because of its conviction of its superiority, justified in trying to impose its degree of civilization on less meritorious nations? Or, to put it more accurately: Has such a superior people a right to impose its culture on less deserving *white* races? (For of course all the Great Powers, ourselves included, do not consider black, brown or yellow peoples in such arguments.) And are nations, accused of inferiority, justified in defending themselves diplomatically, and with arms, against compulsory uplift? On this general issue there is a fairly clear ethical division between the two warring camps of Europe.

I find it hard to see any moral distinction between pan-Germanism and pan-Slavism. I can see little ethical difference between military power on land or on sea. France has little in common with her allies. She more than either of them is fighting consciously in this moral issue of freedom to be yourself, even if others call you inferior. It is for her—Rights of Man against the Divine Right of Kings. But even in her case the issue is bleared by the fact that both of her allies are empires and that her own colonial policy has been smirched by all the vices of imperialism.

Some of the orators of the Entente tell us that it is a conflict between a civilization based on the rights of the individual and a civilization of state control. But there is no inevitable conflict between such theories. No one can deny that a great deal can be said for both ideals. "Individualism" bears one kind of fruit, "collectivism" another. Neither has reached the limit of its development. As long as each was willing to let the other alone there was no inherent quarrel between them. But as soon as either tried to convert the other by force, trouble was sure.

So the question at issue—or rather, the main question, for it is impossible to reduce the politics of nations to a simple formula—was: Will Germany preserve the peace at the cost of abandoning her large claims to leadership? Will the rest of Europe preserve peace even at the cost of accepting the overlordship of the Germans?

In the summer of 1914 both these questions were answered by an emphatic "No."

But before discussing the events of the Fatal Year, there is one other point to deal with, one other obscuring contention to be cleared up.

The Germans claim that they are fighting a defensive war—a claim echoed by all their opponents. Once more it is rather a quarrel over words than a rank hypocrisy. If you are accused of killing a man it is not sufficient to say that you did it in defence. The judge will ask what you were defending. The only valid plea is *self*-defence. It is not permitted in law to kill in defence of your opinion. Although it was once not only good form but highly pious to kill in defence of your religious beliefs, it is no longer legal.

When a Belgian speaks of a defensive war he means that he is fighting to defend the political existence and territorial integrity of his country.

In the summer of 1914 neither the political structure nor geographic frontiers of Germany—the Deutschreich nor the Deutschland—were in danger. England certainly did not want to dismember the German Empire, it would have been hard to recruit a corporal's guard for such an enterprise. France was not preparing to attack Germany, not even to recover Alsace-Lorraine. The Germans had more reason to fear Russia. If the Tsar and his mystical reactionary pan-Slav friends stayed in power, there was certainly a possibility that when they had completed their military reorganization they might have attacked Germany. But there was no immediate danger. All the Liberal elements of England would have repudiated a Russian attack. It is very doubtful if France would have joined such an aggression.

Austria-Hungary, to be sure, was in a more difficult position. But the dangers which threatened her were as much internal as external.

But this discussion of the extent to which the territory of the Central Empires was threatened would probably have seemed an insignificant quibble to most Germans. What they worried about was the prestige of the Deutschtum. There could be no possible question but that it was threatened—worse than threatened: it was doomed. Nothing but a successful war could revivify it. It is evident, from the

German press, from the speeches of her statesmen—the Kaiser included—that it is not the German soil they are defending, but this German Ideal—this Mission in the world which God has laid upon them!

If it is assumed that rather reluctantly the Kaiser and the real rulers of Germany were convinced—largely by the results of the Balkan wars—that it was necessary to draw the sword in defence of the Deutschtum and that, once convinced, they planned in cold blood to do so at the first favorable opportunity, almost every event preceding and following the outbreak of the crisis, falls into orderly place. And facts, which in any other hypothesis, are inexplicable, become simple. If for instance, one assumes that the Kaiser always wanted war, how is it possible to explain that he did not draw the sword before at more favorable moments?

I will develop my hypothesis—repeating the warning that it is a personal opinion and that proofs are lacking. It is entirely possible that any day some new document—a secret treaty, for instance—may throw an entirely new light on the subject.

The great military law which passed the Reichstag in June, 1913, contained several novelties besides the unprecedented increase in the size of the standing army. The most interesting were the financial arrangements. The immense sum of money required was to be raised by a new and unnecessarily quick method. The technical working out of the law would require several years. In the ordinary course of events the money would be raised in instalments as it was needed. But this new war tax was to be realized at once. It was to be turned into the state coffers and held there—part of it inactive—till needed. Most military writers commented on this novelty at the time. The event has proved the sagacity of their suspicions. Germany would have a very large war chest at the beginning of 1914. And there is every indication that this money voted to be expended over a course of several years, was used at once for accumulating stores.

In choosing the moment and the manner of drawing the sword the German war-council must have had two considerations in mind. First, haste. Every month that passed was more than a mere waste of time. The Russian army reorganization was progressing apace. Towards the end of 1914 some of the new strategic railroads would be opened. And every year, almost every month would see new developments along this line. So far in the actual progress of the war the Germans have owed their successes in the East very largely to their superior railroads. They certainly had this in mind in their pre-war theory. In France the law for three years' military service was just going into force. There was difference of opinion as to how much eventual increase of force would come to France when this law began to work smoothly, but it was quite certain that its first effect would be a tangle of disorganization. And every delay meant that Franz Josef might die and a revolution break out in Austria.

Secondly, the *casus belli* should be sought in the Balkans. Great Britain seemed ready to make any quarrel over Morocco her own, but reluctant to be drawn in over a dispute in the Near East. It is the first principle of diplomacy in preparing a war to isolate or divide the enemy. Bismarck had always done so successfully. The Germans believed that England would surely fight if any issue mentioned in her ententes was touched. There was at least a chance that she would stay out—or hesitate too long—if the row started in the Balkans.

A further point in support of my theory is that in the spring of 1914 for the first time the "conversations" in Berlin on the subject of an Anglo-German Entente took on a hopeful tone. Neither side has yet published any full account of this diplomatic event. It is uncertain what happened, but there are indications that the subject of barter was the Bagdad Railroad. For a long time the British government had been trying to reach some sort of entente with Germany, her proposals had generally centered on the naval situation and had seemed inadequate to the Germans.

Suddenly Wilhelmstrasse took notice of the hand which was held out from Downing Street. It may be that the British offered new and more acceptable terms. It is more probable that Germany had made up her mind to a war, which she hoped to limit to Russia and France, and was trying to disarm British suspicion.

So I believe that, even if the Archduke had not been assassinated at Sarajevo, there would have been "trouble in the Balkans."

These considerations were fully discussed in the European press. A great many well-informed people were holding their breath, expecting a new crisis in the months between the midsummers of 1914 and 1915. It was often said: "If Europe lives through this critical year in peace, Mr. Norman Angell will be proved right—that, after all, war is the great illusion." The supreme bluff was due.

And although I believe that from 1913 on the rulers of Germany were planning for war—in defence of the Deutschtum—I think it was largely in bluff. They knew it was to be a very critical bluff, the most serious they had yet tried. They were "prepared" to back it up, "prepared" for the "showdown." But I believe that in their hearts they hoped to get what they wanted without fighting. I think that Austria hoped Serbia would give in, that Germany hoped Russia would give in—that what they wanted was not war—but the spoils of war.

It is impossible to believe that the Foreign Offices of England and France and Russia ignored these indications of an impending crisis. It is not probable that they were caught as unawares as they would like to have us believe. I think they saw that Germany was preparing for a new and more stupendous bluff. It is hard to believe that Sir Edward Grey and his colleagues in Paris and St. Petersburg were less well informed about the symptoms of approaching storm than the writers of newspaper articles. But many crises had passed without bloodshed—perhaps this one would.

In the spring of 1914 people, interested in the international situation, who believed in peace, based that belief on the fact that Germany had let slip so many better opportunities to fight.

But it was obvious that if Germany was going to war, she could not postpone it much longer.

On the 28th of June, 1914, the heir to the Hapsburg throne was assassinated. It was a better pretext for action than the warriors of the Deutschtum had had any right to expect. President Poincaré of France, his prime minister and foreign secretary, were away from home on a visit to the Tsar. King George of England had failed to reconcile the hostile factions in Ireland. Civil war was imminent. Great strikes, which might develop into revolution, had broken out in Russia. The occasion was as good as the pretext.

BOOK II

THE NEW ELEMENTS OF DIPLOMACY

CHAPTER XI

THE RIGHTS OF NATIONS

In the last forty years several new ideas have been born, or have grown to maturity, which will influence the work of the diplomats. There will be many things discussed in the peace negotiations to follow this War, which were not mentioned at the Congress of Berlin in 1878. Among others is the theory of the rights of nations.

It is too new an idea to have become well defined. It has never been put into practice, so no "technique" for its application has been developed. The phrases used to express the ideal are vague and it is evident that its advocates are even vaguer in their conceptions of what the ideal implies. Nevertheless, it will be an important factor in the settlement of the War—if the Entente Powers win. All their statesmen refer to it in their speeches. One speaks of "The rights of small nations," another of "The legitimate aspirations towards national unity," and a third condemns Germany or Austria for their treatment of "subject races." It is rather hard to be sure what they mean and it often looks as if they did not quite know themselves.

The phrase "The theory of nationalities," was first given governmental approval by Napoleon III. He saw that it was a weapon against his principal rival, Austria. The expression "pan-Slavism" had a very similar history. The man who popularized it at the Russian Court was not a Slav, but the Armenian Loris Melikov. By marked personal ability, in spite of his race, he had won his way to the favor of the Tsar. With a very realistic sense of politics he saw that the pan-Slav idea was a valuable asset to the Autocracy. It was a fine-sounding slogan, like "Patriotism." It would rally to its support a great many high-minded men and behind it all sorts of scoundrelism could find refuge. It would increase the prestige and solidify the rule of his Imperial Master; it would foment discontent and insurrection in the rival realm of the Hapsburgs. So, Napoleon III. saw that if Italy and North Germany realized their ambition for national unity, it would be at the expense of Austria.

But at this period when the Germans were breaking away from Austrian predominance in the North and the scattered Italian States were uniting under the House of Savoy, no one spoke of this "right to national unity" as inherent. In the official mind, such "rights" had no *a priori* foundation, they depended upon and grew out of "might." Individual idealists like Byron might enlist in the cause of Greek independence but the governments of the Great Powers did not recognize any "rights" in the case, until the Greeks had shown that they were strong enough to set all Europe by the ears.

This attitude dominated the diplomats at Berlin in 1878. No one had a right to national unity unless they had won it, and to only so much of it as they had won. The diplomats recognized certain *faits accomplis*, fragments of several nations had won their independence, Turkey was not strong enough to re-conquer them. But aside from such cases, they drew frontiers to suit themselves without any concern for the facts of ethnology nor for the wishes of the populations so summarily disposed of. It would have seemed grotesque to Bismarck and his colleagues at Berlin, if anyone had suggested that Serbia—for instance—had a "right" to have all the people who spoke her language united under one government. And in 1878 no one was shocked at this attitude of the diplomats—except the poor people who were personally disappointed by being thrown back to the Turks.

But in the last generation there has been growing in Europe a feeling that there is an "inherent right"—or at least a "manifest expediency"—in the matter. It is pretty widely admitted by the younger generation that there is a grave tendency towards disorder wherever national aspirations are arbitrarily thwarted. We, in America, are so used to the idea that the "consent of the governed" is implicit in any government, that it is hard at times to remember that it is a brand new idea in Europe and by no means universally accepted.

It is necessary to remark parenthetically that the theory of national rights applies only to white men. The English do not approve of the nationalistic aspirations of the Egyptians. The French do not apply the theory in Morocco. Nor have we shown any inclination to worry over securing the consent of the Porto Ricans or Filipinos.

However, the idea as applied to "civilized" people has been gaining ground. The English have nearly made up their mind to apply it to Ireland and are quite united in the desire to impose it on Germany and Austria. Russian statesmen are very emphatic in their conviction that "oppressed nations" have a "right" not to be ruled by Germans. As the French were the first to formulate the rights of man, so they have been clearest in their statements of the rights of nations. Their statesmen and publicists speak and write as if ethnological groups, with the same language, customs and traditions—even if they are too weak to assert it—have a right to independence or at least to a large degree of autonomy and self-government.

Monsieur Arthur Chervin, formerly President of the Statistical Society of Paris, in his study of the race question in the dual monarchy—"L'Autriche et la Hongrie de Demain" gives as sharp a definition as I have found of this idea. "This phrase (*le principe des nationalités*) implies the right which human groups, large or small, but united by a community of origin, of language, of customs, of tradition, of historic relations, of social and political aspirations, have to group themselves in order to escape from a foreign yoke, and to constitute a nation, a fatherland in the most modern and elevated acceptation of these words."

The Germans do not accept this principle. They have an indisputable right to national unity because they can show the record of three victorious wars which they waged to win it. But the people they conquered, Danes, Poles, and the inhabitants of Alsace-Lorraine, just as manifestly have no such right. Of course the admission of such a theory as that proclaimed by the French would be suicide for Austria-Hungary or Turkey.

So, if the non-German forces win in this War, they will be influenced in the redrawing of the map by this theory of the rights of nations.

The problems raised by this theory are far from simple. First of all, there is the question of fact. If an entirely disinterested Census Commission studied the disputed districts for ten years they might be able to reduce the problem to something like scientific terms. But all "official" statistics are suspect. The Austrian census is notoriously faulty. All sorts of intimidation is used to secure "favorable" figures. In a land of such mixed races the number of people who speak more than one language is large. The personal preferences—or the "instructions"—of the census taker inevitably falsify the results. The Roumanians lay claim to the Province of Bessarabia on the ground that seventy-five per cent of the population is Roumanian. The Russian census states that less than fifty per cent speak the Roumanian language. One figure is quite as likely to be true as the other. The most notorious instance of conflict in the statement of "fact" is furnished by Macedonia. The Serbian, Greek and Bulgarian governments have been for years "cooking" statistics to prove their claim to this territory.

The more thorough-going advocates of the rights of nations propose to decide such uncertain cases by means of referendum. But even if a large corps of trained and honest election officials were at hand, it would often be found hard to apply this solution. In the best of circumstances the diplomats will have a very thorny problem on their hands in determining which of the conflicting claims it is wisest to accept as true.

Secondly, it frequently happens that ethnological claims to national unity come in direct conflict with other considerations equally as important. In the old days, the drawers of frontiers gave great weight to strategical considerations. In 1870 the Germans annexed part of French Lorraine in order to secure the fortress of Metz. Today the region inhabited by Poles stretches westward dangerously near to Berlin, and to the northward the Poles—on the basis of ethnological rights—would cut Prussia in two. Economic considerations—as I will show in the next chapter—are also often in hopeless conflict with the rights of nations.

Thirdly, ethnological and language frontiers are rarely, if ever, sharply drawn. If on a map of the world you painted black every acre where ninety per cent of the population is Polish, you would get four or five fairly large but not contiguous spots around Warsaw, Posen and Cracow, and spots in Paris, London, New York City, and Buffalo. If you painted red every acre which contained Poles to the extent of seventy-five per cent, you would probably join the black spots in eastern Europe. But there would be many blank spaces left and the result would not look like a country—the outline would be fantastically jagged. If you then painted blue the acres with fifty-one per cent Polish population, it would give you a territory twice or three times as large, it would color some, but not all of the blank spaces in the midst and the outline would still be too irregular to serve as a practical frontier. It would be impossible to decide on a boundary which would include all the Poles without including a great many non-Poles.

The same problem of racial mingling is encountered everywhere the attempt is made to apply the theory. In the Tyrol, the Italian population shades off gradually into the German. Along the dividing line there is a broad strip where it would be difficult to find a single family which was not a hybrid of both races. And the ethnological map of south eastern Europe—Austria-Hungary and the Balkans—is tremendously confused.

Remembering that if the Germans win they will ignore this theory of national rights, let us take up the ethnological problems the diplomats of the Entente will have to face in case they win.

"Italia irridenta" has played so large a rôle in popularizing the idea that people of the same race have a right to the same rule, that it naturally comes first. Italy was not able to complete her unity in her wars of independence. About a million—here again the statistics are uncertain, the Austrian census of 1910 gives the figure 768,422—Italians were left under the Hapsburg yoke, principally in the province of Tyrol and on the Istrian Peninsula at the head of the Adriatic. There is also a scattering of unredeemed Italians up and down the eastern coast of the Adriatic. The Austrian census of 1910 gives these figures for the Province of Dalmatia: Total, 645,666; Serbo-Croat, 610,669; Italian, 18,028, or Slav, 96.0%; and Italian, 2.8%. In the days of Venetian greatness all this coast was under Italian rule. The language is still current in the ports but the Hinterland, as these figures show, is overwhelmingly Slav.

The Italians, in case of victory, hope for much more than in the way of spoils. But the neighborhood of Trieste and the Province of Tyrol is all they can claim on the basis of the rights of nationalities.

There is also an "oppressed Latin race" in southeastern Europe. In Austria-Hungary—mostly in the Provinces of Transylvania and Bukovina—there are many Roumanian peasants. The Austrian census admits somewhat more than three millions. The Roumanians claim more. There is also the Roumanian problem in Bessarabia. But only the most ardent advocates of the theory of nationalities suggest applying it to the victors. If the Entente wins, there is small chance of Russia giving up her Roumanian subjects.

According to the "theory" all these "unredeemed" Roumanians ought to want to be united to the kingdom.

There is, however, wide and bitter difference of opinion as to their real desires. In Transylvania they are certainly discontented with Hungarian rule, but the lot of the peasantry in Roumania proper is far from enviable. It is quite possible that if the unredeemed Roumanians were allowed to do as they please, they would form an independent government of their own.

In the same neighborhood there is the equally complicated question of the Southern Slavs. The population of Austria-Hungary is divided roughly into three groups: Germans, eleven millions; Hungarians, ten millions; and Slavs (including the Bohemians and Poles of the North), twenty-two millions. The Southern Slavs—between six and seven millions—are more nearly related to the Serbs than to anyone else. A large section of them came under Venetian rule in the Middle Ages and were converted to the Catholic Church and write their Slavic language in Roman letters like ours. Culturally, they are more closely related to the Bohemians and Poles than to the Serbs. The rest of the Southern Slavs belong to the Orthodox Church and use the Russian alphabet like the Serbs. It has always been the Austrian policy to fan these religious discords in order to divide their subjects. It is an open question whether the religious or racial principle is stronger among these people. And the economic life of all this Southern Slav group looks towards Austria rather than towards the Balkans. All this great plain is agricultural and drives a thriving trade with the industrial districts north of the Danube. The economic interests favor the status quo.

A project has long been current of transforming the Dual Monarchy into a Triple State, that is, to create a Southern Slav Kingdom which would have the same sovereign as the other two nations, Austria and Hungary. Undoubtedly a great many of the Southern Slavs would prefer to be incorporated in a greater Serbia. But undoubtedly some of them would have preferred to form a separate kingdom within the far more prosperous Austrian Empire. Which, if either, of these tendencies is in a large majority is at present uncertain. The progress and outcome of the war will undoubtedly influence the public opinion of these Slav populations.

It is fairly certain that at least a minority of the Croats will be opposed to any union with Serbia which did not give them a very large degree of autonomy. And unless Austria is so badly defeated that it becomes decidedly unfashionable to belong to it, the Slovenes farther north will almost certainly object to Serbian rule. Even the most exalted advocates of the rights of nations—the pan-Serbs excepted—do not believe in forcing national unity on people who do not want it.

These problems of national unity affect directly the Dual Monarchy. The German Empire contains three groups of "subject people,"—the Danes of Schleswig-Holstein, the inhabitants of Alsace-Lorraine, and the Poles.

To a certain extent the annexation of Schleswig-Holstein by Prussia in 1864 was in accordance with this theory of national unity. A very large part of these two Danish Provinces were inhabited by Germans—approximately eighty per cent. All the southern section of this annexed territory, well up above the present line of the Kiel Canal, has spoken German for many centuries. But Bismarck was not content to stop at the ethnological frontier and annexed close to a million Danes.

The memory of that war is as remote as that of our Civil War. Few of the generation which saw the conquest are still alive. There has been a steady emigration of Germans into the Danish section—especially the towns—and the digging of the Kiel Canal has brought an immense stimulus to business—which has been shared even by the Danish element. A strict application of the ethnological rule would return Northern Schleswig to Denmark. It is probable that the population of this territory would vote for the change, but it is not certain. Certainly the German population of Holstein and Southern Schleswig would bitterly resist being separated from Germany. The Danish government would probably not welcome any such gift. Those who propose it are not influenced by the theory of national rights, but by a desire to punish Germany by taking from her the strategic and economic advantages of the Kiel Canal.

Alsace-Lorraine presents a different problem. In 1870 the people of Lorraine were indisputably French. But the peasants of Alsace spoke German and were ethnologically closely related to the Teutons. However, they were a liberty loving people and had enthusiastically embraced the political principles of the French Revolution. They were as much opposed to the annexations by Germany as were the French speaking people of Lorraine.

Ever since the treaty of Frankfort the victors have tried to change the nature and constitution of the population. In the early years of the new *régime* a great many inhabitants of keen French sympathies were driven out of the district by carefully planned persecutions. Strenuous efforts have been made to Germanize those who remained. The government has encouraged Germans to emigrate into this Reichsland and colonize it. How far they have succeeded in changing the composition of the population is a subject of bitter discussion. In some places, notably the new industrial centers, the Germans seem to be in the majority, and other sections, especially the countryside, are vehemently anti-German.

The French are not willing to allow the matter to be decided by a referendum. They are certainly right in saying that if the Germans who have come into Alsace-Lorraine since 1870 were disfranchised, and if all those French sympathizers who have fled from the conqueror were allowed to go home to vote, the result would be overwhelmingly in their favor. They have a plausible argument that there is no reason to allow a burglar to keep his spoil, simply because he has frightened away the original owner. If a referendum were taken the actual population would, in some places, vote in favor of Germany.

Here, as in Schleswig-Holstein, the Germans have brought a great prosperity—such as Alsace-Lorraine never knew under French rule. This is partly due to the German genius for organization and intelligent, forward-looking state help in developing industrial life. And it is very largely due to the fact that the annexation of these provinces gave Germany control of both banks of the Rhine.

There are many considerations which make a river a poor frontier. Valleys tend to unite, while mountain chains divide. From a purely geographical point of view the crest of the Vosges—or the mountains of the Schwartzwald—form a better frontier than the Rhine. There is always communication between the inhabitants of the two banks of a river. A glance at an ethnological map shows that peoples of similar civilization tend to group in valleys.

For the technical development of a river as an economic unit—a trade route—it is evidently better to have both banks under one authority. (With us, the central government has charge of all water routes. It is easy to imagine the haphazard and inefficient results we would get if we entrusted the development of the Mississippi to the states which border it.) The Germans have made of the Upper Rhine a model of economic development. A good many of the old stock of Alsace-Lorraine would, for sentimental reasons, prefer French rule, but would at the same time regret to lose the prosperity which the Germans have brought.

As among the Southern Slavs, so here, there are a great many who would prefer to establish an independent government. And there is at least one committee which is advocating a union with Switzerland.

Nowhere is the German rule of a "subject race" so entirely unsatisfactory as in Prussian Poland. The program of Germanization had failed completely. After more than a century of administration here, the Germans are more hated by their Polish subjects than by their Danes and French. As so often happens the worst accusations against the Germans are to be found in their own apologies. Prince von Bülow, the former chancellor, in his book

"Imperial Germany" discusses the Polish problem at length. His argument boils down to this very simple proposition: If the Poles are allowed to enjoy prosperity their women bear too many children. The Prussians have been installed in Poland for a long time, but the proportion of Poles in the population of these provinces increases. One of the grounds on which the Germans base their claim of racial superiority over their neighbors—especially the French—is their fecundity. They cannot tolerate being surpassed in this matter by a "subject race." But unless something strenuous is done, Prussia is doomed to become Polish.

After a period of relative tolerance under the Chancellor Caprivi (which the ungrateful Poles utilized in restrained breeding) the Prussian policy has changed to one of ruthless—and scientific—repression. Just as some of our more rabid Southerners have advocated the checking of the negro birthrate by surgical operations, so similar means have been suggested against the Poles. But von Bülow believes that the same results can be obtained by economic pressure. In 1888 the Prussian Landstag created an *Ausiedielung-kommission* (Board of Colonization) to buy out the Polish landlords and resell their estates in small plots to German colonists. As the Poles generally refused to sell, a new law was passed in 1908 which gave the commission the right to buy land without the owner's consent. Polish children were flogged in the public schools if they spoke their mother-tongue. Everything was done to break the spirit of nationality. Everything was arranged with Prussian thoroughness to make it not only very unpleasant but also very unprofitable, to be a Pole. The fight has been bitter in the extreme. How long the Poles could have kept up their resistance in the face of overwhelming odds is uncertain. Few people in Europe deserve more pity than the Poles of Germany.

But the Polish "nation" was not even permitted to be oppressed in common. When their independence was overthrown—by a combination of external intrigue and internal dissension—there was a series of "Partitions" between Prussia, Austria and Russia.

The Poles of Russia are little more fortunate than those of Germany. The phrase "Bleeding Poland" has generally referred to the Tsar's share of the spoils. And, if his rule has been preferable to that of the Kaiser, it was not because he was more tender towards his "subject races," but only because he was less efficient. The process of Germanization has been orderly, scientific and inexorable, that of Russofication has been brutal, bungling and haphazard. The Russian Poles have always felt that there was some chance of a successful revolution. But it is hard to convince either a Russian or a German Pole that anything could be harder than their present lot.

The Austrian Poles have been in a very different position. They are better off than either of the other two sections of their brothers and also in a much more tolerable position than the other "subject races" of Austria-Hungary. After the Hapsburgs had been crushed in 1866 by the rising power of Prussia a reorganization of their empire was necessary. A compromise called the *Augsleich* was reached between the German and Hungarian elements which resulted in the constitution of the present Dual Monarchy. This arrangement has been called "a conspiracy between the two strongest nationalities in the Hapsburg empire for the concerted oppression of the rest." While the Hungarians could claim very near, if not quite, a majority of the population of Hungary, the German element was in a decided minority in Austria. The census of 1910 gives them 35.58 per cent of the population. And "official" statistics are nearly always padded. The rest of the "Austrians" belong to one or another of the Slav families: Bohemians (or Czechs as they call themselves) Poles, Ruthenes, Slovenes, etc. It is evident that the German element could not hope to govern Austria unless they made accomplices of one or another of these

Slav groups. They chose an alliance with the Poles. The province of Galicia was given a large measure of home rule. The Polish language was put on a par with German.

At least one of the reasons why the German politicians of Vienna selected the Poles for their allies in internal politics was that they could count on them as "reactionaries." The Austrian Poles are, to a large extent, feudal landlords. They form a privileged minority of the population and are sure to oppose any such subversive ideas as universal suffrage. The mass of the people in Austrian "Poland" are Ruthenians of the Uniate Religion, an heretical, hybrid sect, which bears some resemblance to the Greek Orthodox Church but recognizes the Pope at Rome. The House of Hapsburg very cleverly won the loyalty of the Catholic Polish nobility by allowing them to oppress their "subject race" to their hearts' content. The landowning class of Galician Poles would much prefer to retain their favored position in the Dual Monarchy rather than to enter into a reconstituted Poland which implied any democratic liberties for their peasants.

The problem of Poland represents several of the difficulties which will arise in any attempt to apply the theory of nationalities. In the palmy days of their national glory the Poles were among the worst offenders against the "rights" of other races. They conquered and embodied in Poland large sections of Ruthenia, Russia, Lithuania and Prussia. Never in history have their political frontiers coincided with their ethnological frontiers. Poland cannot be "reconstituted" without violating the rights of some other national group.

I have already referred to the difficulty of establishing any absolute ethnological frontier for the Poles and to the fact that strategic and economic considerations are likely to seem quite as important to the peace negotiators as the theoretic rights of nations.

The only thing one can hope from its application—provided that the Powers who believe in the theory win—

is a rough approximation to ethnological justice. With
the best will in the world there will inevitably be unsatisfied minorities. But such difficulties are very much reduced if they are frankly faced. Large facilities for cross
migration could be easily arranged. If, for instance, the
Italian frontier in the Tyrol is to be changed, those Germans contained in the newly acquired territory who did
not like the new *régime*, could emigrate and the Italians
left out by the new frontier could immigrate. Many other
practical expedients to reduce the inevitable friction of
change will suggest themselves. And every sincere effort
to give people the form of government they covet will tend
to make Europe a more orderly and livable place. It
may be accepted as a maxim of statescraft, that trouble
is threatened wherever one group considers itself oppressed
by "foreigners." It is Utopian to hope to eradicate all
the discontent which has grown up about these aspirations
for national unity, to satisfy everybody, but an immense
amount might—with sincere effort—be accomplished.

The extent to which any effort towards the application
of this theory will be made, depends of course on the outcome of the War. Neither Germany, nor Austria-Hungary,
nor Turkey accept the theory. In case of their defeat,
we may expect Great Britain, as she has few claims on the
continent, to be the most disinterested advocate of the
rights of nations. She would probably think it was overdoing the "theory" to apply it to her island possession in
the Mediterranean or to Gibraltar, but aside from these
cases her vote will probably be cast in this sense.

France, aside from Alsace-Lorraine, where she puts
historic above ethnological considerations, will probably
support this theory in every case where it is not prejudicial
to her ally, Russia. If the German defeat is overwhelming,
she may be able to free her foreign policy from Russian
influence and give unqualified support to this theory. In
general the French are more interested in such abstract
principles than their allies and the idea of the rights of

nations has undoubtedly caught a firmer hold on public opinion in France than elsewhere.

Russia will certainly believe in freeing all subject races from German or Austrian rule. She may, if pressed by her more liberal allies, live up to her promise to give some sort of autonomy to the Poles. But—unless there is a fundamental revolution in her politics—it is improbable that she will extend this theory of the rights of nationalities to her internal affairs. The fact that her other subject races will certainly clamor for all the concessions she gives the Poles, will influence her—if her reactionaries stay in power—to reduce the autonomy of Poland to a minimum.

Italy and Serbia can be counted on to favor the theory wherever it means an increase to their territory. There is no reason to believe that either of them would show any loyalty to the theory if it stood in the way of their "legitimate aspirations."

The rights of nations was not even mentioned at the Congress of Berlin in 1878. The idea has grown to the point where it has forced itself on the attention of "practical" statesmen. Some of them, with every show of sincerity, have accepted it as a watchword. But it has not yet grown to full maturity. No government of Europe accepts it without qualifications. Some reject it absolutely. But if the Powers of the Entente win, we may expect to see the theory given official sanction. Violations of it by the diplomatic map-drawers, instead of being the rule, will be the exception.

CHAPTER XII

DOLLAR DIPLOMACY

At the Congress of Berlin very little was said about "business." A generation ago such considerations were beneath the dignity of diplomats. Today every embassy has its "commercial adviser"—quite as important a personage as the military attaché. *La diplomatie des chemins de fer*—the French equivalent for Dollar Diplomacy—has now become respectable and ambassadors are expected to know something about "tariffs" and "cost of production" and "trade development."

The two main economic considerations of modern diplomacy are (1) access to raw materials and (2) trade routes.

Russia, with her immense expanse of territory, holds a favored position in Europe. She is an almost complete economic unit. As her industry develops and—largely under German leadership—it has been developing rapidly, she finds most of the raw material she needs within her own borders. Such tropical products as rubber are all she lacks. She has a wealth of minerals and timber, exceedingly fertile farm lands, great grazing expanses which furnish meat and hides and wool. In the Transcaspia fine cotton is being grown. For fuel she has abundant coal and oil—and almost limitless waterpower. In regard to natural resources her position is as promising as was ours at the beginning of the last century. Her immense territories are under-populated and under-developed.

The situation of Germany is the reverse. Her lands are already over-populated, her fields do not normally produce enough food to feed her, and her birth-rate is dangerously high. Her population increases about 800,000 a year.

This increase must be absorbed by industry. If there are no jobs for her children in the factories they must emigrate or starve. And industry, always expanding to meet this increase, demands an ever larger supply of raw material. The actual frontiers of the Empire do not contain enough to meet the present need.

Their deservedly famous steel industry is an example. The Krupp armament works at Essen, of which we hear so much these days, are only a small part of the immense and steadily growing metallurgic industry of the Westphalian Rhine. The supply of German ore is notably insufficient. Across the neighboring frontier in eastern Belgium, Luxembourg, and northeastern France are great fields of low-grade iron ore. The Germans developed a process of working this ore profitably. And there, in the heart of French Lorraine, are little villages, like Saint-Pierremont, which German brains, German money, and German labor have turned into thriving mining towns. The ore goes to feed the great iron mills of the Rhine.

The French did not need this raw material. Their own iron industry had naturally centered around their older and richer mines. It had not begun to run short of raw material. If the Germans are kept from their source of wealth by exceptional laws or by tariff barriers—if the price of steel rails is arbitrarily increased by a chance political boundary—they and all the world are suffering an economic wrong.

France on the other hand lacks oil. Italy lacks both fuel and mineral wealth. There is hardly any industry in England—except coal mining—which is not dependent on imported raw material.

Russia and the United States stand quite by themselves in this matter. But in both these countries the importance of foreign trade tends to grow. The situation in regard to dye-stuffs is typical. I am told that even our government Bureau of Engraving was embarrassed for lack of red ink to print our postage stamp. The other countries less fortunate in the possession of natural resources are to a very much greater degree dependent on imported raw material.

In times of peace it would seem that free trade would greatly ease the situation. It would matter very little to the German ironmongers where their ore came from, if political frontiers did not tend to increase its cost. But much of the discussion on this point is vitiated by the assumption that it is simply an economic affair. Almost all professors of political economy are in favor of free trade, but their scholarly arguments have as little practical result as those of the enthusiasts for disarmament. As a matter of fact other considerations are at stake besides those of "pure economy." We, in America, know that often one of the considerations in tariff discussions is simply "graft." The high tariff *régime* in Russia was primarily a financial measure. Count Witte wanted to put the Empire's currency on a gold basis so as to improve Russian credit in foreign banking circles. He pushed up the custom charges in order to gather the necessary "gold reserve." He was relatively uninterested in the effect on the economic life of the country.

The principal motive of high tariff in Germany has been political, in a narrower sense dynastic. As Professor Veblen very clearly indicates in his "Imperial Germany and the Industrial Revolution," the ruling class in Germany has intentionally manipulated custom barriers—from the days of the Zollverein to the present—in order to weld together the German "race" and to sharply differentiate it from its neighbors. The German universities have devolved a "school" of patriotic economy, which is not "economy" at all, but a most uneconomic industrial nationalism.

As long as—from various reasons—tariffs remain in fashion this question of access to raw material will be a serious concern to statesmen. And a diplomat who was inspired by the desire to reorganize Europe with the sole intention of facilitating the greatest industrial production at the lowest possible cost, would advise endless changes in the map. But of course he could not realize his ideal without violating the rights of nations and many other sacred interests.

However, when the soldiers finish their job, and the diplomats begin work, the "commercial advisers" will make themselves heard and the phrase "access to raw materials" will come up frequently in their discussions.

The second economic consideration of diplomacy—"trade routes"—is of far greater importance. This is primarily a matter of the sea. Almost every important trade route leads to salt water. Easy circulation—cheap transportation—is the most vital need of modern life. In spite of the marvellous progress in the means of transport by land, water traffic is cheaper. It is slower, to be sure, but the larger and heavier the produce, the greater is the saving in carrying it by sea.

Before we opened the canal, most heavy freight from New York or Europe to Panama City on the Pacific was shipped clear around the Horn, although a very good railroad—only forty miles long—existed across the Isthmus.

Much of the prosperity of England is due to the fact that it is so small an island. Land transportation—the bringing in of raw material, the exporting of the finished product—is reduced to the minimum. It is typical that even in inland commerce we speak of goods as "shipped" not "trained." No matter how highly a nation has developed its railroads, its canals and rivers, it is at a very real disadvantage if these routes do not lead to the ocean.

Russia and Germany both suffer from the economic wrong of not having sufficient access to the ice-free seas.

All the great rivers of Russia run to the South. And the Black Sea is landlocked. Its commerce is at the mercy of whoever holds the Dardanelles. The insufficiency of the Baltic and Antarctic Seas has been demonstrated by this War, and Vladivostok is a long way off from the center of Russian life.

The Germanic peoples are grouped geographically about the upper waters of the Rhine and the Danube. They have given these rivers immense industrial importance by the most modern and scientific development, but the mouths of neither of them is in German control. The Danube, like the Russian rivers, empties into the Black Sea. The mouths of the Rhine are Dutch.

During the last generation half a hundred treaties have been signed in regard to trade rights on these important waterways. It has been accepted—in principle—by international legists that no single state can exercise unlimited sovereignty in such cases. "Geographical accidents" of so great importance belong to Europe as a whole. An international commission has been established to regulate traffic on the Lower Danube. (It has not worked very well, because the hostility between the various governments of the Balkans has been too great to allow them to coöperate whole-heartedly on anything. But in spite of this ill-will a good deal has been accomplished in improving the traffic route and the principle of such control has been clearly enunciated.) Holland has escaped this "international *régime*" by making large and frequent concessions to all interested parties. The German trade rights in the Dutch Rhine have been continually expanded.

But still all the Rhine-borne traffic suffers vexatious handicaps. German industry has brought great prosperity to the Dutch ports. An arbitrary political frontier forces the Germans to share the normal profit of their labor with foreigners who have not coöperated in its production. The Dutch—rather like "absentee landlords"—get rich by sitting still.

The Germans have tried to persuade the Dutch to enter the Empire voluntarily. They offered them a position on a par with Bavaria, second only to Prussia. It was rather like offering the landlord a job on the farm. The Dutch refused.

Even if Holland should be absorbed by the Empire, German industry would still be handicapped in comparison to that of England or France or Italy. Even the mouths of the

Rhine, while a great advantage over all her present watergates, could not equal the exceptional facilities of her trade rivals. That this situation should be irksome to the Germans is natural, but it is hardly possible to remedy it without sweeping reforms in the geological formation of the earth.

Austria-Hungary was in a more fortunate position. She had fine ports on the Adriatic, at Trieste, Fiume, Pola and Cattaro. These harbors, especially Trieste, have been very important factors in her industrial development. The Austrian Lloyd, the finest fleet in the Mediterranean merchant service, carries most of the Adriatic trade, runs an express service to Constantinople and the Black Sea ports and another to Egypt, Suez and the Red Sea. Trieste is the window through which all the Germans and Slavs of the Upper Danube look out on the world. But the possession of Trieste and these other ports, while entirely justified by economic considerations, is in rank violation of the rights of nationalities.

"Trade strategy" has taken on a new and vast importance in this War. The closing of the Dardanelles has paralyzed the grain and oil trade of the Black Sea—to the immense advantage of Austria and Germany. The Russian Caucasus and Roumania are the two principal petroleum centers of Europe. The output of these two oilfields is now lying idle or going to the Germans. This is certainly true of the Roumanian oil, and some at least of the Russian oil is probably going to the enemy. The immense quantities of grain which normally come down the Danube and the great Russian rivers to the Black Sea and out through the Dardanelles, are now rotting on the wharves—or going up the Danube. The Germans with this easy access to grain and oil can afford to laugh at the "impotent" blockade of the Entente. The desperate effort to force the Dardanelles—condemned as foolhardy by most neutral military and naval authorities—is motived by the desire to open the sea route to Russia and also the hope of intimidating the Roumanians into stopping their trade with the Germans.

Italy, in the early months of her "neutrality," seized the harbor of Avlona on the Albanian coast, and so, by controlling both shores of the narrow straits of Oranto, can close the Adriatic. The British at Suez and Gibraltar hold both outlets of the Mediterranean, and by their geographical position across the mouth of the North Sea can "bring pressure to bear" on all the sea-borne commerce of northern Europe. The possession of these strategic points is of great importance quite aside from the old and well-established principles of naval strategy, *i. e.*, the interfering with and sinking of the enemy's warships.

Unfettered, cheap transportation—free use of the sea—is as important to modern industrial life as the circulation of blood to the body. The nations like the United States and Russia which can live without international commerce are rare exceptions. The industrial revolution—the invention of steam power, and the division of labor which followed—has completely changed the manner of life of the nations. It has put them at the mercy of anyone who controls the sea. It is no longer necessary to send an army to devastate the enemy's country. It is possible to lay waste its industry by closing its sea-gates. It is not even necessary to declare war. By a judicious scattering of mines and by declaring fresh air contraband, it is possible to smash the industrial life of a "neutral" nation. This War has demonstrated that belligerents will do all in their power to crush the enemy's industry; that, in this effort, they will ignore the rights of neutrals, that they will use the economic power given them by sea-control to force neutrals to join them, and that in the heat of the conflict the governments will not have time to restrain their own citizens from reaping private and not very honorable profits from the situation. The English shippers, for example, have utilized the opportunity of the War and the extraordinary rules of their admiralty to cut in on the carrying trade of Holland to an extent they never were able to do in what is called "fair competition."

To pretend—as the English do—that Germany had no

reason to be uneasy over British navalism, that the rest of the world should have trusted them unquestioningly with this great power, is a proposition hardly worth discussing. The dominant sea power will always be able to collect any tax it cares to on the water-borne commerce of its rivals. And year by year civilization becomes more dependent on world-wide exchange. The English claim that they have never abused this power. They are sincerely convinced of this themselves. But it is hardly a question to be left to the decision of the person who wields the power. There are very few people in the world who agree with them in this matter.

The German criticism of the British position would be unanswerable, if there was any reason to believe that they objected to such arbitrary power *per se*. But their record on land indicates that it is not the *ding an sich* to which they object, but to the fact that their rivals, the English, possess it. They do not want to abolish sea-dictatorship, but to wield it themselves. Their talk about the ruthlessness of the British sea-tyranny is not very convincing. However, most of the neutral nations which are pro-German in their sympathies have taken that side because they would—or think they would—suffer less from German sea-rule than they do from that of the English.

But no matter whether there is any justification for sea-rule or not, it is certain that in the liquidation of this War—whichever side wins—great stress will be laid on the possession of these strategic points which dominate the sea-routes. And, as old-fashioned naval warfare seems to be going out of fashion, the diplomats will consider these points not so much as "bases" for the revictualing and repairing of warships but rather as gates which in the event of a new war can be closed to the detriment of the enemy's commerce.

We may hope, however, that the diplomats will not entirely subordinate their economic discussions to the point of view of war. After all—at the very worst—there will be intervals of peace, and the needs of civilization in such times will deserve some consideration. And this brings us back to the problem of ocean gateways. The freedom of the seas will be of small value to a nation without ports.

Neither Germany or Russia can be given sufficient access to the sea, nor Austria allowed to retain her present harbors without violation of the theory of the right of nationalities. The conflict between these two principles—economic and ethnological—can be intensified or mitigated by tariff arrangements.

The industrial life of a community can be thrown entirely out of gear by customs regulations. A striking example of this was furnished by the Balkan Wars. Salonika is the one really good harbor between Athens and Constantinople. It is the natural water gate for import and export for Macedonia. Under the Turkish rule it fulfilled this function and enjoyed a large prosperity. The treaty of Bucarest divided Macedonia into three sections. The northern part went to Serbia. Salonika and a narrow strip of hinterland went to Greece: eastern Macedonia and the undeveloped harbor of Dedeagatch went to Bulgaria.

At once customs houses were erected along the new frontiers. Goods imported into Bulgarian Macedonia via Salonika had to pay two taxes, the Greek tariff when it was landed and the Bulgarian tariff at the frontier. Produce brought out had to pay the Greek tax before it reached Salonika to be shipped. Inevitably all the trade of Bulgarian Macedonia was diverted to Dedeagatch to avoid the Greek tariff. Salonika, now a port only for a narrow strip of Greek territory, is doomed to lose much of its former prosperity. A new town is growing up in the swamps around Dedeagatch. This dislocation of established trade routes, the ruining of one city and the building of a new one, is pure economic waste. It has no excuse but reverence for the hoary tradition of customs houses.

In theory, free trade would completely solve the problem. If there were no custom barriers, it ought not to make any difference what flag flew over a port. And there is no doubt that every reduction in such mediæval trade restrictions—and they may take the form of freight rates, clearing-house charges or harbor dues—tends to unify the economic life of the world and to remove the causes of friction. But even if all tariffs were abolished—a most unlikely proceeding in the face of such ancient traditions—the problem would not be entirely solved. In practice "human nature" is not yet perfected. And "good will" is quite as important as "free trade" in equalizing economic opportunities.

Some years ago, on a long sea trip I chanced to have many conversations with a German merchant who, after twenty years, had given up his business in Hong Kong—"chased out," as he said. His story illustrates a frame of mind which is almost, if not quite, as important as tariff laws. He had gone out as a youth to act as clerk in a German importing and exporting company in the English "open door" colony of Hong Kong. At that time—twenty years ago—there was only one other German firm in that port.

He had small respect for English traders. They drank too much whiskey, he said, and wasted time playing games. They did business by means of native middlemen. He and his countrymen took the trouble to learn Chinese. He had prospered and in time established a business of his own. Other Germans had come to Hong Kong and had followed his example of hard work and had also prospered. About 1900 half of the business of this British port was in German hands. Then there was a change.

"At first," he said, "the English treated us pretty well. They would not have anything to do with us socially, but they were fair enough in trade. But at last they became scared, they woke up to the fact that we were beating them in every department of business—and then things changed. They did not alter any of their laws—no—they did not have to. If a British and a German ship came into the harbor together, the British ship was docked first. You

see, the harbor master was an Englishman. I have seen
German ships, with consignments on board for me, held
up for two weeks, waiting for a chance to unload. They
have good sanitary laws in Hong Kong. They ought to be
carefully observed, although they cost money. Well—
German merchants in Hong Kong have to live up to the
letter—to the dot on the i's. The English inspectors are
not so severe on their countrymen. One day the representative of the electric company—an Englishman—called on
me and said he would be unable to renew my lighting contract. He was polite about it—very sorry and all that—
technical difficulties. But it was a lie. We, German merchants, had been trying, for a long time, to get a franchise
to install a rival electric plant, we could have furnished
light and power at a big saving—their system was antiquated. But of course we could not get the franchise. We
had to go back to oil lamps. The thing which finally drove
me out was that my lease expired. The owner would not
renew it; no one who owned a decent business place would
rent or sell to a German. The English do not like competition. Of course I subscribe to our Navy League."

Later I talked this over with an Englishman, who had
been in Hong Kong, and he admitted the substantial accuracy of this story, but his reply to it was fairly plausible.
The English have expended an amount of blood and money
on developing their colonial markets which is quite in-
calculable. They resent outsiders coming in to reap where
they have not sown. "Why," he asked, "did not your
German go to his own colony of Kiau Chow? No! They
much prefer ours where all the most dangerous and expensive pioneer work has been done."

It is the same elsewhere. Legally a *régime* of equal
opportunity for all nations has been established by the
French in Morocco. But everywhere the non-French
merchants are closing up their businesses and leaving.
Once upon a time—not so very long ago—there was a
considerable export of goat skins from Mogador to our

glove factories in Philadelphia. Now, a native who sells to an American buyer is not well looked on by the French officials of the port. This trade has been diverted to Marseilles. The central government at Paris and the French people as a whole would undoubtedly disapprove of this interference with American commerce (especially as we stood beside them loyally at Algeciras and refused to protest when they tore up that treaty), but what can they do to restrain the petty officials? The French in Morocco, colonists, civilian administrators and soldiers, reason as did the Englishman about Hong Kong. "Here, we are spending our money and blood to open up Morocco to commerce. Why should foreigners, who bear none of the expense, get the profit?"

If, as a result of this War, Trieste is given to the Italians, German and Austrian trade, no matter what the tariff laws are, will be at a disadvantage in this port.

Although "free trade" will not entirely solve the problems of this conflict between economic and nationalistic interests, it will certainly tend to lessen them, high tariffs will as certainly embitter them.

The considerations of economic interest, of access to raw material and open trade routes, will occupy a large share of the attention of the Peace Congress to come. If the diplomats are inspired by a desire to heal as quickly as possible the wounds of this War, to give to the industrial development of Europe the best facilities, a great deal can be done by commercial treaties. But, on the other hand, the victors can, if they wish, use economic measures as weapons to further abase and paralyze the vanquished.

CHAPTER XIII

THE COLONIAL WORLD

More and more European diplomacy becomes occupied with non-European subjects. Of course the idea of colonies is as ancient as history. But at the Congress of Berlin in 1878 there was hardly any reference in the official sessions to territory outside of the Continent. Russia was pushing her frontiers beyond the Caucasus into Asia, but this was expansion, not colonization. In the corridors Disraeli was offering Tunisia to France but there is nothing about this or similar deals in the official records.

Times are changing. At the Conference of Algeciras in 1906 it was just the opposite—European frontiers were not even mentioned. It is a typical fact that while all we know of the Triple Alliance (the complete treaty has not been published) indicates that it is exclusively continental, all the published texts of the ententes—the newer forms of diplomacy—are exclusively colonial.

There are few points where the political ideals of Europe and America are more sharply differentiated. We are not a colonizing people. The few colonies we have we acquired more by accident than by reasoned design. We do not enjoy them. When we boast of our national riches, the colonies are the last thing we think of. The great mass of our people would rack their brains in vain to discover any way in which they were better off because our flag flies over Porto Rico or the Philippines or Alaska—or Guam. We all pay taxes for their support and very few of us profit by them.

It is entirely different in Europe. In each country one finds colonial societies organized by people whose livelihood directly depends on the colonies and who continually urge their government—even at the risk of war—to increase the overseas domain.

Very few of us receive letters which bear one of our colonial stamps. The colonial mail of Great Britain, France, Holland, and Germany is immense.

We have no grounds to pretend to a high morality on this subject; when we wanted Panama we took it. But as a general proposition the forces which push the Old World into colonial adventure do not operate in the New World. We have no need of colonies.

There are three main causes for the European policy of colonial expansion. (I) Surplus population. (II) Hunger for raw materials. (III) The need for sales-markets.

We may be sure that this War will greatly stimulate the scientific study of the "laws" which govern the birth rate. About all we know of the subject now is the depth of our ignorance.

Parts of the world which are today almost uninhabited once supported dense populations. Not so many centuries ago central Europe was a vast forest which hardly knew the sight of man. Today it is overcrowded. Evidently the number of inhabitants per square mile does not depend on locality—geographical environment.

Occasionally, to one tribe or another—to some branch of the great human family—there comes a spawning impulse. And just as inexplicably this impulse suddenly dies out. Some nations, which for centuries have fairly balanced their deaths and births, begin to grow, some nations, which were once prolific, begin to decline. The matter does not seem to be determined by race.

It certainly is not a matter of political organization or material prosperity. For several generations the Germans have had a noticeably high birth rate. The ups and downs of fate do not seem to have influenced it at all. The devastation of the Thirty Years War and the Napoleonic adventure marked the lowest ebb of their national prosperity, but apparently the degree of their fecundity was not affected by hardships. Since they founded their empire and have achieved wealth they continue to increase and multiply tremendously. On the other hand, in spite of centuries of persecutions, poverty and dispersion, the Jews have grown apace. They are immensely more numerous now than in the days when they lived in the Land of Milk and Honey under the rule of Solomon the Magnificent.

The English had a period of great fecundity which coincided with their burst of colonial enterprise in the seventeenth and eighteenth centuries. Whether one of these phenomena caused the other, or whether they chanced to come together we do not know. While the great excess of births over deaths has diminished, the acquisitive instinct persists. Surplus population cannot be given as an explanation of the British "forward" policy in South Africa or Persia.

That colonial enterprise does not depend solely on the pressure of population is also proved by the case of France. The great colonial empire which was lost by the kings before the Revolution, had not been built up nor accompanied by any large emigration from France. Only parts of Canada and a few points along the Mississippi show signs of French colonization. And certainly surplus population is not the explanation of the new colonial empire which has been founded by the Third Republic. No other country of Europe is in so marked a period of population decline.

The reasons for such a decrease in the birth rate—which may lead to national extinction and may be only a beat in the mystic rhythm of life—are obscure in the extreme and certainly complex. The causes of excessive fecundity are equally unknown. But the "balance of population" has seemed to be of importance in this tragedy of War. As soon as scientists can spare time from high explosives and asphyxiating gases they will give this subject of the birth rate, and its control, new and more intense study.

In the Europe of our day three branches of the family are especially prolific: the Slavs, the Italians, and the Germans.

For Russia this is not a disturbing phenomenon, but on the whole a marked advantage. She has three ways of absorbing this increase of population: (I) the opening up of undeveloped territory, (II) the improvement and intensification of her agriculture, and (III) the growth of industry.

There are vast expanses of Siberian steppes which have never been ploughed, provinces as big as Texas, which are practically fallow. The degree of farm culture in the "developed" districts is very low. The land already under exploitation could, with irrigation, farm machinery, greater capitalization in the way of live stock and scientific methods, support twice or thrice the present population. And every sign points to an imminent and immense industrial awakening. When Russia begins a serious effort to work her national resources—her fields, her mines, her forests and waterpower—she will need to triple or quadruple her supply of workers. At the present rate of increase her population will not press on her frontiers for a hundred years or more.

The situation of Italy is the reverse. There is hardly an acre of her soil which has not been tilled and over-tilled since the days of Romulus and Remus. There is practically no fallow territory. The degree of culture varies from district to district. In some places it could be improved, but on the whole Italian agriculture cannot be counted on to support much more population than it does at present. The raw materials of modern industry are scant in Italy. There has been considerable development of this kind in the northern provinces. But the Italians have to import most of their coal, all of their fuel oil and a great part of their mineral ores. To at least as great an extent as in England, their industry depends on the importation of raw material from overseas. Italy is a poor country and there are probably more people living on these meager resources than at any time in recorded history. But the number of births greatly exceeds the number of deaths. There is nothing to do but emigrate!

The emigrant may find a larger and more satisfying life for himself under a new flag, but he is lost to the Fatherland. And those Italians whose patriotism is racial rather than geographic, who think of their nation in terms of Italian blood and not in expressions of frontiers, regret this loss. They see the little British Isles creating new Englands in Canada and Australia. In this War they see these other Englanders rushing to the defence of the Mother Country. They regret the millions of Italians capable of bearing arms who—citizens of other countries—will not come home to help in the present crisis. So for many years there has been a colonial party in Italy which demanded a colony to absorb their surplus population. They have hoped to turn the current of emigration from the Americas to their new domain in North Africa and to build up there on the southern shores of the old Roman Sea a new Fatherland, where Italians could be Italians still.

This argument of surplus population which has pushed the Italians into their Tripolitaine adventure applies with even greater force to Germany.

Central Europe also is relatively poor in natural resources. Agriculture is more highly developed than in any other large country, but its product does not suffice. In the first decades of the last century the high birth rate served to fill the gaps made by the Napoleonic wars, but in the 'forties and 'fifties the Germans could not find enough food at home and this was the period of greatest emigration to the United States. Then came Bismarck, the economic unity of the Zollverein, successful wars, national unity, the great French indemnity and industrial development. Emigration to America practically stopped. The birth rate had not fallen—in fact the population of Germany has nearly doubled since 1870—but industry absorbed the increase.

However, this marvellous industry has its monstrous side. It has a terrible law of life—it must grow. If it stops for a minute, if it declines or even if its rate of growth decreases, the population problem at once becomes acute. In the years before the outbreak of this War, this was a constant preoccupation of thinking Germans. What would happen in case of an industrial depression? Thousands—perhaps millions—would have to starve or emigrate. By heroic means the government has to a large extent prevented such economic crises as have been known elsewhere. But there was a hectic tendency towards overexpansion in German industry which has worried many observers. It was mortgaged to the knobs on the office doors. They were playing for immensely high stakes, but if luck went against them their loss would be catastrophic. Always of late the need of a reservoir into which they could pour their surplus population, in case of a crisis of unemployment, has been one of the bases of their colonial policy.

It is of course evident that we do not have this motive for colonial expansion. Our situation is more like Russia's. We have need of immigration to people our undeveloped districts.

Colonies also have a definite value to European countries as a source of raw material. The higher the industrial development of a country—the larger the proportion of its population engaged in manufacture—the more imperious becomes the need for a regular supply of the products which feed its machines. British industry would be wiped out if access to its colonies was interrupted. It is often said that Great Britain must control the sea in order to assure her food supply. But even if there were plenty of food for her people, a shortage in raw material for her factories would starve her just as surely.

During the interruption to the cotton trade caused by our Civil War, the textile districts of England suffered immensely. Since then the empire has experimented in cotton growing in all its domains. The regular supply of raw cotton is so important to her, that she cannot trust it to the good will of foreigners, she must control the source. The British government has spent a great deal of money in developing the cotton fields of India and Egypt.

German experiments—for Germany also imports her raw cotton—have shown great promise for cotton production in Mesopotamia, along the route of the Bagdad Railroad. At this moment the cotton spinners of England are watching with especial interest the progress of the British army in the Euphrates campaign. The "cotton interests" of any country would be glad to know that their flag was flying over these promising plantations.

We see exactly the same rivalry for the control of the petroleum supply. The perfection of the "gas-engine" is almost as revolutionary as the development of steam-power. Especially since oil has been successfully applied to land and sea locomotion, the demand for it has gone up by leaps and bounds. The world's supply is limited to a few scattered localities. The oil wells of the United States, the Russian Caucasus, Galicia and Roumania are at present the most productive, but their ownership is fairly well established. Potential oil-fields, whose present owners are weak, are storm centers. An immense amount of international intrigue—a hopeless tangle of finance and diplomacy—has been caused by the discovery of oil in Mexico and Colombia.

But probably the richest undeveloped oil-bearing district today is that of Persia. The Bagdad Railroad would have taken the Germans very close to it. It is quite as much for oil as for cotton that British soldiers—who might be, from a military point of view, more profitably used in European battlefields—are fighting in the deserts of Mesopotamia.

The Italians and French hope to grow cotton in North Africa. Germany, perhaps more than her rivals, is hunting for mineral resources. And all the world is hungry for rubber. The governments of Europe have scientific missions at work in their various colonies studying the mineral and vegetable products and developing practical means to increase the output of such raw materials as can be used by the home industry.

Hardly one of our big, vital trades in the United States is dependent on imported raw material.

Of equal, if not of greater importance, is the fact that the colonies offer a favorable sales-market for the products of industry. Almost without exception the industrialized states of Europe manufacture much more than their citizens can consume—or rather, more than their citizens can afford to buy. This is a phenomenon which the professors of political economy mis-name "overproduction." It is an absurd term. France, for instance, never manufactures more lace and ribbons than her women-folk would like to wear, but normally she manufactures more than they can buy. The wages of the German toy-makers of the Schwartzwald are so pitifully low, that they cannot afford toys for their children. Even the children themselves must work long hours to gain a bare living for the family. So there is "overproduction"—a need for foreign markets.

Some years ago I was told by an American automobile manufacturer that his trade was suffering from "overproduction." I found his statement hard to believe as I had always wanted a motor car and knew no end of people who did not feel that they were suffering from owning too many. I was greatly pleased to read later on of the exploits of Mr. Ford. The trouble with the trade had not been that too many automobiles were being made, but that too few people could afford to pay $5,000 for one.

This technical term "overproduction" does not mean that more of a given article is being made than the community could use, but more than the community can buy. As wages are uniformly low in Europe the per capita buying capacity is small, and "overproduction" is chronic. Unless external markets can be found the factories must close down. This has been especially true in England, where, in times of peace, the problem of unemployment has reached tragic proportions.

There are three classes of foreign markets: (*a*) at one extreme is the relation between one industrial community and others. It is not very profitable. The ironmongers of the Rhine do not make great sales in Pittsburg. (*b*) At the other extreme is the relation between an industrial center and a savage community. It is not very profitable either. The same German ironmongers cannot sell much of their wares to the negroes of equatorial Africa. To savages you can only sell grog, and bibles and glass beads and silk hats. (c) For an industrial nation the most profitable markets are in semi-civilized countries. In China, India, North Africa and Turkey there are railroads and bridges to build, harbors to equip, armies to furnish. It is a trade proverb that you can sell anything to a Turk.

Here again it is evident that the situation of the United States is quite different from that of the European countries. Of all the wealth our industry produces in normal times, less than 10 per cent goes abroad. The sum total of our agricultural export seems gigantic, but it is very small in comparison with the amount of food stuff we consume at home. In only a few highly specialized industries do we find our home market insufficient. All over the world you find our Kodaks, and fountain pens, American harvesters and sewing machines. Even in these products the foreign trade is very much smaller than the home consumption. Many of these things with American names are actually made abroad. Northampton in England is the center of a large shoe trade. On the main street there are half a dozen factories which turn out "American" shoes. They have bought our shoe-making machines and imitated our "trade-marks."

Even given the largest definition to our foreign trade it is a mere bagatelle compared with our internal commerce. At the outbreak of this War our sea communications with Europe and Asia were reduced by more than one-half. But the industrial depression which hit us was very much more due to the disturbance of finance than to the paralysis of the sea routes. The various new forms of "naval blockades" which the belligerents invented so busily hurt the neutral countries of Europe—Holland and Scandinavia and Switzerland—infinitely more than they did us.

Wages are relatively high in America, and our "buying

power" is much greater per capita than in Europe. One trivial, but striking, example is furnished by baby-carriages. An American visiting the parks of the popular quarters of London, Paris, Vienna or Berlin, is struck with the number of women and men who *carry* babies. The wives of working men and small shopkeepers would think a baby-carriage was a frightful extravagance. The kind of people, who consider a porcelain bath tub a necessity in America, regard it as a luxury in England. These are small indications of a big fact. Man for man, the Europeans probably produce more than we, but they buy less. To an extent which we can hardly realize European industry depends for its existence on foreign markets. And, properly managed, a colony offers especial profits.

In judging the value of a colony it is necessary to take into consideration much more than its mere size. Does the climate permit of a large scale immigration from the home-land? Does it produce needed raw material? Will it buy the surplus product of the home factories?

Germany—compared to her principal industrial rivals, France and England—is noticeably poor in colonies; she gets little value from her immense African territories. The climate is deadly to Northerners, they do not to any great extent—rubber is the one exception—supply her lack of raw material, and they are not heavy purchasers of her principal products. An analysis of the custom returns for Southwest Africa and Cameroon shows that most of the articles brought out from Germany were on government orders, for the public works and for the needs of the garrison. Germany's best colonial enterprise was Kaiu Chow. It gave her access to minerals and silk and tea, it was a doorway by which she could pour into China the surplus of her "overproductions." But it was far away and entirely at the mercy of her enemies any time they wanted to exert their "sea-power."

Quite aside from political designs, it was economically logical for Germany to seek trade outlets in Turkey. Here—

at no great distance—she found immense resources of raw material and an eager market. Anton Sprenger in his book on Babylonia speaks of Asia Minor as "the one part of the globe which has not been seized by the nations ambitious to own the earth. But it is also the most favored zone for colonization; and if Germany does not let this opportunity slip before the Cossacks put their hands on it, she will have the best part in the partition of the world." Paul Rohrbach, one of the mildest and sanest of the German writers on such subjects, has also pointed out the exceptional advantages which Asia Minor offers as an ideal field for German enterprise, especially emphasizing the fact that none of the other nations had a prior claim. There were also those in England—I have referred above to the writings of Sir Harry Johnson—who advocated a policy of friendly coöperation in the German efforts in this direction. But the British government did all in its power to thwart the Bagdad Railroad project. It was not till too late—the spring of 1914—that they decided to get out of the way.

The colonial problem has been one of great and growing interest to the Germans in recent years. They are at a marked disadvantage as they entered the field late. For this their national hero—Bismarck—is largely to blame. He was a Prussian junker, a landlord, a magnified peasant. He had no feeling for modern industry, and when at the height of his power he failed to foresee the approaching importance of colonial markets. There were long years when he could—if it had occurred to him—have secured for his people all the colonies they could want. But he was a "European," he thought in terms of "the continent." Colonies appealed to him as apples of discord to keep his enemies divided. It was only reluctantly that he gave heed to the clamor of the growing group of "exporters"—the German Colonial Society was founded in 1882—and gave his consent to over-seas adventures. And by this time there was little left worth taking.

In face of their increasing need for foreign markets there has been a growing discontent in Germany over their meager share in the colonial world. Inevitably their attention has turned enviously towards the prosperous colonies of their weaker neighbors. Little Holland and little Belgium are more fortunate in these matters than great Germany.

It was not only the mouths of the Rhine which the Germans were trying to get when they asked Holland to come into the Empire. They also wanted to share in the rich Dutch colonies. They have also tried by honorable offers of purchase to get hold of the Portuguese and Belgian colonies. The most common criticism of Bismarck is that he did not take Algeria from France instead of Alsace-Lorraine. And the Germans have been quite frank in saying that if they win in this War the main compensations they will demand will be colonial.

That they should covet their neighbors' wealth is not surprising. No country of Europe suffers so acutely from overproduction—of manufactured goods and babies. No country is in such real need of raw material. With considerable reason they can claim that they would make better use of Walfish Bay, Portuguese Angola or the Belgian Congo than their present owners do. And the "official" German doctrine teaches that "needs" and "abilities"—and "might"—give them a "right" to the goods of their weaker and less deserving rivals.

There are two systems of colonization. The one, exemplified by the old Spanish *régime* in America, was frank monopoly. The colonies existed for the benefit of the mother country. Trade with outsiders was absolutely forbidden. Royal edicts forbade the manufacture of hats in Mexico, so that the hatmakers of Madrid could charge what price they liked. Another edict forbade the wine-growers of Peru to sell their product in Panama, because the Spanish merchants did not want competition.

The French practice is derived from that of the Span-

iards, it presents a modernized and mitigated monopoly.
Here and there—as, for instance, in Morocco—the French
have been led to a reluctant promise of the "open door."
But they are hostile to the idea, and in general French trade
has a real advantage—legal or extra-legal—in the French
colonies.

The other system is that of free trade—or at least of
allowing the colonies to arrange their tariffs to suit their
own interests. In some of the British Crown Colonies there
is practical free trade. The self-governing dominions of
the Empire are permitted to decide on their own financial
policy. As a general rule the merchants of the home
country do not enjoy any trade privileges—beyond a vague
"good will"—over their rivals of other countries.

There has, however, been a noticeable tendency of late in
the British Empire towards a sort of economic "nationalism"—very similar in theory to that of the same school of
German economists. The "tariff reform movement,"
led by the Tories, is an effort to establish a Zollverein of
the various units of the Empire and to "protect" British
industry by a high customs wall against the foreigner.
This tariff reform agitation was frankly a weapon against
Germany. Whether or not it would have materialized
(the dominions had nothing to gain by subordinating their
interests to the mother country) the Germans considered it
a serious threat. Their own colonial markets were not
nearly sufficient, and if they had been shut out of the
British Empire it would have been ruin.

However, there is a large school of writers on economics
and politics who maintain that the "rage for colonies"
is unjustified. And nowhere else have I found such tren-
chant and thorough-going attack on the theory of colonization as among some German writers. Perhaps Bismarck was more right in this matter than those to whom
he gave in. Certainly the faction in Germany who are
opposed to colonial enterprise are an unpopular minority,
but their argument is worth summarizing.

The English are the classic example of successful colonizers. Their ventures fall into several classes. First there are the colonies they have peopled with their own stock. At the end of the eighteenth century her most promising colonies in America revolted. Taught by this bitter lesson, she has conceded and conceded to her other English speaking dominions until their actual value to the homeland is at least problematic. In this War, for instance, Canada has rallied nobly to the mother country. But it is hardly conceivable that the help she will bear in this European War will be commensurate to the energy,—money and men—which England has spent in Canada. In times of peace, Canada has not shown any self-sacrificing inclination to favor England in economics. As a source of raw material and an outlet for the products of industry, Canada is more of an asset to the United States than to England.

When you leave out the English speaking dominions, the British Empire is—from a commercial viewpoint—an even more doubtful investment. Of what value is the piece of Central American swamp which is called British Honduras? The Island of St. Helena made a good jail for Napoleon, but does it pay a modern state to hold such possessions? Great Britain, these Germans say, is overweighted with such dead wood.

A great deal can be said for the commercial value of Egypt and India. But remember the Sepoy Rebellion. In both of these territories, the English are sitting on the crater of a volcano. The "nationalist" movement is well developed. The English will have to use a mailed fist policy, definitely crush the revolutionary movement—a policy which for years on end will stop all commercial profit from these colonies—or, by gradually granting ever new concessions, give away all the advantages she has spent so much to win.

Next in order as "successful colonizers" come the French. They began their second colonial period with the annexation of Algeria in the thirties. Now, after more than eighty years, a small band of territory along the coast has been organized into a "civil zone"; it has recently reached the self-supporting stage and is no longer a drain on the Republic. But back of this civil zone, way down into the barren desert, is the military zone where it is all outlay and no profit. The very expensive conquest of Algeria entailed that of Tunisia and more recently launched the nation on this Moroccan adventure. The best that can be said of this North African colonial empire is in the future tense. It may—possibly—pay in the distant future. But for the next few generations it means an immense drain on the French treasury. In a report on the colonies which M. Pauliat presented to the French Senate in 1901 his figures showed that as recently as 1897, in all the colonies—Algeria and Tunisia excepted—there were 4,327 French colonists and 10,097 "*fonctionnaires*." That is, there was a little more than one government official for every half of a colonist. It would not take a great deal more colonial expansion of that kind to ruin even so rich a country as France.

Certainly a small—a very small—section of French business men have made fortunes out of the colonies. But all the nation has paid excessively for this gain to a few individuals. This is also true of "our" enterprise in the Philippines. It is impossible to get accurate figures, but it is evident that if you could find a record of all the profit which has come to Frenchmen—or to "us"— from the colonial policy it would be much less than the vast amounts which the government has sunk in colonizing. It is like a high tariff to protect "infant industries," all the citizens are heavily taxed to make a few individuals rich.

Germany actually has developed profitable markets under other flags. Their colonial trade was infinitesimal compared to their total external trade. The Englishman in an English colony certainly has some advantages over the German trader, but German trade is not being taxed for the expenses of the colony.

The same school of anti-colonial economists argues that it

is no loss to have Germans emigrate and become citizens of another country. Every German who settles in a foreign land—whatever his business—is a sales agent for German commerce. The very profitable export trade in Munich beer is an example often cited.

From a military point of view—for even the anti-colonial economists of Germany always have considered the possibility of war—a far flung colonial domain presents positive disadvantages—which are not counterbalanced by the few colonial troops it is possible to bring to Europe. In this War the Germans did not have to worry about a pan-Islamic revolt. They did not have to suppress a rebellion in South Africa nor send troops to defend the Suez Canal. Their lack of colonial dispersion allowed them to centralize their efforts.

These writers sum up their case with the statement that the development of international finance and industry tends surely to break down all trade monopolies; that gradually but inevitably all countries will be forced to give up their special commercial privileges at home and abroad; that the epoch of high tariffs is only a passing phase in the development of civilization and that as free trade increases the nations which find themselves burdened with the expense of colonial administration will be to that extent at a disadvantage.

It is idle to prophesy, but it is at least possible that future generations will decide that Bismarck was right in not wanting colonies. But in the midst of the industrial stage, which our civilization has at present attained, there are certainly strong arguments in favor of colonial expansion. And every argument which Italy or France or England uses to justify their colonial policy, applies with double or triple weight to Germany. The peace congress to follow this War will give a great deal of attention to the colonial world.

CHAPTER XIV

THE GROWTH OF PUBLIC OPINION

VERY few people in Europe followed with interest the proceedings of the Congress of Berlin in 1878. There is scarcely a word in the *compte rendu* of the sessions nor in the memoires of the delegates to indicate that the diplomats gathered there gave any heed to public opinion.

There was a journal published in Paris—*Mémoires diplomatiques*, which reported such events, but it was a technical review and its editors no more thought of influencing the opinions of the general public than do those of the *Journal of the Society of Physiological Chemists*. The regular newspapers had little to say on the subject. The better informed people knew that Russia had defeated Turkey, that Austria and England wanted to keep the Sick Man alive a little longer, that hostility was running high and that a great war was possible.

At the Conference of Algeciras, one of the delegates protested angrily: "There are more newspaper men here than diplomats." It was true. And the newspaper men were nearly—if not quite—as important as the diplomats. All the great dailies of Europe were publishing long—if not always truthful—accounts of the proceedings. Most of them went to the trouble of sending highly paid men as their correspondents, men who had been trained in the diplomatic service. The public was interested. The French diplomats could not have held so firmly to their position—a firmness which brought them very close to war—if they had not known that public opinion at home was back of them, that the position they had assumed seemed just to the people.

At the Peace Conference to follow this War there will be more newspaper men than diplomats.

Crispi has left an interesting account of one of his interviews with Bismarck. The Italians, worried over the threats of the French catholics to restore the temporal power of the Pope, wanted a Dual Alliance with protestant Germany. Bismarck wanted Italy to join his existing alliance with Austria. Crispi objected that public opinion in Italy would be opposed to any *rapprochement* with Austria—the hereditary enemy. Bismarck gave him a scolding. No government, he said, could successfully fight against public opinion, but a statesman was culpably careless who allowed public opinion to oppose him. He advised Crispi to go home and "prepare"—nowadays we would say "fix"—public opinion.

The force of public opinion, which the Iron Chancellor recognized a generation ago, has grown immensely. All the governments of Europe, by various means and with various degrees of success spend considerable energy in "preparing" it. The governments could be divided with some precision into two classes: those who tell the newspapers what they must print, and those who only tell them what they must not print.

The Ballplatz—the Austrian foreign office—has the reputation of employing the crudest and most unscrupulous means in imposing its point of view on the public. This is so true, that intelligent Austrians, who want to know what is happening in Europe, subscribe to foreign newspapers. *Le Journal de Génève*, published in Switzerland, circulates all over Europe. It gets news from all sides and is almost entirely free from governmental pressure. So it is a good standard by which to check up the truthfulness of the home papers.

Public opinion is much more skilfully handled in Germany. Most of the important newspapers boast of their "official" connections. One is known as the organ of the Navy Department: another of the Agrarian League. Several regularly print articles on foreign affairs which are edited in Wilhelmstrasse. But the effort to make the people "think governmentally" goes much further than the elaborate control of the press. The children in the primary schools, the young men in the universities and in the barracks, the godly when they go to church, rarely heard a word which would displease those higher up. The same precise discipline which makes the Germans march so well, also rules their thinking. The school teacher, the drill sergeant, the professors and pastors, share with the newspaper editors the work of "forming" public opinion.

But, if the German press is thoroughly "harness-broken," the British newspapers "stand without hitching." The political genius of the English consists in governing without seeming to. To take one instance: The organizing Germans, the systematizing French, long before this War broke out, would have had done on paper something about the exact number of soldiers Canada would be required to send to Europe in case of war. There was no document which bound the British Colonies to send any troops to defend the mother country. But during the spring of 1915, there were at times more colonial troops than English in the first line trenches of Flanders.

In the same way the British press, although there is no formal machinery for its control—the military censorship under the Defence of the Realm Act is a special war measure and only preventive—has always been proverbially docile. No one can explain exactly how it is done, but the British Foreign Office can always count on the newspapers following its suggestions. The German government, with all its elaborate "press laws" is not able to get such results as Sir Edward Grey has done in the last few years.

With impressive unanimity the London papers have threatened war with the United States and have thrown us bouquets. At one moment they were all agreed that the Dutch people were a nation of heroes, and with equal unity of thought they suddenly decided that the Dutch were the scum of the earth—who had the turpitude to sell food to the enemy. Almost every English newspaper man I have talked to during the War is convinced that the

Italian policy has been one of crude blackmail. But they do not say this in print. The daily "leaders" call them noble descendants of Julius Cæsar.

It was by watching the newspaper comment on the Balkans that it was most easy to see how Printing House Square takes its tips from the Foreign Office. As the British fleet cannot get through the Dardanelles to threaten Roumania, the policy of Downing Street has been to coax her into refusing to trade with the Germans. The press has not been as violent towards her as towards the other small nations which are exposed to naval action. Bulgaria was first ignored, then flattered, now cursed. The Greeks do not know when they go to bed whether the London papers in the morning will be calling them cowards or comrades.

There is not a foreign minister in Europe who does not wish that the press of his country was as well-behaved as that of England.

In France complete freedom of the press is the peace-theory. During the Algeciras crisis it was "common knowledge" that M. André Tardieu in his daily articles in *Le Temps* was an unofficial spokesman of the Quai d'Orsay. But his position was exceptional. As an extreme comparison one could say that while there are a few newspapers in Germany and Austria which claim to be independent, there are one or two in France which are suspected of being official. Even in the midst of this War, the French newspapers are relatively free. The censor frequently forbids the discussion of certain subjects—slashes out columns of interesting news—but there is no visible effort to force the papers to publish articles which will please the government.

But in no country—not even in England—is the effort to control public opinion entirely successful. Never in history has there been a period when the general public has been so keenly interested in foreign affairs. The governments do not want a discussion of the diplomatic situation. It is in such matters that the censor is most severe. None of the governments are giving to their people the information on which a really enlightened public opinion could be based. No one in France, for instance—outside of the government—knows on what terms Italy joined the Entente. The diplomats do not like to commit themselves to anything definite in the way of terms—some lucky chance may permit them to ask for more than they expected. So, whatever enlightenment public opinion may have, on the problems involved in the peace proceedings to follow this War, will have been gained in spite of, not because of, their diplomats.

But in this matter, the diplomats are waging a losing fight. Even the military censor cannot suppress the discussion. The various governments can expand false information, suppress disagreeable facts, but they cannot repress the curiosity of the public. It is harder to censor books than newspapers. Even in England books and pamphlets circulate which the foreign office would like to suppress. "Nationality and the War," by Arnold Toynbee, is one of a hundred volumes intended to enlighten public opinion. The noticeable weakness of this book is that the author evidently did not get any help from his foreign office. It is a weakness which any book written today must share. The diplomats do not want the public to know what they are trying to do.

It is hard to censor books, it is harder to censor the spoken word. In spite of the diplomats, the discussion goes on—not so healthily as it would in the open—underground. As the months lengthen out, just as happened in our Civil War, the people are getting a clearer and clearer vision of the issues at stake. It is certain that the moment the War is over—perhaps before—these discussions will break all artificial bonds. A public opinion will not only be formed but it will make itself heard in the hall of the Peace Conference. There will be more newspaper men than diplomats at the Congress. Whether they like it or not, the diplomats will know that every important word they say, every important vote they cast, will be reported in the home papers within a few hours.

The governmental effort to mislead public opinion—to trick it with false news—is in itself an admission of the force of public opinion. The most remarkable thing about this War, to me, is the way in which all the governments involved recognize the necessity of convincing their citizens of the justice of their cause. It never occurred to Frederick the Great to tell his subjects where he was leading them. Napoleon began his campaigns with resounding proclamations in which eloquence took the place of reasoned arguments. Today the various governments are spending millions and infinite pains on a detailed presentation of their case. None of them have shown any disposition to tell the truth of the whole-and-nothing-but variety. But all this "campaign literature"—even the official falsehoods—is added proof of the immense interest which the public of Europe is taking in the causes, the progress and the outcome of this War.

The press censorship will probably go by the board as soon as the fighting stops. The official newspapers will go on publishing the truth as their governments see it. The independent press will discuss things more freely. Myriad pamphlets will appear on every phase of the subject. Wherever the Peace Conference is held there will be a swarm of newspaper men. The state of public opinion at home will influence the delegates throughout their labors. And, when they have signed their names to a new map of Europe and return home, they will have to report not to kings but to Parliament.

Public opinion, as it strives to form itself—in spite of the censorship—is evidently very much preoccupied in the problem of peace—a permanent peace.

Most professional diplomats will say that the ideal of permanent peace has nothing to do with their trade; that they must be "realists" dealing only with actualities;

that they must not even try to look down the dim vistas of the future. Such an attitude is entirely in accordance with their traditions. Bismarck and his colleagues about the green table at Berlin in 1878 scoffed at the idea—it was something to interest a theological seminary—not serious minded statesmen. And few European diplomats today will admit that the laying of the foundations of permanent peace is any of their business.

But it is quite certain that public opinion has very different views on the subject. Whatever the diplomats may say about it, almost everyone else thinks that it is one of their main duties to work for peace.

This new ideal about the business of diplomacy has received sanction from the highest quarters. It would be hard to find a single recent speech by a king or a prime minister which does not definitely promise his people that the object of this War is to end war. "Not peace, but the peace" was a phrase which made the rounds in the summer of 1915.

A very interesting collection of reports from the school teachers in a mountain district of France has recently been published. The Minister of Education has instructed all his staff to keep diaries of these stirring times. It will furnish rich material for future historians. The first section to be printed contains the reports of the "mobilization" in the province of Dauphiné. The school teachers tell how the news of the declaration of war reached their Alpine villages and how the "reservists" set out "to join the colors," and what the villagers had to say about it. It is impressive how often the same phrases came to the lips of these peasants as they sought words to comfort the wives they must leave to bring in the harvest and care for children. "It is best so," they said, "we will finish it up, so the children will not have to fight."

If—as some prophesy—this War is only a prelude to a long series of wars, there will be a profound disillusionment all over Europe. Millions of men, from one end of the continent to the other, are fighting bravely, uncomplainingly, but on the whole, regretfully. More or less clearly they feel that the men they trusted with this business of diplomacy did not measure up to their duty. And every statesman, who listens to the voice of his people—whatever his theories in regard to permanent peace—knows what is expected of him.

The diplomats have considerable justification in maintaining that it is not their business to establish peace. They are very much in the position of the lawyer, and no one is so optimistic as to expect lawyers to abolish litigation. The diplomat is only an agent. He follows, according to his abilities, his instructions. He cannot abolish war as long as his clients want to fight.

There are two conceptions of peace, and in neither case can the diplomat do much about it single-handed. The first is the pax Romana. It is victorious warriors who erect that kind of peace. Today, a sort of pax Britannicæ reigns on the Seven Seas. Except in a few clearly defined areas there is no naval warfare. Such a peace is of course quite satisfactory to the English. But no one has been able to establish anything like such a predominance on land since the Fall of Rome. It is even doubtful if England can—in case of victory—maintain her undisputed rule of the seas. It is entirely improbable that any such peace of domination will result from this War.

The only other kind of peace, which is not a mere truce, an arming for a new war, must be based on mutual justice. Peace, for instance, is a mirage between the Tsar and his people. There may be armistices now and then, but when a hundred million people feel themselves the victims of a raw and blatant injustice—typified in one man—there can be nothing but war. There can be no hope of peace between capital and labor as long as either side smarts under a manifest injustice. It is the same between nations. If the ideal of justice is unrealizable, war is inevitable. The diplomats by themselves cannot eliminate the injustices which are at the roots of conflict.

It is quite fantastic to expect peace to grow out of war. War inflames the passions—with vile lusts as well as with noble enthusiasm—and justice must be the work of cool blood. About all we can hope for from the congress to come after the War is that the diplomats will avoid the obvious mistakes which will render it difficult or impossible to do real work for peace in the years to come.

It is fairly obvious that there is something too real to be ignored back of this theory of the rights of nations. People with the same language and traditions tend to develop a sense of nationality and an aspiration to group themselves in an independent political organization. The denial of their "right" to realize their aspirations seems to them an injustice—a *casus belli*. Any flagrant violation of this principle on the part of the diplomats will be planting the seeds of a future disaster.

It is also evident that economic considerations have a great deal to do in precipitating war. Any attempt to crush the industrial life of the vanquished—any effort to cut them off from raw material or markets, to smother them by tariffs or to interfere with their free use of the trade routes of the sea—will be planting the seeds of new discords.

It is also fairly well demonstrated that no people are so cowardly as not to fight to preserve their existence. In the reactionary circles of France and England people talk— and even write articles—about how to annihilate Germany. The Tories of Germany say that Belgium no longer exists and that France and England must be rubbed off the map. Any effort to annihilate the vanquished—unless it is done thoroughly by preventing the production of a new generation—will make peace impossible.

But it is not too much to hope that the statesmen of Europe may have learned this lesson. Russia and Germany have both tried to eliminate the Polish question and both have failed, just as England has failed to dragoon Ireland and as our first "reconstruction" policy failed in the South.

If half the threats which are commonplaces in the European press are carried out—no matter which side wins—we can bid good-bye to the idea of peace.

The British experiment in South Africa gives us reason to hope. If the governments of Europe, when they give their instructions to their delegates at the peace conference, have that lesson in mind, the future of Europe may be better than most of us dare to expect.

It was the most remarkable example in the records of practical politics of what can be done for the peace of the world. The Boer War itself gave England very little to be proud of. But the Tory Government which had engineered and conducted it—misconducted it—gave place to a Liberal Ministry, which earnestly—and as the event has proved, wisely—set to work to heal the wounds of that conflict. There is very little in the history of the world of which Liberals have more right to be proud than of this settlement. It is one of the most shining examples of British political genius. In very much less time than it took the United States to rewin the loyalty of the confederacy, the British empire won a surprising degree of loyalty from the defeated Boers.

If the European Congress, which is to liquidate this War, is held under the auspices of governments which are inspired by an equally wise liberalism—for the diplomats will obey instructions—there is reason to hope that no cause for immediate hostilities will be left and that the friends of peace will be able to go on working for their ideals untrammelled by diplomatic blunders.

This is the one real basis for the hope of better times. The issues will not be fought out solely by the diplomats grouped about their "green table." The real decisions will depend on public opinion at home.

No diplomat, returning from this congress, will ride up the avenue of his capital, waving his silk hat to an uniformed, admiring crowd, who shout approbation to such a vague and bombastic phrase as "peace, with honor."

The coachman will turn about in his seat and say: "Your Excellency, why did you annex all that African swamp?" A newsboy from the sidewalk will cry: "Why did you abandon that railroad concession in China?" The papers of the opposition, and hostile members of Parliament will ask similar and more searching questions. The diplomat who cannot answer them will be in a bad way.

It is a tradition among the diplomats—a tradition shared by M. Delcassé and Sir Edward Grey among others—that the people are not intelligent enough to understand foreign politics. But the gory head of more than one statesman has decorated a lamp post because its owner did not understand the people.

It is rather dangerous business to ask men to leave their farms and workshops, their wives and children, to fight for peace and then, when the war is over to say, "We were only joking. You are so stupid we had to lie to you. Peace is a mirage, an illusion. Now you must go home and pay heavy taxes to arm for the next war. And you must begin at once to teach your children how to fight."

There can be no doubt that the people of Europe—on both sides of every frontier—have taken their statesmen seriously when they promised to lay the foundations of permanent peace. "Not a peace, but *the* peace."

BOOK III
THE LIQUIDATION OF THIS WAR

CHAPTER XV

THE MILITARY OUTCOME

Obviously the diplomatic settlement of the War depends first of all on the fate of the armies in the field. And no phase of life is more proverbially uncertain. Of the myriad factors which determine the success or failure of a campaign, a large share are so confused and obscure that they are generally called "luck." Napoleon is said to have lost the battle of Waterloo because of a bad map and a fit of indigestion.

There are two extreme possibilities. (1) A complete triumph for the Deutschtum. (2) A crushing defeat for the Germans. But nothing is more improbable than an extreme decision. All things are possible, but it is hardly likely that the Germans will dictate peace in Paris or Petrograd or London, or that the armies of the allies will enter Berlin.

There is a chance of a drawn game, resulting from mutual exhaustion. But this assumes a perfect equilibrium of force—like that of the two Kilkenny cats. The balance will probably swing definitely to one side or the other.

If we figure these possibilities graphically, as though represented on a globe like our earth, with a complete allied victory for the North Pole and a German triumph for the South Pole, and the equator for a dead-lock, we can say with some certainty that the future peace congress will meet in one of the Temperate Zones, that the War is more likely to end in the Tropics than in either the Arctic or Antarctic circles.

To discuss the diplomatic problem to be met after the War, we must arbitrarily assume a decisive outcome. The more definite the victory of one side or the other, the simpler these diplomatic problems become. It does not matter very much which side we choose, for if we guess wrong the considerations at issue will not be changed, only the method and direction of their application will be reversed.

Although the memoirs of all great generals tell us that we must always leave a large margin for chance, it is possible to state some of the factors of the military struggle— the factors which appear to be the dominating and determining ones.

In the spring of 1914—just before the outbreak of the War—the resources of Germany were less than those of the coalition which opposed her. Aside from her own forces, Germany could count with certainty only on the help of the tottering empire of the Hapsburgs. Their combined strength was notably less in men, in money, in industrial resources, than those of Great Britain, France, and Russia. Her disadvantage at sea was even more striking. But because of immensely superior organization, she could utilize a larger percentage of her strength at once; she entered the campaign very much stronger than her enemies.

The Powers of the Entente were stronger—on paper. But no one of them was organized for war. Marcel Sembat was right in the book to which I referred above. A republic cannot compare with such an organization as the German empire in creating a fighting machine. France and England, because of their more liberal *régime*,—Russia because of her mediæval reactionary autocracy and system of Grand Ducal corruption, could not throw anywhere near as large a percentage of their strength into the first clash. It was little short of miraculous that France was able to concentrate enough force at the Marne to win that battle and check the first drive of the Germans.

The Allies suffered another serious handicap—what is called *la maladie des coalitions*. They had no centralized command. While the German war council had all of its forces obedient to a single will, the Allies, before any serious decision, have always had to waste time coördinating the views of Petrograd, Paris, and London.

On the whole, during the first year of the War this lack of coördination was more manifest in diplomatic than in military matters. Great Britain, following her own naval policy, did much to alienate the sympathy of the neutrals. She so angered the Swedes that the railroad which connects Russia with the Atlantic across Scandinavia was sometimes closed. The French, Russian, and English diplomats between them succeeded in bringing in Italy. But this has been more than offset by the entry of Turkey on the side of Germany. Italy has not as yet accomplished anything for the Entente Powers to compare with their loss of prestige at the Dardanelles. And the entry of Italy into the coalition made it necessary to consult Rome as well as the other three capitals.

But it was in the fall of 1915—the beginning of the second year of the war—that this lack of coördination in the councils of the Allies became most apparent and most disastrous. Their diplomatic fiasco in the Balkans bids fair to be followed by a military disaster. And of greater seriousness than this is the marked tendency of the Allies to say that the others are to blame. Such recriminations at the very best weaken the coalition—at the worst, they may ruin it.

But the resources of the coalition are so much greater than those of the Germans that they can afford a certain amount of bungling. Even if the German drive towards Constantinople is entirely successful, even if all the Balkan States join the Germans, even if Egypt and India revolt, the odds are still in favor of the Entente Group—*provided* they stick together, *provided* they improve their fighting organization, *provided* their will to conquer is as strong as that of their enemies.

Undoubtedly these "ifs" are big. It would take a bold prophet to answer "yes" decisively to all of them.

However, it is not probable that the Entente Coalition will break up during the course of the hostilities. Modern war is a great national effort. It develops a national enthusiasm which acquires a sort of momentum. As recently as the Napoleonic wars it was customary for nations to change sides on the eve of a battle and go over to the enemy. Such bold treason is not likely today. The danger is rather that one or another of the members of the coalition may think that it is doing more than its share and content itself with a "platonic war." There is a very common belief among the French that they are doing more than their share. With a large part of their own country invaded, there was in some quarters a strong feeling against sending troops to the Balkans to protect the British colonies of India and Egypt. But all of the Entente Powers have so much to lose by defeat, and their hope of victory is so dependent on common action, that there is little chance of any of them playing their allies false.

They are improving their organization. In this field France has immensely surprised her allies. There are even some neutral observers who say that she has as large a percentage of her potential force in the field as Germany. This is an exaggeration. But she is gradually climbing up towards an equality with her rival. If one could grade the German organization at one hundred per cent—and it was certainly the best the world has ever seen—the French were perhaps at fifty per cent at the outbreak of the war and have now attained seventy-five per cent. In some developments—such as the organization of the munition industry—she has possibly reached one hundred per cent.

In regard to Russia there is very little accurate information. They have never even dreamed of utilizing in war as large a proportion of their men as Germany has. In mere numbers they are richer than anyone else. The problem with them is the efficiency of their officers and the adequacy of their supply of munitions. Their command was generally poor at first. But they have shot a good many traitors and have disgraced a great many incompetents and are undoubtedly much better commanded today than at the outbreak of hostilities. As their industries are hardly more than rudimentary, their munitions problem depends mostly on their transportation facilities. As long as the Dardanelles are closed, these will be very limited. But they can always put as many men in the field as they can equip.

Reliable information is also hard to secure about Great Britain. The large optimism of some of their official spokesmen is disproved by the meager results they have obtained on land. They were prepared for naval work and have done it well. They have probably increased their predominance over Germany in this matter. Their mobilization of industrial resources was very slow. Few people in England were prepared for the idea that modern warfare is a national affair. In previous conflicts the navy and army had done the work and the mass of the people carried on business as usual. But "business as usual" is a slogan in direct antithesis to the needs of a modern war. The nation which can get the greatest amount of sacrifice out of the greatest number of its citizens is best prepared for war. A realization of this fact grew slowly in England. By a strange paradox the British, while reluctant to adopt compulsory military service or to interfere with business, have gone farther than their allies in the compulsory mobilization of finance. France has relied mostly on voluntary loans "*Les Bons de la Défense Nationale.*" The English have commandeered private wealth by heavy direct taxation. While they have not yet put into the field anything like as large a percentage of their potential strength in men as Germany or France, their army is certainly stronger than at first and can still be increased. In short, their "organization," far below that of the enemy at the outbreak of hostilities, has improved and it is to be expected that a larger and larger proportion of their strength—industrial, financial, and military—will appear in usable form.

The overcoming of the lack of coördination between the Allies is a more difficult and delicate matter—and in this problem no visible advance has yet been made. But in these days of wireless telegraphy, it is not an insolvable problem. While the Allies will never enjoy the great advantage of a centralized command in the affairs of war and diplomacy, they must, through bitter experience, learn to ameliorate the situation.

Questions in regard to the will to conquer are too subtle to be given any definite answer. However the defence is generally more grim in its determination than the aggressor. As long as the Allies are fighting on their own soil for its liberation they are more likely to have the "superiority in morale." The French soldier in Champagne or Artois is more likely to fight furiously than the Bavarian soldier in the heart of Poland. To the Germans, with their amazing record of victory, peace must look more tolerable than to the Allies whose territory is invaded. It is hardly possible to imagine a Belgian wanting peace at present. For the Entente Powers to stop fighting short of victory—or a crushing defeat—would be to admit German superiority, while they still have a chance of disproving it.

Considered from a purely military point of view the outlook for the Allies is good. In this sense time fights for them. If they stick together, if they learn from experience to overcome the faults of their organization, if their will to win does not weaken, they get stronger with each passing month. The Germans will be doing marvels if they keep up their present power. It took the North four years to discover Grant—*i. e.*, the organizer of effort, the centralized command, the grim determination to fight it out on this line if it took all winter.

It is a race between superior organization and superior resources. And while it is not possible to increase resources, it is possible to improve organization. If the Allies stick together—and do not throw it away—victory is theirs. I think they will win.

So—disclaiming any pretence of prophecy—I will first assume the definite defeat of Germany. This is of course an arbitrary assumption. It is quite possible that the outcome will be the reverse. I will discuss that possibility separately. But it is necessary to assume one conclusion or the other in order to simplify the diplomatic problems.

I assume that the armies of the Allies cross the Equator (which is, of course, "an imaginary line" and does not correspond with any existing frontier) and fight a victorious battle in the German tropics and are pressing on towards the Temperate Zone. They cannot hope to advance much farther without a series of bloody battles, they cannot increase their advantage without great effort and expense, and in the army and at home everyone is tired of war. But the generals and statesmen are confident that—in spite of the cost—they can press onwards towards the Arctic regions and even to the Pole. The last victory has heightened their confidence.

On the other side, the German General Staff, the Kaiser and his ministers, know that they are not completely beaten, that they are still in a position to organize a stubborn defence and can make the enemy pay a frightful price for every advance, but they have given up hope of a complete victory. They know in their hearts that the enemy has the upper hand, and that—if the war goes on—their only hope of escaping hopeless defeat lies in some chance collapse of the enemy's will. But the reports from home speak of increasing poverty in the means of life and the munitions of war, while their spies tell of the determined enthusiasm of their opponents. They know that they will be able to get better terms of peace now, when there is much fight left in them, than they could hope for at a later period when they had reached the end of their resistance. Under such circumstances they would, in all probability, let it be known that they would listen to a proposal for an armistice.

The history of recent wars shows that the old idea of an armistice is dead. No one, any longer, is willing to trust the word of his opponent. They will not even grant a few hours truce to bury the dead. The Allies will be reluctant to stop their military operations for fear that the Germans would use the interval to reorganize their force. At the time of the first Balkan war, this problem was met by one of the Allies—the one with naval power—refusing to sign the armistice. Bulgaria, Servia, and Montenegro stopped fighting, but Greece kept up the war right through the peace proceedings at London and, by her control of the sea, was able to keep the Turks from importing coal or bringing troops from Asia Minor by water. So, in the situation I have suggested, it is probable that England would refuse to sign the armistice and would maintain her blockade.

At all events the Allies would not agree to a cessation of hostilities, except on terms which would grow more and more onerous for Germany with the passage of time and so prevent them from dragging out the proceedings indefinitely. Whatever the terms of the armistice, this will be their main purpose—to put the enemy in a position which will automatically get worse and worse and so bring increasing pressure on him to accept the demands of the victors. A naval blockade is an obvious means towards this end.

Among the terms of the armistice will be the choice of a place for the Peace Conference. This may seem at first thought a small matter, but there will be a tense struggle of will on this point, and the result will be something of an indication of the relative strength of the two parties.

Some of the enthusiasts of the Entente—confident in an overwhelming victory—say that the Peace Conference must be in Brussels, or Louvain. There is, probably, no spot on earth where the defeated Germans would feel themselves less among friends. If they consent to come to a Belgian city to discuss the definite terms of peace, it will mean that they are very thoroughly beaten. They will probably suggest Stockholm—a place where the Russians are feared and the English are hated. The Allies, if victorious, certainly will not accept a city where the British policy of blockading Europe has made them so unpopular.

Some place in the United States is a possibility, but

hardly a probability. It is generally felt in Europe that our influence will be towards compromise, that we will try to make the victor moderate in his terms. We are supposed to have a penchant for the under-dog. So, while the defeated may suggest Washington, the victor will probably insist on a European city. Also all the more democratic elements in Europe will want to keep the proceeding as close to home—as nearly in touch with public opinion—as possible. A compromise on Switzerland is probable and again the choice between German speaking Zurich and French speaking Geneva will be indicative.

The augurs will also draw prognostics from the interval between the signing of the armistice and the date set for the opening of the congress. It is a fair assumption that the victors will arrange the terms of the armistice in such a way that from a purely military point of view delay will weaken their enemy and strengthen them. So, if the diplomats of the Allies show haste or the German statesmen try to delay the proceedings, it will indicate that non-military forces are at work. It would probably mean discord among the Allies.

CHAPTER XVI

DIPLOMATIC TACTICS

If the German armies are destroyed—or threatened with destruction—the future of the German people will be in the hands of the Imperial Diplomatic Corps. And they will center their efforts on trying to sow discord among the victors.

This is the one "defensive" tactic of diplomacy. The classic example of what can be accomplished in this manner was furnished by the activity of Talleyrand, the French delegate to the Congress of Vienna, after the crushing defeat of Napoleon. This most astute diplomat saved much more out of the wreckage than anyone dreamed could be saved and he did it by fanning jealousies and stirring up disputes between Russia and England and Prussia and Austria. The fundamental maxim of diplomacy—at which Bismarck was quite as clever as Talleyrand—is "Separate your enemies."

The German diplomats were signally unskilful at this in the years before the War. The grouping of their enemies became closer after every crisis and the only "separation" they managed to achieve was that between their friends, Austria and Italy. But as soon as war broke out they tried openly—rather too openly—to regain the ground they had lost. In the first days of September, 1914, when the German armies were threatening Paris, tentatives were made to separate England and France and to make a separate peace with the latter. Continuous efforts have been made to bribe or frighten Russia and Servia into deserting their friends.

The Allies responded to these "tactics" by the Declaration of London, in which Great Britain, France, and Russia pledged themselves to prosecute the War and to make peace in common. It is interesting to note that the Balkan Allies before attacking Turkey—in 1912—reached an agreement similar in spirit, if not in wording. They kept it throughout the First War, but, as soon as Turkey was disposed of, they began to quarrel among themselves.

It is no longer probable—as happened so often in the Napoleonic period—that a nation will suddenly change sides in the midst of a war. It is, of course, still a possibility, but the chances are that the signatories of the Declaration will live up to their word. But the momentum which tends to keep them united during the war will slow up when the fighting stops. As the exaltation of conflict subsides the common interests seem relatively less important than individual interests. It is after the war that these tactics of sowing discord have the greatest chance of success.

Every historic crisis which has any resemblance to this War indicates that the success of such tactics is well within the realms of possibility. To reduce these risks of discord to the minimum is the present preoccupation of all the more broad-minded diplomats of the Entente, and, doubtless, how to use the fear of such discord to the advantage of their own government is the present preoccupation of the more narrowly patriotic diplomats.

There are many joints in the armor of this anti-German Alliance. None of her Allies, for instance, have any interest in seeing Great Britain increase her naval supremacy. The English seem to find it hard to realize why anyone objects to their ruling the waves. But, as a matter of fact, almost everyone does. If the neutral nations have a voice in the Congress they will all side with Germany in a seditious demand for freedom of the seas.

The American attitude on the matter is typical. In times of peace, when the British did not bother us by abuse of their sea power, we hardly noticed that they had it, we had no objections to their pretensions of "a divine right." But when, at the outbreak of this War, they began to violate all the accepted ideas of international law and to interfere with our commerce in non-contrabands with neutral nations, we began to ask: "Why should the English rule the waves? How much effort on our part would it take to dispute this high-handed domination?"

The discomfort which British navalism, and their bizarre blockades have caused us is very small compared to what Holland and the Scandinavian countries have suffered, and, as far as we are concerned, it is likely to grow less. For nothing could be more senseless than for the English to drive us to dispute their sea-rule. We are in every way better situated to do so, if we really set our mind to it, than Germany was. Every argument points to the probability that Great Britain will seek our friendship on the sea rather than our hostility. But the smaller nations of Europe would all—if allowed a vote—support a naval code which would limit the arbitrary power of the English fleet.

While her present allies are glad that Great Britain is strong at sea—for the first months of the war it was the only help she could bear them—they have no interest, once Germany is defeated, to see that power grow. Russia is, to a large extent, disinterested in the fate of the seas. It was mostly due to English influence—after the Anglo-Russian Entente—that she began building her anti-German fleet. Her future is manifestly on land. France and Italy, however, are maritime, colonial nations. Once this War is over they have no interest in seeing British navalism strengthened.

On the other hand Russia, France, and Italy have interests which are opposed to the traditional policy of the British empire. Nothing is more clearly indicated by history than that it is instinctive for British statesmen to oppose the expansion of their neighbors in the direction of English colonial possessions—and they have colonies in every direction. For a long time, especially since the cutting of the Suez Canal, the English have considered it a vital necessity to dominate the Mediterranean. The "regularization" of their situation in Egypt has not lessened their stakes in this neighborhood. The English also expect to inherit all the German developments in Asia Minor and especially the famous Bagdad railroad. They have already occupied the shores of the Persian Gulf and are pushing up into Mesopotamia.

Now the Russians lay claim to Constantinople and the Straits. The French intend to "protect" Syria and Lebanon. The Italians claim Alexandretta. This means the establishment of three—possibly rival—powers in the Eastern Mediterranean, three places where European armies can be concentrated at the gates of Egypt. It also means sharing the profits of the Bagdad railroad, for the Mediterranean terminus will be in Russian, French or Italian hands. Great Britain fought one war (the Crimean) and threatened another (The Congress of Berlin) simply to keep Russia away from this district. If her allies get what they expect from victory British naval dominance in the Mediterranean is over.

Now, these considerations are not secrets, they are commonplaces. The German diplomats know them by heart. It is evidently a field for defensive tactics. They will offer to back French and Russian and Italian claims at the expense of Turkey, if they, in turn, will promise to vote against England in naval questions—if only they will vote to make it a World Congress, including the neutral as well as the belligerent powers, *i. e.*, to increase the number of anti-English votes on naval matters. There are opportunities for endless intrigues on this subject.

No one knows, with any certainty, what is going on in the diplomatic councils of the Allies. And it is one of the most obvious arguments against such secrecy that it encourages all sorts of rumors, invites all the most sinister forms of intrigue. The Germans are, of course, taking advantage of this and are doing their utmost to shake the confidence of their enemies in the loyalty of their Allies.

One such rumor was current in Paris in June, 1915. There was a very detailed story going the rounds that a secret accord had been signed at London between Italy and Great Britain by which they bound themselves to vote together in the future Congress against France and Russia in the Near East questions. So definite an "entente" is highly improbable, but unfortunately it is a possibility. And this story—very possibly started by a German agent to demoralize the public opinion of France—had as a sort of sequel all the history of the British diplomatic controversy with Portugal over their conflicting claims in South Africa. I heard this rumor in Paris from two quite different sources. In both cases, when I said that I did not believe the British government would be quite so base, the reply, in almost the same words, was: "Do you know about their ultimatum to Portugal? (11th January, 1890.) I thought the Austrian ultimatum to Servia was pretty bad till I read this English ultimatum."

An inexplicable mystery has surrounded the entry of Italy into the War. First she declared war on Austria-Hungary. Months later she declared war on Turkey. Whether or not she is at war with Germany is uncertain. That intrigue is rife over this equivocal situation is certain. The lack of frankness lends itself to the most sinister suspicions. Such *mal-ententes* are promising soil for German diplomats to plant the seed of discord.

Unfortunately diplomatic history is only too full of rank treacheries and brutalities, and some—like this Anglo-Portuguese affair—are so recent that it takes a very large optimism to hope for a complete reformation in so short a time.

All that can be said with certainty is that no disloyalty between allies would be so raw as not to find ample precedent in history, that the interests of the Allies—aside from waging this War to victory—are far from identical; that there are manifest tendencies towards discord which increase with time, and may become acute as soon as the fighting ceases; and that it is the obvious thing for the German diplomats to study these tendencies towards dissension and encourage them. It is their one hope to save something out of the wreckage in case of defeat.

And if the military outcome should be the reverse of what I have suggested the situation would be the same. The diplomats of the defeated Entente would attempt to sow discord between Germany, Austria, Bulgaria, and Turkey, and, by sacrificing their former friends, try to make better terms for themselves.

As the "tactics" of the defeated are obvious, so the "tactics" of the victors are clear. It will be to the interest of the diplomats of the Entente to divide the peace proceedings into two sharply separated sections; first, the presentation of their united demands on the Germanic alliance; second, a conference of the victors to divide the spoil—a conference from which the defeated will be excluded. In no other way could they so effectively counter German intrigues. If Talleyrand had not been allowed to sit at the Congress of Vienna he could not have saved so much from defeat.

Nor could the Allies, by any other means, so strikingly demonstrate the importance of their victory. From one point of view the cause of this War is typified in the German challenge: "Nothing can happen in Europe without our consent." It would be a triumph—perhaps sentimental, but certainly impressive—if the victors could arrange a new map of Europe without even consulting the Germans.

Nothing is more unlikely than that the actual peace proceedings will follow this formula, but, in so far as they depart from it, it will be a diminution of the Allies' victory. Unless they can do things in this way there is grave risk—even a probability—of disastrous dissension in the face of a half-defeated enemy. Nothing less than a most improbably overwhelming success on the field of battle will allow them to arrange things so simply as I have suggested. The chances are here—as in the past—that the diplomats of the defeated will regain a good part of what the soldiers have lost.

But it will simplify the discussions of the diplomatic

problems involved if we assume an extreme issue—having suffered some notable reverse, the Germans sue for peace, an onerous armistice is signed and two weeks later the plenipotentiaries of the belligerents meet at Brussels: as soon as the opening formalities are over, the Allies present their united demands in the form of an ultimatum, requiring within a specified time a "yes" or "no" answer: A negative answer breaks the armistice, and the allied armies are ordered to continue their march towards Berlin. Sooner or later—unless the military tide turned—the Germans would have to submit. Then the diplomats of the Entente could meet by themselves about a green table in some other hall to divide the spoil with less fear of German intrigue.

There never has been such a solution to a previous war. No matter which side wins, it is improbable in this case, but I assume it for the sake of simplification.

CHAPTER XVII

THE DEMANDS OF THE ENTENTE

A WELL-KNOWN proverb advises against counting one's chickens before they are hatched, but the statesmen of the Entente are convinced of their ultimate victory and have begun to discuss among themselves the terms they will demand of the Germanic alliance. They have not, however, taken the public into their confidence. They are probably far from agreeing among themselves.

In their speeches and statements to the press, the prime minister and diplomats have agreed on only one clear-cut proposition. Alsace-Lorraine is to go back to France. The inhabitants of this district are not to be consulted. It has been decided for them at London, Petrograd, and Paris.

The other formulæ on which they have publicly agreed are vague—as for instance reparation for the Belgians. They have pledged themselves to make the first condition of peace, the evacuation of Belgium and restitution for all the damage done. But whether they mean an indemnity in money or territory, colonial or European, has not been announced.

The former Commander in Chief of the Russian armies, the Grand Duke Nicolas, issued a proclamation to the Poles, promising them reunion in one political group under the Russian scepter, and certain vague liberties. This proclamation has not received the public sanction of the Tsar nor of his government. But the French and English statesmen seem to have taken the Grand Duke's promises seriously, and have frequently spoken as if the victory of their arms meant the creation of a united and autonomous Poland.

Russian officials have been reticent in the matter—and the reason is not far to seek. There was a certain grim logic in the old autocratic *régime* of oppressing everybody. It will be inconsistent to give "liberties" to the Poles which are denied to the Finns, the Letts, the Ruthenes, the Georgians, and even the Russians themselves. But the public opinion of the Tsar's liberal allies will be sadly disappointed if the Grand Duke's promises are not kept. If they are kept it will mean new hope for all the peoples of all the Russians.

But there has been no published statement as to the frontiers of this proposed national unit, nor as to the theory on which they are to be drawn. A military strategist would draw the frontiers in one way; a political economist would certainly give the Poles an outlet to sea along the lower Vistula and so cut Prussia into two separate parts; an ethnologist would draw quite another shape on the map; a historian, who tried to "reconstruct" Poland would reach still another result.

On this delicate question of what territory they mean by "New Poland" the diplomats have observed a discreet silence. When the time comes for them to draw the frontiers they will be influenced by the extent to which they want to hit Prussia. If they decide every disputed point against the Germans, Poland will be very large.

Servia has also been assured that her "legitimate national aspirations" will be realized. But there is a large difference of opinion as to which of her national aspirations are "legitimate." The Serb race, like the Polish, has vague outlines. On all sides it melts into and mingles with other races: Roumanian, Bulgar, Greek, Albanian, Italian, Hungarian. But the expression "realization" of her "national aspirations" can hardly mean less than that Austria will have to abandon to her Bosnia and Herzegovina—perhaps all her southern Slavs. The Serbs also expect to receive an ample coast line on the Adriatic.

If the Roumanians decide to join forces with the Entente

Group—and her action is very uncertain—she will be encouraged to claim all the provinces of the Dual Monarchy where her language is spoken.

Italy is offered her "unredeemed" territory in the Austrian provinces of Trentino, Istria, and Dalmatia. And it is probable that she has been promised territories in this last province—the coast of the Adriatic—where her language is not spoken.

Italy—and Greece, if she decides to join the Entente—are also offered large shares in the spoils of Turkey.

It is generally agreed that Turkey is to be cut to pieces.

In these territorial changes the German Empire would suffer less than its allies. The Powers of the Entente will ask Turkey to cease to exist and Austria-Hungary to abandon many rich provinces. Bulgaria will be heavily penalized. This last cannot be done without violation of the theory of the rights of nationalities. But if the Powers of the Entente owe their victory to Greek help they will probably allow them to annex even more Bulgarian population than they took by the Treaty of Bucarest in 1913. Their territorial demands on Germany would be limited to Alsace-Lorraine, Poland (an elastic term), possibly Schleswig to the Danes, and some of the Rhine provinces as an indemnity to Belgium.

But the statesmen of the Entente have agreed on another very vague formula. German militarism must be destroyed. It is said that three times in the last fifty years Germany has disturbed the peace of Europe and that it must be made impossible for her to recommence. How this result is to be achieved has not been disclosed.

No one seems to put much confidence in arbitrary limitation of armaments. No one feels bound to keep promises made under duress. Even her enemies would feel that Germany would be justified in trying to get around any such regulations which might be imposed on her.

All of Germany's enemies have an especial hatred for Prussia. There is a very general feeling that the other Germans are not—naturally—so bad and would not be so strong in military organization, would not be so hard to defeat, so hard to keep in order, if it were not for Prussian leadership. There may be some effort to break the Hohenzollern domination in the German Federation. The Powers of the Entente would like to see the imperial crown pass to the less able dynasties of Saxony or Bavaria. It is probable that an effort will be made to exaggerate the differences between the North and South Germans and, while treating the latter with some consideration, to make the cost of defeat fall heaviest on the former. It has even been suggested that it might be well to refuse to recognize the Empire and to deal separately with the half-hundred sovereign states which existed before the Union.

The Prussia of Frederick the Great was a very small affair compared to the Prussia of today. The Allies, if victorious, would like and possibly may try to reduce it in one way or another to its former size and importance. A number of articles have been written in France—and allowed to pass the censor—which advocated separating the Rhine provinces from Prussia and making them into a "neutral" buffer state, or giving them to Belgium. Many similar schemes, all having the intention of decreasing the importance of Prussia in the structure of the Empire have been unofficially suggested. Perhaps something will be attempted in this sense—possibly something accomplished—but success would depend mainly on the frame of mind of the Germans at the end of the war. Some people prophesy that in case of defeat the Germans themselves would throw out the Hohenzollerns and repudiate Prussian ideals. But there are no symptoms of such a reversion of feeling as yet. It is at least probable that the hope of revenge would make the defeated Germans more inclined to a military dictatorship than ever.

The more liberal writers of France and England are inclined to let the German people solve their own internal problems. If Toryism is triumphant in the home politics of the coalition, it is more probable that some such effort to impose "constitutional reforms" on Germany will be made.

But in this commercial age it is probable that the most important elements in the terms of peace will be economic and financial rather than geographical and political. There is much talk in the English, Russian, Italian, and French newspapers of "the other war," the war on German industry. There is little doubt that the Germans hoped to demand commercial advantages if they won, and if defeated they will have to suffer similar disadvantages.

First of all Germany will have no colonies except those the victors care to give her. By the middle of 1915 she had lost all her overseas domains except parts of her African colonies, where small forces of her troops—without hope of reinforcement—were still keeping the field against rapidly growing odds. But the German colonies were more significant as a future asset than as present wealth. The oldest dated from the early eighties and such enterprises always have to pass through a long, barren period of development. The loss of her colonial possessions will hurt the next generation much more than this one.

However, if the diplomats of the Allies are ordered to strike at her industrial life—to break her "militarism" by rendering her too poor to buy arms—they will find many other weapons at hand besides confiscating her colonies. They may turn against Germany the weapon she used against France with such cynical cruelty in 1871 and inflict on her a crushing war indemnity. Bismarck made no secret that in demanding five milliard francs (a thousand million dollars) he intended to "bleed France white." And he expressed his regret to his friends that he had underestimated the amount of blood there was in French veins. He was disgusted that they were able to pay the indemnity so quickly. The Germans will be in a poor position to protest if they are similarly treated. If the Allies decide "to bleed Germany white" they are not likely to repeat Bismarck's mistake by fixing the indemnity too low.

They will have other economic arrows in their quiver. A tendency to boycott things "made in Germany" will be an inevitable result of the hatred engendered by this War. The diplomats can intensify this tendency if they want to. They can encircle Germany with prohibitive tariff walls. They can take the German merchant fleet as part of the war indemnity; they can arrange railroad agreements which will stop, or seriously slow up, German trains at their frontiers, they can revise the treaties which govern navigation on the Danube and the Rhine.

But, of course—and it is not an altogether Utopian hope—the Allies may be sincere in their statements that they intend to lay the foundations of a permanent peace. Instead of despoiling the vanquished to the limit, they may instruct their diplomats to moderate their demands so that the Germans can develop in the paths of peace.

But there is very little hope for a peaceful future unless the diplomats of the victors can reach a substantial agreement on the terms to be imposed on the vanquished and so be able to present their demands in a coherent form and with at least the appearance of unity.

CHAPTER XVIII

THE DIVISION OF THE SPOILS

KEEPING to our arbitrary assumption that the armies of the Entente have forced the Germanic alliance to sue for peace, it is evident that their diplomats will have only begun their task when they have agreed on what they will take away from the vanquished enemy. They will have endless thorny questions to settle among themselves about the division of the spoils.

There is a very delicate problem involved in the sharing of the war indemnity. Whether they decide to moderate their demands in the hope of future peace or decide to use the indemnity as a punitive measure, there will be trouble in dividing it. No sum which Germany and her friends can pay will be large enough to repair the devastation of the War. It is extremely doubtful if any indemnity can be squeezed out of Austria-Hungary, Turkey, or Bulgaria. If the War lasts a few months longer, no matter which side wins—these countries will be "bled white." And real money will be rare in Germany.

If a commission of experts went through Belgium, the invaded districts of France and Poland, and made a modest estimate of the cash value destroyed, as the agents of an insurance company visit the scene of a fire, and if to this sum was added the extraordinary expenses which have been forced on the Allies by the War, the figure reached would be staggering—past any possibility of Germany paying it with the wealth of the present generation. And for the immediate reparation of damages the taxes which the Allies may decide to inflict on the generations of Germans yet unborn will hardly count.

So the creditors—the victors—will have to accept the

fact that their debtor is bankrupt. They will have to content themselves with a few cents—a very few cents—on the dollar. But how is this sum to be divided among the creditors? Will Great Britain, France, and Russia keep their pledge and fully indemnify Belgium before they enter their own claims? And to what extent has Belgium a first lien over Serbia? If there is anything left after these two claims are settled, how are the Great Powers to divide the remainder? Will this financial plum be shared according to needs or according to service rendered? Certainly Great Britain has put more money into the war chest of the Entente than Russia. But the Russians have more freely poured out their blood.

The theory of the rights of nationalities is not easy of application. Even if the three original Powers of the Entente—Great Britain, France and Russia—have agreed on a frontier and a form of government for the New Poland, there remain a number of obscure and intricate problems in southeastern Europe.

Assuming that the Dalmatian coast of the Adriatic is to be freed from the yoke of the Hapsburgs, it has to be divided between the Italians and the Slavs. Italy, not content with redeeming the province of Trent and the purely Italian districts of the Istrian peninsula, makes large claims in Dalmatia. She bases these claims partly on historic tradition. But the fact that once upon a time the Venetian flag floated on all the coasts of the Adriatic is no more firmly established than that the British flag—and before it the Dutch—floated on Manhattan Island. The Italian claims are partly—and more reasonably—based on present desires, economic and strategic. She insists on indisputable predominance in the Adriatic—in short she wants to make it an Italian lake.

This ideal cannot be realized without gross violation of the theory of the rights of nationalities. The amount of pure Italian blood on the Dalmatian coast is small, the number of the inhabitants who show some trace of Italian parentage is large, but the great proportion is Slavonic. It is the same with the language test. The number who speak only Italian is very small, the bilingual population is large in the ports, but back from the coast the great mass of the people speak only one or another Slav dialect.

The Italian government has made no official statement of its claims in this district. Their minimum is probably four out of five of the practical harbors, and all the islands which can be turned into naval bases. Judging from unofficial newspaper articles and the poems of d'Annunzio their maximum claims will be the reëstablishment of the Venetian domain and the Latinization of a large section of Slav hinterland. Their claims will be largely influenced by the success of their army and they will certainly ask for more than they expect to get.

The Slavs of this district are divided into three main groups, Slovenes, Croats, and Serbs. They are already protesting wildly because there are indications that the Powers of the Entente have promised Italy—when they were trying to persuade her to declare war on Germany—parts of this Adriatic coast which the Slavs think is theirs.

The conflict of interests in the Adriatic is not confined to Latins and Slavs. The Teutons, who are weak in these parts on "historic" and ethnological claims, have very vital commercial interests at stake. Their problem is typified in the case of Trieste. Nearly 75 per cent of the population of this busy harbor is Italian, close to 20 per cent is Slav (Slovene) and less than 5 per cent is German. But this small number of Germans and Austrians—and very cordially hated they are by the great majority of the population—represent the economic force which has transformed Trieste from a half-dead Italian town into one of the world's great mercantile ports. It is not only that the Germans to the north, who use Trieste as the outlet for their commerce, would suffer, if they were shut off from it by political frontiers, but the Dalmatian coast would suffer too. What little civilization these Slav populations have, they owe to Germanic business enterprise at Trieste. If the Austrian Lloyd Steamship Company stopped its mail service, they would drop back into the lethargic isolation which marked their history in the centuries before the Teutons came to the Adriatic.

It will be a serious misfortune to a great many people who do not speak German, if the German speaking people are shut out of Trieste.

The claims of the Serbs are likely to be quite as hard as those of Italy to reconcile with common sense. First of all the Serbs think that all the southern Slavs of Austria-Hungary should be united to their monarchy. But it is very uncertain if all these Slavs want the union. The Bosnians will probably welcome the chance to come in under one flag. The chances are about even in regard to the catholic Croats. Both of these racial groups have been suffering heavily under the Hungarian yoke and any change will probably be welcome. But there is an independence party in Croatia. However, the Slovenes have not had such a hard time. Their economic interests are closely tied up with Austria. If they are given an opportunity to vote they will have to choose between a sentimental attachment to their "race" and the dollar and cents advantages of being part of a paying partnership.

The Serbs also have "historic traditions" (quite as good as the Italian claim to Dalmatia or the Dutch to New York) which they feel justifies them in violating the theory of the rights of nationalities. The "Greater Serbia" of their dreams includes a large sprinkling of "subject races": Bulgars, Albanians, Greeks, and Roumanians.

The Roumanians—if they decide to come in on the side of the Entente—will also advance embarrassing claims. Their problem is intricate. Their people are massed in an irregular group, densest in the rich grain lands of the lower Danube, scattering out on both sides into the mountains and gradually mingling with their Slav and Hungarian neighbors.

If they join the Entente—and nobody knows which side they will join—they will be told to go ahead and redeem their brothers of Transylvania (the Hungarian Province) but the problem of Bessarabia remains. Both the Russian and Roumanian statistics in regard to this district have been falsified, but it seems that much of the lower valley of the Pruth which is now the boundary, has Roumanians on both banks. The Allies may try to persuade Russia to cede this territory to Roumania. In other words, her "legitimate aspirations" imply the giving up of territory by both sides. To further complicate matters—probably as an excuse to remain neutral—Roumania is formulating "demands" in return for her intervention which far exceed the territory inhabited by Roumanians. However, it is quite possible that she may remain neutral—and so simplify the diplomatic problems.

The theory of the rights of nations is a new idea: it has not progressed to the point of working both ways. After all it is no more fantastic for the Roumanians to want to annex a few million Tartars, Russians, Ruthenes, Hungarians, Germans and Serbs in the name of this right to free their "unredeemed" brothers than it is for the Italians to claim the Slav populations of the Adriatic or for the English, French and Russians to demand territory in Turkey.

A problem, almost equally difficult, will face the diplomats of the Entente as soon as they have succeeded in dividing the indemnity and the territory they will have taken from Germany and Austria-Hungary—the colonial world. I will take Africa as an example. Of course the theory of the rights of nations does not extend to black folk. At the outbreak of the War the German flag flew over two and a half million square kilometers, with a population estimated at 11,000,000. It is probable that most of the heritage will fall to France and Great Britain. All forecasts would be thrown out if Russia suddenly showed a desire to become an African power, but her traditional policy is to annex her neighbors, to push out her frontiers, not to seek far-away colonies.

Great Britain "needs" parts at least of German East Africa in order to build her "all red railroad" from the Cape to Cairo. The forces of the South African Union under General Botha have conquered Southwest Africa, and it is improbable that the imperial government will intervene. The Union will do what it likes with this territory. A German official coming from this colony summed up his impression of it by saying: "If a dog saw it he would howl." But diamonds have recently been discovered in the southern part. The government of the Union would like to operate these mines in order—by competition—to break the dictatorial influence of the De Beers Diamond Company in their internal politics. There is also talk of trading off the northern part—the part a dog would howl at—to Portugal in exchange for southern Mozambique and Delagoa Bay, a deal to which the Portuguese will never consent if they feel strong enough to resist it. As France has adjacent territory she will probably lay claim to Togoland and Cameroon. The Belgian Congo may also benefit by some "frontier rectifications" at the expense of German East Africa.

The Liberal element in the Entente Powers will oppose any annexation of German colonies. It will prove that the Tory Imperialists are in power if Germany is driven out of Africa.

But while, in Liberal circles, one hears a good deal of argument against depriving Germany of all colonial outlets, hardly a voice is raised in behalf of Turkey. Far and away the most delicate problem in the division of spoils is furnished by the remnants of the Ottoman empire. The Turks are not quite "white," in the European sense of the word, so no one will feel restrained by the theory of the rights of nations. Everyone is planning to take a share of the Sick Man's inheritance. The conflicts are so acute and so numerous between what each nation calls its "legitimate aspirations" and its allies call its "exaggerated ambitions," that the subject deserves a chapter by itself. It typifies to a greater extent than any one other problem, the danger which will threaten the Entente Powers in the moment of their victory.

CHAPTER XIX

THE FATE OF TURKEY

All the Powers of the Entente—and some of the neutrals—have staked out claims in Turkey. If they win, the Ottoman empire will pass away. The Turks will probably be driven back into the mountains of Asia Minor and lose not only their last province in Europe but all their coast line. *Sic transit gloria mundi.* No one who believes in a reasonable organization of the world will regret to see the irrational Turkish adventure—the most amazing epic of rapine the modern world has seen—come to an inglorious end.

Even as the northern barbarians overthrew the civilization of Rome, so the hordes of Pagan Mongols swarmed down from the steppes of Central Asia and overwhelmed the brilliant culture of the Caliphs of Bagdad. For a hundred years or more there was tense competition among the three religions of the East as to which should convert the invaders. The Jews and Christians failed, and the horde became Mohammedan.

One of the lesser chiefs of the Mongols—Osman or Otman—founded an independent dynasty in Asia Minor. His tribe increased: it enjoyed a large endowment of what M. Bergson has called the *élan vital.* The Otmanli were nothing but warriors; at this trade, however, they had no rivals. They crossed the Straits into Europe, gave the death-blow to the moribund Greek empire, conquered Syria, Egypt, Mesopotamia, Arabia, and all the northern coast of Africa to the borders of Morocco. They won the Greek Isles, most of the coast of the Black Sea, all of the Balkan Peninsula and they twice besieged Vienna.

The Turks have never lost their essential quality of

"invaders." Even in Constantinople they have lived as a strong garrison in a conquered city. Suleimon, the Magnificent, was magnificent only in the amount of his spoil.

In "the good old days," when muscle and individual daring and lust for conquest won victories, they were a Great Power. Their decline began when it was discovered how to fight with machines and chemicals. When, before the Pyramids, in sight of forty centuries, French infantry with muskets defeated the Mamelukes, who charged with scimitars, the military power of the Sons of Otman was broken. The Sick Man has been left alive these hundred years—to the shame of Europe—because the christian nations were too jealous over his heritage to allow him to die. But now—if the Powers of the Entente win—his estate must be probated.

Great Britain, without waiting for the final settlement, has begun to cash in, by "regularizing" her situation in Egypt and Cyprus. Her troops—which her allies would like to see in the main campaign—are conquering Mesopotamia and so approaching the precious oil and cotton districts and tightening their grip on the Bagdad railroad.

Her naval forces have already occupied some of the Greek Isles. Tenedos, commanding the mouth of the Dardanelles, is the most important from the point of view of naval strategy. No official statement has been issued as to the British intentions in regard to Tenedos. But in spite of the best intention the English found insurmountable difficulties in the way of observing their promise to evacuate Egypt, and Tenedos is too valuable to be abandoned lightly.

The fact that Great Britain has so large a number of Mohammedan subjects gives her "special interests" in Arabia. She cannot tolerate any other Power gaining control of the Holy Cities of Islam. An ounce of prevention is worth a pound of cure. A stitch in time, etc. She already "protects" certain points on the Arabian coast: Aden, Muskat, Koweit. So she may decide to "regularize" her position here and change this "zone of influence" into a protectorate.

The British diplomats will come to the peace conference with a certain number of *faits accomplis*—which cannot be discussed. They can hardly ask for much more of the Turkish spoils than they have already so thriftily taken. What further demands they make will probably be limited to the Bagdad railroad.

There is a wide difference of opinion in England as to the best policy in Mesopotamia. Those Liberals who before the War were in favor of encouraging German enterprise in this district, probably think still that it would be wise. But to say so at present would lay them open to unpleasant suspicions of being friendly to the enemy.

One section of opinion wants to annex the valleys of the Euphrates and Tigris and the Mesopotamian desert up to the confines of Syria, which is to be French, and to push forward the construction of the Bagdad railroad under British auspices. This would mean the rapid economic development of one of the most promising sections of the earth. The rails from the Mediterranean to the Persian Gulf would shorten the route to India and so draw the empire closer together.

But another section of the public—led by the "shipping interests"—are opposed to the opening of the railroad. It would compete with the Suez Canal. With the German merchant marine crippled by the War, the Oriental trade will be a practical monopoly for the English. If they keep railroads out of the Near East, the growing commerce of Mesopotamia will follow its natural course down the great rivers to British ports on the Persian Gulf, and so to European markets in English bottoms. If the railroad is built, much of this trade will be diverted to non-English ports in the Mediterranean, and non-English traders and shippers will cut in on the profits. But when the interests of political reaction conflict with those of economic reaction, the former generally win. It is probable that the "railroad" party will defeat the "shipping" party and that Mesopotamia will be annexed.

The French claim a protectorate over the undefined territory inhabited by the native christians of Syria and the mountains of Lebanon. Their "interests" here are derived from some industrial developments such as railroads and the work done by their catholic missionaries. While bitterly fighting the church at home, the republic has been jealous in protecting the rights of her Jesuits abroad. It was Gambetta who said that "Anti-clericalism is not an article of export." The other Powers of the Entente will hardly question French claims here, as, having borne so much more than their share of the War, they are plainly destined to reap the smallest territorial gains from victory.

Italy wants some of southern Asia Minor. Her claims are on a par with those of other nations in such colonial matters: they are solely economic. In recent years some Italian financial groups have secured concessions from the Sultan in and about Alexandretta, and considerable Italian money has been invested. No official statements have been issued in regard to the extent of their claims, but it is probable that definite treaties have been signed with some or all of her Allies. The Italian government took rather more pains than were necessary to assure the world that it was being guided by "*l'égoisme sacré*." And Egoism, no matter how sacred, is hardly likely to be contented with vague promises. Italy probably hopes to control the coast from Alexandretta to the new Russian frontier somewhere south of the Dardanelles. This would include the rich and important city of Smyrna. How far inland her claims go is uncertain.

The Greeks also have large claims in these parts. Once upon a time Greek civilization was supreme along the Ionian coast. But there seems little chance that Greece will have any voice in the councils of the Allies.

Ethnologically the Greek claims in Asia Minor, while

slight, are very much better than those of any other European nation. But economically Greece is in no position to administer this territory. Smyrna is very largely Greek, and it promises to become a more and more important commercial center. But Turkish misrule has largely devastated all this territory. Greece itself is a poor country; the large increase of territory due to the Balkan Wars was more than the home country could stand. The new provinces in Epirus and Macedonia are not yet assimilated. The annexation of any large territory in Asia Minor would be a disaster. But there is a party in Athens who talk seriously of reëstablishing the Glorious Greek Empire of Byzantium, forgetting of course—as is generally the case in such "historic arguments"—that the eastern empire was scarcely glorious after it ceased to be Latin. However, neither one of the groups of Great Powers—although they are bidding heavily for Greek support in this War—want to see the Greeks at Constantinople. There is no immediate prospect of the creation of a new Byzantine empire. The Greeks will be fortunate if they live through this War without losing territory.

The entrance of Turkey into the War on the side of Germany, and the closing of the Dardanelles—a great victory for the German diplomacy—was a very sad blow to the Powers of the Entente. It was much more serious than the purely military result of closing the route by which munitions could best be sent to Russia. It also made a desperate confusion in Russian finance, for in normal times she pays for her imports by the grain and oil she exports by the Black Sea and the Straits. There is a large element of poetic justice in the present predicament. If Britain and France and Russia had loyally stood by the Balkan alliance in 1912, it might not have broken up. Turkey would not have dared to enter the War in the face of such a united bloc. As a result of this Balkan diplomacy in recent years the Entente had only one sure friend in the Peninsula, Servia, the weakest of them all, and the most exposed. For, not having had the imagination and moral authority to solve the Balkan problem, Britain and France and Russia find themselves drawn into a war on behalf of Servia.

Russia is pushing her army of the Caucasus down into Persia (with whom she is not technically at war), into Turkish Armenia and along the Black Sea coast towards Trebizonde, and it is her hope to reach by this route the Bosphorus. She lays claim to all this coast and an undefined hinterland.

There are endless opportunities for disputes over these ill-defined, sometimes conflicting claims. French Syria will have English Mesopotamia to the east and Italian Asia Minor to the north. Italy and Russia will probably have a common frontier somewhere along the coast. Perhaps in the interior Britain and Russia will meet—for the first time in their history. This is the best hope the Turks have in case of defeat. England and Russia have always disliked the idea of being neighbors, so perhaps they will be inclined to make a fairly large nation out of the remnants of Turkey, to serve as a buffer between them.

But of course all these problems, intricate as they are, and serious as they may become, are the merest bagatelles compared to the question of the Straits.

Many books have been written about the Dardanelles. Their importance in the history of Europe can hardly be exaggerated. From the time when people fought with stone hatchets till today, when the mightiest guns of the world's mightiest armada are thundering there in vain, the Dardanelles have been the strongest naval base on earth. From a military point of view neither Gibraltar nor Heligoland even compare with Gallipoli.

The economic importance of the Straits is even larger. The greatest rivers of central and eastern Europe feed the commerce of the Black Sea, and the nation which holds Constantinople is not only sure of free passage for its own fleets but can lay whatever tax it pleases on the fleets of others.

The Turks realized the surpassing value of the situation, and to a larger extent than anywhere else in Europe they settled in and about Constantinople. In the five centuries they have been there they have taken root and today no one but the Turks can rule the Straits without flagrant violation of the rights of nations. But, as I said, most Europeans feel that the Turks are not really white, so their rights will not be considered. If, in spite of victory, the Powers of the Entente allow the Turks to remain in Constantinople, it will be for other reasons.

It is generally believed that the English and French have formally promised Constantinople to Russia. But there is a Latin phrase much used in diplomacy to crawl out of embarrassing promises—*rebus sic non stantibus*. It means: "things have changed." It would not have much weight as a defence for violation of contract in civil laws but it still is in usage in international relations. The last time the English and French fought side by side (the Crimean War) it was to keep Russia back from the Straits. Neither of them would really welcome Russian war-ships in the Mediterranean. Circumstances may arise which will lead them to champion the right of the Sick Man to stay alive a bit longer.

There can be no doubt that if the guardianship of the Straits is to be given to any one of the European Powers, Russia has the first claim. Any *régime* at Constantinople which does not give the Russians a "most favored nation" guarantee, which does not amply assure her against having her commerce in grain and oil smothered by a closing of the Straits, is iniquitous and contains the certain germ of future trouble. Russia's need for free access to a warm sea is so great as to equal a "right." But Roumania certainly has an equal "right" to a "most favored nation" clause.

It is probable that if the Entente wins, we will see Russia installed at Constantinople. The situation has changed in many ways since the Crimean War. The long alliance has greatly decreased the French distrust of Russia. The digging of the Panama Canal has somewhat lessened the value of the Suez route to the British. Even if they have to give up their predominance in the Mediterranean (and it is already a fiction in the face of the combined Italian and French fleets) they will still have a sea-route to the Pacific and India. And if the British establish themselves permanently at Tenedos, the concession to Russia would be greatly mitigated.

But, looking at the question in a broad spirit—not merely as a part of the tactics of carrying on this War—it is to be hoped that Constantinople will not be given to Russia nor any other nation unconditionally. The Straits are of too great a public importance, they belong to the world at large. With every industrial development of the Near East their importance will grow. It is not only the nations with a frontage on the Black Sea who have an interest that free trade shall rule over this water-way, but also every nation that buys their grain and oil and sells their goods in exchange. No nation should be given unlimited sovereignty and so be allowed to favor its own commerce at the expense of its rivals.

Here more than anywhere else the diplomats will be faced by an economic problem. It will be most unfortunate if they allow their decisions to be swayed by considerations of naval strategy or political expediency.

No one who has passed through the Straits—the Dardanelles and the Bosphorus—can have escaped the impression of great natural wealth utterly undeveloped. The last time I was there I was fresh from a winter in Panama. The difference was appalling. Even so important a thing as the upkeep of proper lighthouses was neglected. At this great shipping center there was no adequate wharfage, no modern dry docks, no sufficient warehouses, no well equipped marine repair shops. The coaling facilities were mediæval. Nothing better could happen for the great interests centered in the Straits than to have them administered for ten years by a board of civil engineers, like our late Isthmian Canal Commission. It will be unfortunate to see them entrusted to the most corrupt and backward of the Great Powers. Of all the European nations Russia is the least prepared to do such necessary engineering work.

If the armies of the Allies prove victorious, their diplomats will deserve great credit if they can reach an amiable and workable settlement of the intricate affairs of Turkey.

CHAPTER XX

IF GERMANY WINS

THE war will not be over till the last cannon is fired. And, while from a purely military point of view the odds seem to be heavily against the Germanic forces, any serious discord among the Powers of the Entente would assure their victory. With the best of luck they can hardly hope for an overwhelming triumph. But once more in order to simplify the diplomatic problem, I will assume a decisive victory for their armies, which carries them through the Tropics and well into the Temperate Zone of their enemies.

In that case we can ignore the theory of the rights of nations, which has no place in their diplomacy. The other problems of economic and colonial considerations would be the same in substance as those discussed above on the hypothesis of their defeat. They would also face the same problems of tactics.

The fact that the German Empire dominates her allies has been a great asset during the war, as it has resulted in a unification and coördination of military action which the Entente coalition did not enjoy. To an almost equal extent this will be an advantage—in case of victory—in the solution of the diplomatic problems. Orders will go out from Berlin. Vienna, Sofia and Constantinople will probably have as little to say in the formulating of the terms of peace as they have had in controlling the actions of their armies.

Still it will be the defensive tactics of the defeated Entente Powers to try to sow discord among their victors. While the Germans can afford to offend any one, or even any two of their allies, they cannot safely offend all of them. Discord with Austria-Hungary is most likely to arise over the division and treatment of Poland. Bulgaria and Turkey have sharply conflicting interests: it will be hard to content both of them. But any dissatisfaction among her former Allies can probably be counterbalanced by hitching to the chariot of the Deutschtum one or more of the defeated nations. Germany might decide to spare Russia and crush France and Italy and Britain. Or she might decide to save Britain for an ally and smash the rest.

Germany would probably not annex any territory on the continent of Europe except on specifically economical grounds. Such considerations would lead her to push out her frontiers on both the West and the East.

She would probably annex Belgium and the North of France with a coast line on the North Sea and the Channel at least as far south as Calais,—perhaps down to Boulogne. She would justify this with two economic reasons. (1) It would give her access to the rich mineral deposits of this territory, which she needs for her metal industry. (2) It would give her much-desired sea-gates.

The fate of Holland would be uncertain. Some of the more rabid pan-Germans are for frank annexation. Almost all the industrial population of western Germany would like to control the mouths of the Rhine. A rather interesting alternative to such brutal annexation of Holland has been suggested. It has been proposed to break Belgium in two, to combine the French speaking section with the to-be annexed territory of northern France, and form it into a *Reichsland*—the *régime* devised for Alsace-Lorraine when it was annexed,—and to offer the Flemish speaking section of Belgium to Holland on consideration that Holland voluntarily enters the empire, or at least comes into the German Zollverein. Whatever the formalities are, if Germany annexes Belgium, the "independence" of Holland will be little more than a fiction.

There are two quite distinct and generally hostile economic groups in Germany. And the industrial group, which would be most interested in this expansion towards the West, was not in power when the War broke out. It is not *their* War. The Junkers, who were in supreme control, are agriculturalists. Far from loving the "industrials" of the Rhine they will be bitterly jealous of any increase in their power. They will demand for themselves compensating annexations to the East. It is the "Conservative" and "Agrarian" newspapers and speakers who have come out most openly in favor of annexations, and their eyes are turned towards the agricultural lands of Poland, Lithuania, and the Baltic provinces of Russia.

During the course of the War there has been much talk in the German papers—and there was a special commission appointed to study the matter—of a unification of the German and Austro-Hungarian tariffs. The advantages of such an expansion of the Zollverein idea would be great from an economic point of view, but it would also have a large political significance. It would stop the rivalry between these nations over the ownership of Trieste. The Germans want this access to the Mediterranean: the Austrians have been reluctant to give it up. If a customs union is reached this cause of jealousy disappears.

The Hapsburgs—in case of victory—will demand a large share of Russian Poland and perhaps some of the Ruthenian provinces of Little Russia. They will also feel justified in taking back some of the North of Italy. Hungary will take Servia, Montenegro and Albania at least as far south as Durazzo.

Bulgaria will insist on Macedonia. Her imperialistic politicians will ask for much more. It is rumored that the Germans have offered them a strip of Albania with the Adriatic coast from Durazzo to Avlona. And it is also said that they are to be given Constantinople:—Turkey to be compensated by regaining Egypt. This last suggestion seems fantastic to me as it is probable that the Germans would prefer to have the most feeble of their allies at the Dardanelles so as to enjoy a more dictatorial influence there. And it is hardly probable that they would repay

Turkey—the most valuable and docile recruit they have yet found—by asking her to abandon her capital.

There would probably be a new and tight alliance of these four victorious states. They would control, even if they did not annex Holland, the North Sea coast from the Channel to Denmark, all the southern coast of the Baltic, a broad strip of territory from the northern seas narrowing gradually through central Europe to the Straits. And in this immense imperial combine Germany would be supreme.

The effect on the colonial world of a German victory would be even more sweeping. Just what the changes would be it is idle to guess. Germany could take what she wanted and have a great deal left to distribute to her Allies. In Africa, Germany would certainly annex the parts of French and Belgian Congo which she needs to connect up her east and west coast colonies. She would very probably take a large share of French North Africa. She might take India. The amount she took would depend largely on the size of the indemnity she could extract. As a general proposition colonies are expensive playthings. Germany's appetite would probably be limited by the amount of resources she could find to exploit the colonies.

What the world would be like if the Germans win is an interesting but futile speculation. Probably neither side will win so overwhelmingly as to be able to realize one-half of its "aspirations." But keeping to the assumption of a complete German victory we can hazard one statement and one query.

The German solution will not bring peace. It would satisfy nobody but the Germans. Aside from the conflict of will in the "annexed territories," there would be discontent—perhaps sullen, perhaps active—among her allies over their vassalage. The Egyptian nationalists—for instance—think they would like the Germans better than their present christian rulers. It is doubtful if they would. Islam, all over the world, looks to Germany for deliverance from French and English and Russian domination. But the Persians—as another example—will not find the Turko-German combine any preferable to the Anglo-Russian. The natives of Algeria and Morocco will find the Germans just as christian, just as foreign, as the French.

And, to come back to Europe, the German solution of the Balkan problem will not bring peace to that unhappy district. The Austrians and the Hungarians, inflated with the pride of victory, will not be less arrogant and cruel to their subject races than they have been in the recent past.

A German victory will not solve the "question of the southern Slavs." It will not solve the "Polish question." The "sore spots" of Europe will not be cured. Their number and size and infectiousness will be increased.

A Germanized Europe will mean an armed Europe.

The query deals with the psychological effect. What would it mean to the European mind to see the Deutschtum triumphant? And this no man can answer.

There are elements of great vigor and great virtue in the German habit of mind. All the world could learn much from them.

But more than once in the long history of the race it has happened that the conqueror has fallen victim to the ideas of the conquered. The Mongol hordes which overthrew the Caliphate at Bagdad fell under the spell of the civilization they destroyed. The Goths became Latinized in language and religion and in political idea. It is not impossible that Germany—if victorious—might become Europeanized.

CHAPTER XXI

THE PROBLEMS OF POWER

ONE of the gravest vices of the diplomatic tradition is exemplified in the history of the Balkan Peninsula.

No group of men take a greater pride in calling themselves "realists" than do the diplomats. If you accuse them of some rank treachery, some violation of common decency, they shrug their shoulders and say complacently that they are "realists." But no group of men— with the possible exception of priests and physicians—are more bound by "obscurantism," catch phrases and meaningless formulæ. Their most sacrosanct dogma is the status quo. Listening to these gentlemen talk, you would think that they had never heard of Darwin and the theory of evolution.

Every time the diplomats have come together to discuss the Near East, they have solemnly decreed a status quo. The one outstanding reality of the Balkans is political instability, a constant bubbling and boiling of development and change.

At Berlin in 1878 the Great Powers were faced by the fact that the Russian armies had smashed up the status quo ante. They went through their ritual and decreed a new status quo. It was not simply a weak, negative, do-nothing policy—it was a vicious effort to avoid change, to stifle life. But the diplomats could not stop the process of growth—they could only impede and distort it. Hardly a decade passed when someone did not pull a prop from under their flimsy structure. But—ostrich-like—they stuck their heads in the sand and refused to look their enemy in the face.

In 1912 when Italy had annexed two Turkish provinces, the Balkan allies decided to settle their old scores with the Sultan—the foreign offices of the Great Powers announced that they would not tolerate any alteration in the status quo. These "realists" could not see that whether they liked it or not—things had changed. When at last there was hardly any Turkey left in Europe, they reluctantly admitted the fact and erected a new status quo. This time it was Albania! The Prince of Wied and his descendants were to rule at Durazzo forever and a day.

When the Balkan states began fighting among themselves the next year and tore up this eternal and immutable scheme, the diplomats, undiscouraged, announced that they were really serious this time and intended to maintain the status quo created by the Treaty of Bucarest.

We may be sure that if, at the Congress to come after this War, they try, as is their wont, to crystallize Europe into a rigid framework, their work will be, at best, laughable,—at worst, tragic.

Sooner or later the diplomats will have to wake up to the reality, which everyone else has accepted, that life is growth and change. Even they admit that the war is going to alter the structure of Europe. The process of change will go on after the peace is signed. A wave of child-bearing—which the diplomats cannot control—may sweep over Spain and upset all their careful calculations. Some apparently trifling frontier alteration, some new tariff law, may completely change the economic relations of two countries—deaden one and give the other a great spurt of activity. No one of the nationalities of Europe will stand still to please the diplomats.

In all the reams they have covered with their careful writing, have decorated with their ponderous seals, hardly a single treaty has ever had so long a life as this Belgian Neutrality Guarantee, signed in 1839, to be torn up in 1914. The Triple Alliance, which Italy denounced last spring, was the oldest in Europe—thirty-three years old.

The solutions they give to the problems raised by this War will be tentative. They will not be able to create any sort of permanent status quo. And their new Europe will be workable just in proportion as they recognize—as they never have before—that flux and flow is the law of life for nations, just as it is for amœbæ.

At all events the post-bellum Europe will be different from the old. The status quo is hopelessly dead. All values are being weighed in this War. Old ideas are being submitted to the test of fire—on both sides of every frontier. Very little will survive just because it used to be. Political institutions and prejudices, among other things, will have to stand the test, and "show reason" for their existence. This is equally true of "hereditary" enmities and friendships.

There will be new groupings among the nations—new alignments, new alliances. The old pact between democratic France and despotic Russia is an anomaly which nothing but fear of Germany can explain. A French writer in *Le Temps*, speaking of the former alliance between Italy and the Germanic empires, described it with the indecent but forceful phrase, *un accouplement contre nature*. But this phrase from the penal code was even more applicable to the alliance of his own country with the Tsar.

For more than twenty years now, France has been pouring her savings into the Russian treasury, and so has been buying the military aid of the Cossacks. While some of this money has been a good military investment, some of it has been spent in maintaining prisons in Siberia for all those Russians who have read and taken seriously the history of France. If the French are relieved of the pressing fear of Germany, they will stop sinking their money in the bottomless pit of the Tsar's misgovernment. The Alliance, if it survives at all, will be greatly modified.

The future of Europe depends very largely on the internal politics of Russia. No one can ignore the possibility that a victorious war may strengthen and revivify the autocracy. With new prestige, with access to the warm seas, which will immensely strengthen her industrial life,

Slavdom may grow—by itself—into a grave menace for the Liberal nations of Europe. But the more immediate danger—in case the Entente Powers win—is a new Holy Alliance,—a new *Dreikaisersbund*. Austria and Germany, if defeated, will—as France did after 1870—seek to form a new combination. A reactionary Russia would be their natural ally. With Prussian brains organizing and disciplining the limitless resources of Russia, this combination of the three emperors would, within a generation, be an appalling force of reaction.

It follows inevitably that all the Liberals of Italy, France, and Great Britain are casting up accounts, figuring out the chances of a successful revolution in Russia. There is much reason to hope for success. Finances are likely to be the key to the situation.

The two classic examples of successful revolutions in Europe are furnished by the beheading of Charles I. of England and of Louis XVI. of France. In both cases the people won by controlling the purse. The popular party overcame the military power of the sovereign because, by refusing to grant him funds, they made it impossible to hire large armies. In 1905 and 1906 the Russian Liberals had quite as tight a grip on the Tsar. But their effort at revolt coincided with the period of international tension over the Conference of Algeciras. The threat from Germany was unusually acute. So, when the Tsar could not get money for his Cossacks at home, he could borrow all he wanted in Paris. It was international capital—largely French—which allowed him to win the victory over his people.

The situation is not likely to be repeated. Once relieved from the immediate fear of Germany, the French will no longer have the same interest in supporting the Cossacks. And after the War—even if victorious—the Tsar will be in more pressing need of ready money than ever before. The Liberals of England and France and Italy—and in this matter they hope to find support in America—are resolved not to lend him a cent except on the condition that he grants to his country a real constitution. If the Tsar is left after the War face to face with his own people he will have to choose—quickly—between large concessions and sudden death. All that the Russian Liberals ask is that foreign capital shall maintain a "benevolent neutrality."

This brings us very close to the center of the problem of peace. Europe will not be set free from war by any clever combination of frontiers or tariff laws. The theory of the rights of nations will not solve the problem. The diplomats are only "agents"—everything depends on the kind of government they represent.

We must not expect them single-handed to regenerate the world. It is quite possible that the new treaty they will sign, perhaps at Brussels, if the Allies win, will be quite like the Treaty of Frankfort which followed the Franco-Prussian War, a new starting-point for a generation of shabby intrigues and complicated coalitions—a new struggle for power.

In forecasting the work the diplomats will do, it would be unjust to expect too much of them. Left to themselves they will follow their traditions—and their traditions are bad. It would be hard to put your finger on any spot on the map of the world where some diplomat has not been "decorated" by his king, or promoted by his government, for a piece of work he would not like his children to know about. Whether your finger chanced to fall on one of the great capitals of Europe or on some distant corner of the "uncivilized" world, China or South Africa, Teheran or Fez, Bangkok or Bogota—there in the archives of the consulates or the legations you could find the same sorry record of broken pledges, bribery, all too often of prostitutes on the pay-roll of the foreign office and not infrequently of murder—all for the greater glory and power of the home land.

It is rather cheap to criticize these resplendent gentlemen in gold lace, their breasts covered with jewelled decorations, for having been involved in such scandalous affairs—

cheap and useless. The important point is that the results they obtained were approved of by their governments—and they were not questioned as to the means they employed.

Black as they are, the records of diplomacy are not especially black. Our "muckrakers" have told us similar stories about our internal politics and "big business." There is no reason to expect a higher degree of morality from diplomats than that which we find among the people at home. Just as long as one merchant or one gas company strives for unfair advantages over his rival in the next street, as long as one political party is not over-scrupulous in the way it defeats the other, as long as hostile competition is our rule of life, it is manifestly unjust to expect diplomats to arrange a *régime* of mutual aid and good will among nations.

The peace of Europe depends on the progress which is made towards enlightened and Liberal national government. The Tories, the Junkers, *les hommes d'ordre*, the pan-Slav bureaucrats, our Imperialists will not give us peace—they are not really interested in it. Russia is not the only country where there is danger of reaction. In every country at war today—in spite of all the talk about *l'Union sacrée* and the "civic peace"—a bitter, if silent, struggle is in progress over the question: "Who shall control the War?" and above all, "Who shall control the peace negotiations?" An optimistic book has been written—to take one example—by Arnold Toynbee, "Nationality and the War." He has the courage to be logical—if not altogether wise—and tries to apply the theory of the rights of nations to the victors as well as to the vanquished. His new map of Europe—in case Germany is defeated—implies an amount of self-sacrifice which has no precedent in international history. He suggests that the people of Alsace-Lorraine should be allowed to determine their own fate by a referendum. He proposes that Russia shall not only keep her informal promises to the Poles, but also give some crumbs of liberty to the Finns and Ruthenes. And—being heavily logical—he says that Great Britain should give Cyprus to Greece—not as a bribe but as an act of justice. There is no doubt that there are very many Liberals in England, who are not only in favor of Home Rule for Ireland, but can also be counted on to resist the old imperial tendencies of their government abroad. They accomplished marvels in the settlement of the South African War.

But the Liberal ministry in England has already been undermined—a ministry which was not nearly so liberal as Mr. Toynbee. Not able to carry the weight of the War alone, Mr. Asquith and Mr. Lloyd George have had to accept the collaboration of the Tories. How far this will affect the internal politics of Great Britain it is still impossible to say, although it looks as if justice to Ireland had been indefinitely postponed. But the influence of this Cabinet change is already manifest across the Channel. All the reaction in France—Royalists, Bonapartists, Clericals—are taking advantage of this victory of their friends in England to demand that they also shall be given a share in the government. Their chance of success is relatively small, the Republic is firmly established on a liberal basis, nothing but a serious military catastrophe is likely to change the center of gravity. But liberalism is not so sure of victory in England.

Even in war, as in times of "peace," the bitter struggle goes on between the two theories of government: the one based on a will to power, the other based on a will to justice. If the more liberal elements win in the internal conflict and are in control of their governments during the peace negotiations the diplomats will be instructed to strive for justice—and they will loyally try to rise above the traditions of their caste and to realize the ideals of those whose agents they are. But if the reactionary elements win out at home, the diplomats will be given instructions—more in accordance with their traditions (a very large proportion of European diplomats are drawn from the old nobility)—

to strive by all the usual and unscrupulous means for power.

One of the strongest indictments which can be brought against war, is that it tends to strengthen the reaction.

In order to be just to the diplomats it is necessary to picture them sitting about "the green table" with a telephone receiver at their ear. The other end of the wire goes to a mouthpiece on the council table of the ministry at home. Their will or their skill matters relatively little in these days of submarine cables and long distance telephones. They will be acting on orders. This is just as true on one side of the barricades as the other. The Germans are just as uncertain about what they are fighting for—what sort of peace they want—as the English or French. No matter which side wins in the War the question whether the tone of the peace proceedings will be liberal or reactionary depends on the fluctuations of politics at home.

CHAPTER XXII

DEMOCRATIC CONTROL

The main hope for a better Europe—aside from the gradual elevation of our standards of morals—lies in the increase of democratic control over foreign affairs.

Publicity will have the same salutary effect on diplomacy that we are finding it has on politics and business. In one realm of activity as in the others, the wicked love darkness. In so far as the public is allowed to know what is going on, their agents in European and colonial affairs will—even if they cannot be better than the ordinary citizen—at least observe the rules of common decency. But the diplomats have always enjoyed the privileges of secrecy, and, like every other group of which history tells us, they think that they have a right to the "privilege" and will fight to maintain it.

They continually assert that democratic control of diplomacy—which implies publicity—would weaken the nation which practised it, in its relation with governments of a more antique and autocratic character. It is—they say—like this Utopian dream of disarmament. If everybody promised to disarm and everybody believed the others, it would be a beautiful arrangement. But unless it could be simultaneous, it would be suicidal. This is their main argument in favor of their special privilege of secrecy. And there is no gain in denying its force, nor refusing to see what they mean by it.

It is as true of states as of individuals that every step up towards a higher ethical standard means giving certain advantages to the less scrupulous. The man who decides to tell the truth is evidently handicapped when dealing with liars. Honest trade methods have a hard fight against "unfair" competition. The man who refuses to shoot his unarmed enemy, certainly runs a chance of getting himself killed for his idealism. And, beyond question, a government which abruptly adopted a new policy of absolutely open and public diplomacy would run a grave risk of being out-manœuvered by its neighbors.

But for the state, as in individual cases, it is necessary to decide which is the more worth while, the advantages which come from a reputation of truthfulness, or the advantages of lying. The advantages of honesty and chivalry must be weighed against those of sneakiness and cowardice. The nations of the world will have to decide which ideal of diplomacy will profit them most.

This issue has been raised with typical Latin clearness in the long debate between the French Royalist, Charles Maurras, and the Socialist (now a Minister), Marcel Sembat. Maurras has been attacking the Republic for many years in his newspaper *l'Action Française*. From the first he has seen that the Achilles' heel of the Republican form of government is its relations with other countries. It was very difficult, if not impossible, for Maurras and his friends to argue that the French would be better off—at home—with a king. It was correspondingly easy to criticize the Republican Ministers of Foreign Affairs. A king at the head of the diplomatic corps can follow a settled policy, but it is difficult to get any coherence out of a foreign office, when the chief may have to resign at any minute because of a cabinet crisis. Some French ministers have been in the foreign office less than three weeks. Hanotaux— the Moderate Republican—had been in office for some time, had steered the foreign policy in the direction of a *rapprochement* with Germany and a conflict with Great Britain. Just at the critical moment in his career, he was thrown out of office by the victory of the Radicals, In the very midst of the Algeciras conference a parliamentary crisis, which had nothing whatever to do with foreign policy, threw out the whole cabinet, and a new minister of foreign affairs had to take office in the midst of a crisis. More than once it has happened that a French ambassador has been working in glaring opposition to his chief in Paris. Maurras had little trouble in demonstrating that a republican form of government was the worst possible foundation for what he called "a strong" external policy.

Sembat replied to these attacks by a remarkable book, with the striking title: *Faites un Roi, sinon faites la Paix.* (Make a king—if not, make peace.) He took the wind out of Maurras' sails by admitting most of his criticism. He said that the Royalists were right in claiming that the republic was a weak form of government for an aggressive foreign policy. If the French cherished the idea of revenge, of regaining Alsace-Lorraine, if they wished to press on in colonial adventures, they had best accept a king at once. He said that the army and navy were not in a condition for a war of conquest and that the Republican majority in the *Chambre* would not grant sufficient funds to make it fit for this task. The Republic, he said, could not endure on the basis of any but a pacific foreign policy. He asked the French to choose a king, who would lead them to a glorious war, or the republic which implies peace.

It is evident that the nation which harbors aggressive designs had best keep them secret. If the Germans are defeated in this War, it will be—to a large extent—because they were so naïvely frank about their ambitions. The "less meritorious" people of Europe had plenty of time to prepare their defence. The French would not have succeeded in gobbling up Morocco without a fight if they had not protested so convincingly that they had "no intention of altering the political status of Morocco." Almost all the governments of Europe have succeeded in realizing their "manifest destinies," their "legitimate aspirations"—thanks to secrecy—in a way their own people would have refused to sanction.

It is not possible to believe—in spite of all the German claims of British hypocrisy—that the English would have approved of the methods by which Uganda was added to the imperial domain, if their newspapers had published truthful accounts of the "pacification" of that African protectorate. I, for one, cannot believe that the people who have protested so vehemently at the suffering of the Egyptian "fellaheen" when de Lesseps was digging the Suez Canal, at the Bulgarian atrocities, at the brutal slavery in the Belgian Congo and the Peruvian rubber plantation, would have silently allowed their government to carry fire and sword through Uganda—if they had known.

I do not want to draw an exaggerated picture of the "crookedness" of European diplomats, nor of the "ruthlessness" of colonial administrators, but I want to draw as close an analogy as the facts permit to some of the familiar phenomena of our own American life. Unfortunately, it is not necessary to distort the facts in either case. In our home affairs we are realizing more and more keenly that secrecy is a dangerous privilege. The stockholder in a large corporation not only has a right—for his own financial protection—to know what his agents, the board of directors, are doing with his money, but it is also his social duty to know. We have found it inexpedient to trust the vast funds of an insurance or railroad company in the hands of men—no matter what their church-standing may be—who know that they will not have to render a detailed account of their stewardship. It is certainly true that it is harder for the "directors" to bribe the legislature, to hire thugs to burn the rival plant, or "private police" to shoot down the strikers and beat them into submission (and all of these operations tend to increase the dividends), if they cannot do it secretly. It is small justification for a person who receives such tainted dividends to say "I did not know." It is his duty to know; and a democracy cannot shirk its responsibilities in foreign affairs by the plea of ignorance.

The analogy between business and diplomacy is strong. There are manifest advantages in secrecy. But we are finding more and more that the advantages of secrecy in business are socially inexpedient. Over against the imperial gains to the credit of secret diplomacy, we must weigh the millions of fresh graves in Europe. It is necessary to strike a balance.

It is not probable that there will be any abrupt revolution in the technique of diplomacy as a result of this War. But, in spite of all the hoary traditions, "the old order changeth." Irrespective of the wishes of foreign ministers, without any formal changes in the rules of their department, the veil behind which they have always hid is wearing thin.

One sure result of this War is that the various Parliaments of Europe will have a much keener appreciation of the importance of foreign affairs than their predecessors had. It was not "laws" which ensured to the diplomats their "privilege of secrecy": it was the indifference of the nations. The Parliaments to which they were supposed to report were preoccupied with internal problems. Like the nations they represented, they gave scant attention to international relations.

At the outbreak of this War, we had the incredible spectacle of three members of the British Cabinet resigning, because they were surprised to discover what their colleagues of the foreign office had been doing. One of them, at least, has said clearly that he had been deliberately deceived, that he would not have accepted a position in the ministry if he had not been formally assured that the foreign policy was different from what events proved it to have been.

The significant thing is that the three ministers who resigned were advanced Liberals, men who had been giving their whole energy to the amelioration of social conditions within the empire. They had thought that old age insurance, factory legislation, etc., were more important than foreign affairs. There has been a marked tendency among the Liberals of all European countries to rather ignore the international situation. The Socialists everywhere—with their dream of internationalism—were more alive to the danger, but they also were busy with "local" questions. Now all their projects for reform—of the Socialists and Liberals alike—have been brought to a sudden stop by this catastrophe of war. The Liberals cannot again afford to be indifferent to diplomacy. It is a fairly safe prophecy that no foreign minister of England or France will ever again be permitted to enjoy such irresponsible power as was given to M. Delcassé and Sir Edward Grey.

It is quite aside from the point to argue whether these gentlemen's policy has been wise or unwise. It is improbable that those who want to impeach Sir Edward Grey will succeed. Apparently an overwhelming majority in England is convinced that Germany had been planning to attack them and that Sir Edward Grey and the "inner circle" of the Cabinet have saved the empire by foreseeing the danger. After the War they will probably give him a splendid monument.

But, granting—as most Englishmen do—that Sir Edward Grey has used his extraordinary power with great clairvoyance and statesmanlike patriotism, the fact remains that it was extraordinary power. Even his most ardent supporters go a little pale, if you ask them:—"What if Sir Edward had been a fool?" It is possible that a "court of honor" might decide that Sir Edward has never technically lied to the House of Commons. But his closest friend would not deny that he has allowed the representatives of the people to deceive themselves. He knew that the great majority of the House of Commons had small interest and less knowledge of the international situation. He knew that the Tories, in so far as they understood his policy, approved of it. He was covered from attack from the Liberal benches because they belonged to their own Liberal ministry.

In the past five years there have been a number of sporadic efforts on the part of various Liberal members to force the Foreign Secretary to give the country a frank *exposé* of his policy. He has always been able to avoid doing so. At the first rumble of such an interpolation the party machinery was set to work. The Liberal whips—and the name the English give to these party agents is significant—went about saying: "If anyone causes a cabinet crisis now over foreign policy it means the end of all the reforms on our program. The cabinet will stand or fall together. If you force out Grey, Asquith and Lloyd George go too. The Tories come in. It will be good-bye to Home Rule, Welsh Disestablishment, and Budget Reform. Any Liberal who attacks the cabinet is a traitor. It is playing the game of the reaction."

If the Liberal member, in spite of this whipping, dared to ask his question—as sometimes happened—Sir Edward Grey made an elegant speech which entirely dodged the issue. The ministry asked for a vote of confidence and got it. There was always some crisis in internal politics which seemed very much more important than Sir Edward Grey's foreign policy. And so, not only the country at large, but Parliament and even three of the cabinet were surprised at the War.

It is not probable that Sir Edward Grey will be impeached. But once the need of union in the face of the enemy is past, he will certainly have to face a bitter attack. It is possible that certain resolutions will be read into the British constitution that will definitely limit the extent to which a secretary of state for foreign affairs can deliberately deceive his colleagues and the House of Commons because he thinks it is for the greater glory of the empire. Perhaps Sir Edward Grey's policy has been wise—but what if he had been a fool?

There is an unfortunate tendency to dodge the real issue by making scapegoats of the diplomats. They are being unduly accused these days. It is unjust to blame them for not having preserved the peace. With the best will in the world they could have done very little better than they did. They are the product of the circumstances of their birth, of their training, of the conditions of their trade. They are agents of their governments. They are supposed to be patriots, not citizens of the world. Their instinct is to strive for a greater Britain, a more glorious France, a mightier Russia, a prouder Austria, a more powerful Germany. They cannot become good Europeans faster than the nations they represent. The ultimate responsibility of this War is not theirs as much as it is that of those who hired them. It is idle to shirk our responsibilities in the matter by trying to shove them off on the diplomats.

What then are the prospects of peace? An increase of democratic control over foreign affairs will reduce the risks of war, but it will not eliminate them. It depends on what kind of a democracy is to do the controlling.

A great many people are talking hopefully of the sweeping social changes, which will follow the War. This is a matter of speculation, a dangerous field for prophecy. About all one can say with any certainty is that the ancient, rigid structure of Europe is being melted in the great heat of this War. It will cool in time, and solidify in new forms, which will probably be better, but may easily be worse.

It will be during this cooling process, before the structure of life has solidified and crystallized again, that the greatest opportunity for work will be offered to all those who desire a better Europe. And this opportunity will be great beyond any possibility of exaggeration.

The peoples of Europe have been shaken out of their ruts. Old prejudices and privileges have crumbled, new duties have been imposed. Everyone has been forced to think. To all has been offered a vivid example of the truths of the old proverb that there is strength in unity. "Co-operative effort" is the dominating note of the day. State socialistic measures are the present strength of Germany. They are being imitated everywhere. Masses of men, women and children—millions of them—are being fed and sheltered and clothed, not as in the old days, by their individual effort, but by the mutual aid of the community.

In the trenches the voting populations of all the great European states are learning daily lessons in pulling together. "Individualism" is at a discount. The old hierarchy is crumbling. A man who started life as a valet, is now Sir John French's Chief of Staff. The immense stress of the moment has forced all the world to realize that "a man's a man."

How much of this spirit of mutual aid, which has sprung up to meet this great crisis, will persist in the everyday life of Europe after the tension is relaxed, no one can prophesy. But of one thing we may be sure; in so far—and only in so far—as the ethics of our national life ameliorate, as the various nations in their internal relations gradually struggle up from the primitive abyss, we will gain in saner international relations. When the individual citizen bases his acts in his family, towards his friends, towards his business rival, his boss or his employees, on a will to justice instead of on a will to power there will be no more any reason for war. The nearer we approach this ideal, the less war we will have.

BOOK IV

THE UNITED STATES AND EUROPE

CHAPTER XXIII

OUR TRADITIONAL POLICY

BEING so young a nation we have few traditions. One of the oldest we have deals with diplomacy. It was our first President, with his warning against "entangling alliances," who laid the foundation of our foreign policy. On the 2nd of December, 1823, President Monroe developed this idea in the Message to Congress, which has become famous as his "Doctrine." It cannot be too strongly emphasized that the Monroe Doctrine was a logical outgrowth of Washington's policy. The two stand or fall together.

The circumstances which led to Monroe's action were peculiar—and transient. The South American republics had fought their wars of independence without our help. We had been "neutral" in the struggle between Spain and her revolting colonies. When at last it was evident that Spain could never reconquer these young republics we—rather tardily—recognized them as free and sovereign states. Spain, realizing her own inability to regain her colonies, appealed to the Holy Alliance—the reactionary European coalition which had grown up after the defeat of Napoleon and which was busily engaged in stamping out republicanism in Europe—to help her re-impose her yoke on South America.

It was to this Holy Alliance that Monroe spoke. He said that any effort to extend their "system" on our hemisphere would endanger our tranquillity and that the intervention of any European Power would be the manifestation of an unfriendly disposition to the United States.

The Monroe Doctrine is rather like the British Constitution. It has never been reduced to a formal written document. The Holy Alliance against which it was aimed has passed away, but the doctrine, changing with circumstances, has shown remarkable vitality.

The people of the United States believe that their interests and security would be seriously threatened if any European Power, especially a monarchical government, extended its political organization to this side of the world. We are on record as determined to fight if necessary to protect this hemisphere from foreign aggression.

We have no legal precedent on which to base this doctrine. In international usage such a proposition must be based either on precedent or force. The Monroe Doctrine has lived nearly a century because we have had—or have been thought to have—sufficient strength to counterbalance the temptation to violate it. The temptation has not been great. The French effort to conquer Mexico—at the unusually favorable moment when we were occupied by the Civil War—was so disastrous to them that it did not encourage others to try. Whenever the temptation to launch an adventurous American policy has grown strong in one or another of the European countries it has always happened that other European Powers were so jealous that the threat has never been translated into action. As no monarch since Napoleon III. has tried to extend his realm in America, our ability to maintain the Monroe Doctrine has never been put to the test.

The justice of our claim is not accepted by Europe. Various governments have assured us that they had no territorial ambitions on this side of the world. Comforting as such statements are, they are not a recognition of our contention. The general attitude of European statesmen, and of writers on such subjects is that the Monroe Doctrine is a bumptious Yankee bluff. They deny its legality and smile at our pretence of power. They do not believe that we would or we could defend it. But few, if any of them, seriously think of challenging us.

This is the real virtue of the Monroe Doctrine. It is not

a question of whether we are the military equal of Great Britain or Germany. At the very least we could greatly increase the difficulties they would have to overcome in any attempt to acquire parts of Latin America. It is cheaper for them to seek colonies elsewhere. The English for instance would not be frightened at the prospect of a single conflict with us. But they would not deny that it would have very seriously embarrassed them if we had joined the Boers in the South African War. It would not be a light undertaking—for example—for even the strongest European nation to attempt the conquest of Brazil. The certainty of having us to conquer too at the very least doubles the difficulties. The Monroe Doctrine—whether it is accepted by Europe or not—has had the result of separating this hemisphere from the colonial world. The path of least resistance has led the modern *conquistadores* to Africa and Asia.

But there are two sides to the Monroe Doctrine. America for the Americans and—the inevitable corollary—Europe for the Europeans. Monroe formulated in 1823 the positive proposition which grows out of Washington's negative advice. In his message to Congress, Monroe was careful to recall the policy of his illustrious predecessor. He insisted that it had always been our practice not to intervene in Europe and this was the foundation on which he based his contention that European intervention in America would be an unfriendly act.

While the "Great Powers" are only scornfully tolerant of Monroe's thesis, they are inclined to be insistent in regard to the Washington doctrine. It has been a maxim of modern diplomacy that the United States is "disinterested," in European politics. We are not expected to intervene. The exceptions when our intervention has been solicited are amusing. The nations which have from time to time invited us to the council table of Europe have done so because they thought we would vote on their side. They have become advocates of a strict interpretation of the

Washington-Monroe Doctrine if we threatened to vote with their opponents.

There has never been a time when the British press has been so friendly towards the Monroe Doctrine as when at the Hague our delegates supported the German contentions in regard to the rules for naval war. At that time the English would have been willing to recognize our protectorate over all the Americas, if we would only have gone home and abstained from voting on this "purely European" issue. Fortunately our diplomacy has never consented to the proposition that the seas are a "purely European issue."

More amusing and more typical was our participation in the Algeciras Conference. Our interests in Morocco were almost invisibly small. Germany, among other things, wanted to get some real guaranty that all the world would be given equal economic and commercial opportunities. As we had said so much about "the open door" in the Far East, they naturally expected us to vote with them, and so they welcomed us to the conference. The cordiality of the Kaiser's telegrams to Mr. Roosevelt in the early days of the crisis indicate that he was sure of our support. Great Britain and France having received "assurances" from us—apparently on the tennis court behind the White House—were also cordial in their welcome.

A few years later when France decided to proclaim a protectorate over Morocco, in spite of her repeated promises not to, Germany tried to get the other signatories of the Algeciras Treaty to join her in a protest. Britain and France abruptly remembered that we were a "purely American" power and had no business mixing in a European and African dispute.

The governments of Europe expect us to live up to the Washington-Monroe Doctrine except when they think it will help their game to have us depart from it.

For more than a century our statesmen, with hardly an exception, were also convinced that we ought to avoid any interference in European affairs. In the 'fifties one of our senators introduced a resolution inviting the nations of the world to establish an international court of justice to do away with the crudities of war. He was voted down by an overwhelming majority. Half a century ago we were unwilling to negotiate even arbitration treaties with Europe.

With the beginning of this century—primarily as a result of the Spanish War—a new tendency became visible in our politics. The conditions on which our "traditional" policy was based have changed with the shrinking of the earth. Steamships, submarine cables, wireless telegraphy, are drawing in the ends of the earth. It is an entirely safe prophecy that the time is coming when a "purely European" policy or an "American" or "Antarctic" policy will be provincial. Local interests are fated to grow smaller and smaller in the face of greater politics of the race. Sooner or later the "Monroe Doctrine"—"American particularism"—will lose all meaning. And with the birth of the new century the problem of our foreign policy was clearly posed: Are we, or are we not a World Power?

As was to be expected our answer was hesitating. There was considerable opposition in the Senate and in the public to our accepting the Tsar's invitation to the Hague Conference. It was overcome by assurances that we would not bind ourselves to anything—that we would remember the advice of Washington. At this First Hague Conference our delegates—acting on their instructions—made it very clear that we were not a World Power.

They abstained from voting on the disarmament resolution on the ground that it was a "purely European issue," and when they voted for the arbitration arrangement, they read into the records this ponderous qualification:

"Nothing contained in this convention shall be so construed as to require the United States of America to depart from its traditional policy of not intruding upon, interfering with, or entangling itself in the political questions or policy or internal administration of any foreign state; nor shall anything contained in the said convention be construed to imply a relinquishment by the United States of America of its traditional attitude towards purely American questions."

The advent of Mr. Roosevelt to the White House brought the question more sharply to our attention. He believes that we are a World Power. One of the most outstanding features of his long administration was his insistence that the time had come for us to play a rôle on the stage of *Weltpolitik*. More infractions of our "traditional policy" occurred while he was at the helm than in all the previous history of the country. We—or he—called the second Hague Conference. We mediated between Russia and Japan. And we were "among those also present" at Algeciras. It is an open question if we accomplished anything for Europe by these interventions which could not have been done quite as well by Switzerland. But we did get ourselves and the world accustomed to hearing our name at roll-call.

It is difficult, if not impossible, to combat the argument that sooner or later we must accept world-wide responsibilities. But even if we admit that proposition we are faced by the more debatable question: Do we stand to gain anything for ourselves or others by a hurried entrance on the stage? It seems to me that the more we succeed in putting our own house in order, the more we can hope to exert an uplifting influence on benighted Europe. Unfortunately we have been rather slack in arranging our own affairs.

There is much to be said in favor of withholding advice and assistance until it is asked for. In a score or more phases of life the people of Europe do accept us as models. They copy our shoes, our dentistry, our juvenile courts, and our hospital organization; but they do not copy our municipal governments nor our administration of justice. They have heard more of our lynchings than of the small parks and playgrounds of our progressive cities. On the whole, they think of us as rather uncivilized; but as fast as we give them something worth copying, they copy it, and much more quickly than we have copied their good points. If we are able, in our dealings with our neighbors on our side of the world, to develop a new scheme of international relations which is as much superior to their antique methods as our sanitary plumbing is superior to the traditional English "tub," they will copy that, too. If in our own bailiwick we practised the "peace of justice" more, and talked about it less, it would be better.

Mr. Roosevelt has not converted a majority of our people to his way of thinking in this matter. His protégé, Mr. Taft, was noticeably less "imperialistically" minded than he. In the elections of 1912—while foreign policy was not an issue—it was certainly no disadvantage to Mr. Wilson that it was notorious that he would incline to "traditionalism" in international relations.

For us to claim rank as a World Power is clearly an abandonment of our oldest diplomatic tradition. We stand pledged to Europe. In return for their abstention in American affairs, we have promised not to mix in theirs. There can be no other meaning to the declaration of our delegates to the first Hague Conference (quoted above).

Even Mr. Roosevelt had to make concessions to this traditional point of view. When Mr. White, our delegate, to the Algeciras Conference, signed that treaty, he made a similar qualifying statement. Our Senate would not have given it their sanction on any other condition. The United States acquiesced in the changes in the status of Morocco which the conference agreed upon, but expressly refused to assume any responsibility for the enforcement of the treaty.

Again and again our government has with extreme care made it clear that we do not consider that the policing of Europe is part of our job. In signing the various Hague Conventions in regard to the methods of war, we have virtually said: If the misfortune of war falls on us we will live up to these rules. We will not use dum-dum bullets, we will not sprinkle floating mines, we will not bombard unfortified cities, we will not interfere with the non-contraband trade of neutrals, we will not violate the territory of neutral nations. We have most solemnly pledged our honor in these matters.

But there is nothing in the records of the Hague conferences to warrant Mr. Roosevelt's contention that we are bound to make other people live up to their pledged word. In fact, the official records and common sense point in the opposite direction. The doctrines of Washington and Monroe would be stripped of all justification if we claimed to be a World Power. We peremptorily tell the Europeans that they have no police responsibilities in the Americas. It is a poor rule that does not work both ways.

In spite of Mr. Roosevelt's excursions into *Weltpolitik* it is beyond dispute that our traditional policy is to keep alive the Doctrines of Washington and Monroe. However, there is no virtue in mere age. Very many traditions are bad and the older they become the more likely they are to prove inadequate. Sooner or later I believe we will have to give up—or at least seriously modify—these old doctrines. It would be most unfortunate to regard them as dogmas. While the "imperialists" and advocates of world politics were undoubtedly growing in number among us, they had not, before the outbreak of this War, seriously undermined the attachment of the nation to the "traditional" policy.

There is one phase of our diplomatic tradition which is often overlooked or misstated in discussion. We are not in any way pledged not to go to war with any one or all of the powers of Europe. Our tradition is not Tolstoian. Monroe made his position very clear in the message which made him famous. He expressed the sincere desire of our government to live on terms of amity with the rest of the world, but with equal emphasis he said that if our security was endangered or our rights infringed, we were determined to defend them. And in this, as much as in announcing that we would resist foreign intervention in the Americas, he was formulating the sentiment of our people.

It would be just as much contrary to our "tradition" to abandon the "rights" which we have always claimed and which have received the sanction of general consent, as for us to enter a European alliance or to acquiesce in a European conquest of South America.

The old revolutionary "snake" flag, with the motto "Don't tread on me," is typical of our traditional foreign policy. I doubt if any citizen of the United States has ever advocated any sort of an armed aggression in Europe. But the great mass of the people would whole-heartedly support the government in a war which was forced upon us—no matter by whom.

Through the dozen odd decades of our national life we have been slow to anger. War has seemed to us not only immoral but unreasonable and stupid.

A few days after this War broke out some of my friends were discussing the situation, and one of them in a very informal and homely phrase summed up the American attitude towards such matters as aptly as any more erudite commentator could have done. We had been talking of von Bernhardi. "The trouble with those Germans," he said, "is that they think War is *right*. We don't. We put War in the same class as lying. We don't like to do it, but sometimes it is necessary." "When we do have to lie," he added, "we try to get away with it. And we fight in the same spirit."

Far and away our most profitable war was that with Mexico. It was also peculiarly unjust. But we gained more by it than Frederick the Great gained by any of his campaigns. It was more profitable than any of Bismarck's wars. It is typical that we never boast of it.

For a generation and more we tried to settle our civil conflict, by compromises. But compromises would not do. At last—regretfully—we had to fight it out.

Our facile victory against Spain went to the heads of

some of us. But in spite of our amateur war lords we are not a bellicose people. It would be difficult to recruit an army corps for a frankly aggressive war. But even less are we Tolstoians. Of the ten million men in the United States capable of bearing arms there are very few who are hungering for military glory—very few who would shirk their duty if war was necessary.

In short, our "traditional foreign policy" has been in keeping with our democratic institutions. Now and then we have departed from it—as in our aggression against Mexico. But on the whole it has been based on a very small offensive strength and great resources for long and determined defence. If we want to be a World Power—if we want to say with the Kaiser that nothing could happen in Europe without our consent—it will necessitate a sweeping revolution in our concept of life. We could not throw an appreciable armed force into an overseas battlefield in less than a year. Before we could live up to such responsibilities we would have to stop work on our internal development and create a large army. Very few of us think it would be worth while. Most of us are content to continue in our traditional policy.

CHAPTER XXIV

THE PROBLEMS OF THE WAR

We, in America, were immensely surprised by the War. They had cried "Wolf! Wolf!" too often. I remember writing ten years ago that a general European war was inevitable. There did not seem to me any other solution of the feverish race in armaments, the hectic diplomatic crises. But year after year passed without a "breach of the peace" and I had begun to think with Mr. Norman Angell, that war was "the great illusion." And then— one summer day—the war cloud broke.

It did not take any special initiative on the part of our government to declare neutrality. It was an almost automatic act, the traditional routine of the State Department.

As a whole the nation approved of Mr. Wilson's attitude in the matter. The opposition came from three sources. (1) The Entente-Americans. (2) The Alliance-Americans, and Mr. Roosevelt.

The sudden development of the hyphenated-Americans was a shock to all of us. It is perhaps the most serious problem for us which has grown out of this War. We have always boasted of our power of assimilation and suddenly we are confronted by the fact that our ritual of naturalization contains very little mystic value. It does not suddenly convert a European into an American any more than a marriage ceremony is certain to make everyone live happily ever after.

The matter was complicated by the fact that you cannot tell whether a man has been naturalized by looking at him. Our loyal American citizens of foreign descent have had to suffer for the misdeeds and tactlessness of people who were not citizens at all. It should always be remembered that there are many thousand aliens who live in America, who have never become naturalized, have never sworn allegiance to our government. Most of the men who have been arrested under the common law for seditious activity are not American citizens. The most un-neutral speeches and writings have been the work of "foreigners."

Because of their difference of language the Germanic element of our citizenry has suffered most. The Anglo-American and the Englishman, no matter how disloyal, passes among us unnoticed. It is difficult to tell whether a news item in our English papers comes from an American correspondent or from London. The source of the "news" in the German papers is always evident.

One thing is worth noting. However frantic some of the Germans in America have been, however misguided some of our citizens of German descent have been, they have not urged us to abandon our neutrality and attack the enemies of their Fore-Fatherland. The Entente-Americans have been more often guilty of asking us to sacrifice our national interests on behalf of lands of their origin.

On the whole, this "hyphenated" trouble has been vastly exaggerated. The Delbruck Law, which encourages perfidious naturalization, is something we cannot tolerate. Unless the Germans repeal this insulting law we will have to make it exceedingly difficult for Germans to receive our citizenship. It is probable that our naturalization laws will be revised all around as a result of this War. If the trouble gets out of hand we could reduce it immensely by expelling all citizens of belligerent countries. On the whole our naturalized citizens are loyal. But the real problem is one of assimilation, much more a social than a legal question. Above all, it is a problem of education. It is the second generation which matters most. And it is our schools, not our naturalization courts, on which we must rely.

The attack on the President's policy of neutrality led by Mr. Roosevelt is quite another problem. It is—so far as it is not simply an incident of our internal politics, an effort to influence "elections"—based on the considerations exposed in the last chapter: Are we or are we not a World Power? Has the time come for us to abandon our "traditional policy"? We will not be able to count noses on this question till the coming elections. Mr. Roosevelt seems bent on making foreign affairs a presidential issue. It is to be hoped that he will succeed, for the country ought to be given a chance to speak clearly on this point. Anything which increases the interest of the electorate in international affairs increases "democratic control."

But there is little indication at present that a majority can be found in favor of *Weltpolitik*. Is there any predominating sentiment in our nation in favor of taking sides on the European issues of the War? I think not. We are all distressed over the fate of Belgium, full of admiration for the plucky resistance of this little people, all profoundly shocked that civilization has proved to be so weak a reed. There is among us an almost equal sympathy for France. On the battlefields of Artois, Champagne, the Meuse and the Vosges we feel that a form of government which is dear to us is fighting heroically in self-defence. Many of our more recently European citizens are on the other side. The Jewish refugees from Kishineff can hardly be expected to wish success to their butchers. Most of our citizens from the smaller European states are bitter against Great Britain. There is hardly one of us who does not know quite definitely which side he wants to win. But there is a long step from such personal partizanship to the desire to see our government identify itself with, and give unqualified support to either the Germanic Alliance or the Entente Group.

The issues involved are far from clear. They visibly change as the War progresses. All the belligerent countries are divided internally over the vital issues of the War. In Germany they discuss the question: Is it a War of offence or defence? In England are we to believe the liberal *Manchester Guardian* or the frankly reactionary *London Morning*

Post? Both try to tell us what Britain is fighting for, but their conclusions are worlds apart. After the War are we to find Russia revolutionized or more deeply retrograde? There are too many unknown quantities—"unweighables," in Bismarck's phrase—for us to form a really united public opinion on the purely European issues of the War.

If we are to fight whole-heartedly, we must be convinced that we have chosen the side of progress. We admire immensely the scientific achievements and social ameliorations of Germany. In the last generation we have borrowed more of value from Germany than from any other European country, but few of us care to risk our lives for the greater glory of Hohenzollernism. We have a century-old tradition of peace with England, but more than once official relations have been sorely strained, and we are often shocked at the callous commercialism of the present ruling class of England. In our home politics we are fighting against, not for, such people. We have several penal laws against the sellers of opium. We would be utterly untrue to our own ideals if we were not keen to help the Russians to their freedom, but it is not our business to pull the Tsar out of a hole.

The issues involved in this War are intricate in the extreme. We would resent any European power taking sides in the Mexican muddle. Our intervention in Europe over the moral issues of this War is equally uncalled for.

Unenlightened public opinion in the nations of the Entente would like to have us protest over Germany's action in Belgium. It is doubtful if their statesmen would. The British Foreign Office is glad that by not protesting on behalf of Belgium we established a precedent which has made it logical for us to turn a deaf ear to the protests of Holland and Sweden and the other neutrals. The French diplomats certainly remember that we did not join the protest when they tore up the Algeciras Treaty. And it is highly improbable that the Russian government would want any neutral nation to begin investigations of "atrocity charges."

The material effects of the War were at once disastrous. But "the hard times" of the fall and winter of 1914 were mostly of a financial origin. Our foreign trade is so small in relation to our internal commerce that the interruption of sea traffic, while ruinous for our exporters and importers, ought not to have seriously influenced our general industry. But "credit" went to pieces. The closing of the stock exchanges everywhere was a desperate measure to prevent a panic. Its result was to allow people to be panic-stricken in private. Perhaps the greatest element in retarding the re-establishment of confidence was the uncertainty as to how long the War would last. This disarray in our financial circles was the result of war *per se*. It could not be blamed on any one of the belligerents.

But before many months had passed a new problem began to clamor for solution. Quite aside from the issues involved between the European groups, there arose the more intimate question of what we were to do to protect our own interests. Philosophically the discussion takes this form: which deserves the more respect, the "rights" of neutrals who are keeping the world's peace, or the "rights" of belligerents who are breaking it? In times of peace, most philosophers take the side of the neutrals. But in times of war the belligerents always claim—as we did in the 'sixties—that their "rights" are superior and the neutrals cannot reply effectively except by ceasing to be neutrals.

The first serious blow to neutral rights was given by Great Britain. The best discussion I have found of the British naval war against neutrals is in Professor Clapp's, "The Economic Aspects of the War." The British "Orders in Council" became the "law" of the seas. The trading rights which Great Britain had insisted on when she was a neutral in the Russo-Japanese War (and which by the way she asked us to help in maintaining) she blithely denied to the neutrals in this War. An important element in the situation was the fact that the small neutral states of Europe

—especially Holland—asked us to defend our rights and theirs, to back up international law at sea as against the British lawlessness.

It is regrettable—to my mind—that diplomatic secrecy, which rules almost as much at Washington as in Paris or London, has prevented the administration from taking us into its confidence in this controversy. A White Book containing all the correspondence on this subject not only with Great Britain but also with the small neutral nations would be acceptable.

In the ordinary routine of international law the procedure of protest is virtually automatic. If a citizen has plausible complaint against some other country, there is little option left to his foreign office. The complaint must be registered. It is the duty of his government to see that his evidence is heard, and if his claims are established, to demand compensation. And the general practice is to err on the side of over-protesting. In a synopsis of all the international protests issued in 1910, a relatively peaceful year, it would be found that a majority was received, investigated, and settled without the least hard feeling. Trouble is more likely to arise from the hostile mood of the contending nations than from the gravity of the complaint. Doubtful and important issues, like our recent controversy with England over the Panama Canal tolls, may be settled by common good will. Insignificant incidents, like the breaking of the cane of a German vice-consul at Casablanca, may lead to the verge of war.

As a general proposition, it can be laid down that no liberal, democratic nation dreams of fighting over a commercial protest which can be arbitrated and settled by an award of damages. Most of our protests addressed to England since the outbreak of the war have been of this nature. If we had been spoiling for a fight, it would have been easy to start one over the bizarre British doctrine that they can, in order indirectly to hurt their enemy, play fast and loose with trading rights of neutrals—rights which they were the first to champion when they were neutral. The idea that, because they do not approve of the way the Germans fight, they can inflict reprisals on non-combatants is as untenable as it is original. At the first opportunity we shall certainly "go to court" about it, and have this amazing pretension threshed out. But if the English are ready to live up to their arbitration treaty with us, we do not want to fight about it.

However, the midsummer of 1915 found us tottering on the verge of a very much more serious conflict with Germany. Apparently it was hard for the Germans to understand our attitude. It is perhaps illogical for us to be more angry at German lawlessness than at that of the English, but there is no doubt that we are.

The Roman church made a very convenient distinction between two grades of unrighteousness, between mortal and venial sin. There are many peccadilloes which, while technically wrong, cannot be taken with great seriousness. There are other acts, which—even if we cannot cite the chapter and verse where they are forbidden—seem at once shockingly wrong; there is something about them which, while it escapes logical definition, is evidently heinous.

Great Britain and Germany have both violated their pledges of The Hague by armed invasion and occupation of neutral territory. Armies have settled down unwelcomed in the little Grand Duchy of Luxembourg, and in the Greek Isles off the mouth of the Dardanelles. Necessity knew no law. In both cases the weaklings submitted sullenly to overwhelming force, and as far as one can discover, in both cases, the aggressors respected all the "rights" of the invaded except their right not to be invaded. The American attitude towards both these affairs was that they were most regrettable.

The case of Belgium was in a different category altogether. It was no more "illegal" for the Germans to enter Belgium than for them to enter Luxembourg. But it was horrible. Perhaps our outrage over the sack of

Louvain was more sentimental than logical. It was none the less real. The ruthless conquest of Belgium, the brutality of the "occupation," is much more serious than its mere illegality. The flames from the burning thatch of Belgian cottages have thrown a lurid light on the ideals of the governing elements in Germany. It is wasted time for them to talk to us of friendship.

A British cruiser fires a shot across the bow of a Dutch or American ship: officers board her, go through her papers, find every evidence that she is bound for a neutral port on non-contraband business. Nevertheless they escort her to an English port and with exasperating leisureliness try to make up their minds whether or not they had a right to stop her. Meanwhile British ship owners profit by the predicament of their rival.

A German submarine shoots a torpedo into a great transatlantic liner on the vague suspicion that she is carrying aid to the enemy. Of the hundreds of passengers aboard, many of whom are strictly non-combatants, women and children, a large number are quite uselessly drowned.

Both acts are utterly illegal. It is impossible to justify the first, but it does not make us as angry as the second.

Our real quarrel with Germany is that her statesmen cannot or will not see this distinction between venial and mortal lawlessness. An enlightened despotism might conceivably follow the dictates of logic. It might act on the basis that law is law, that one illegality is as bad as another, and so expect the rest of the world to be just as indignant over the British immaterial blockade as at the sinking of the *Lusitania*. But democracies are not ruled by this process of mind which the Germans call "pure reason." Our newspapers—as good a mirror of the popular mind as we have—are remarkably unanimous. The British have lost heavily in our sympathy by a policy which has seemed to us stupidly illegal, arrogant and decidedly unsportsmanlike. The German methods have seemed to us inhuman and horrible.

The clash is more formidable than the immediate hard feeling caused by specific "incidents." The solution of the "*Arabic* affair"—unless it indicates a very sweeping change in their policy—does not solve anything. The fundamental difficulty is a difference in the habits of mind of the two peoples. If we come to a rupture with Germany, it will not be because she has infringed on our rights—Britain also has done that—but because the *way* the Germans did it was unbearable.

So, after a year of this European War, there seems small chance of our becoming involved in serious trouble with any of the Powers of the Entente. But there is a depressingly grave possibility of continual friction with Germany.

The export of munitions of war to the belligerents has also been the theme of heated controversy. There are two arguments against it. The first is purely ethical. A literal interpretation of the Scriptures—such as that of Tolstoi or the Quakers—condemns the giving of any kind of assistance to anyone engaged in bloodshed. This is true beyond any dispute. But the same literal christianity condemns riches, condemns the entire structure of our individualistic, competitive civilization. There is no more reason for us to obey the advice of Jesus in foreign affairs than in internal politics.

A more practical argument against the export of munitions is offered by those who believe that the manufacture of arms and armament should be a government monopoly and that no state should permit the fabrication of weapons within its borders, except such as it needed for its own military establishment. The scandals in regard to "armament trusts" have broken out in every country. The individuals who make profits from the production of military equipment have so evident a pecuniary interest in "militarism," that it is not surprising to find Krupp agents buying space in the French newspapers to launch war-scares. The manufacturers of armor plate can always be counted on to subscribe heavily to the Navy Leagues of their own—and other countries. Every anti-Japanese speech in America is money in the pocket for our "Krupps."

If private profits in the machines of death were abolished it would certainly knock one of the props out from under militarism. Those who argue in this sense have no better text books at hand than the writings of two Englishmen: Mr. Wells and Mr. Brailsford. But it is doubtful if they would care to have their arguments applied to the American situation.

The weakness of this argument is that it is desperately hard to define "munitions of war." Access to our markets for food and cloth and shoes and raw minerals has probably benefited the Entente Powers more than their purchases of things ordinarily ranked as contraband by civilized nations. Until the Socialists succeed in abolishing private profits altogether, it will be difficult to pass discriminative legislation against munitions of war.

The arguments in favor of continuing the export of military supplies are stronger. First of all the trade is profitable. The great mass of our people are not financially interested in it. But the number and power of those who are making money out of this indirect slaughter is greater than of those whose consciences are shocked by it. Secondly, the precedent in international law is precise. The Austrian notes protesting against the export of munitions have asked us, not to observe established rules of neutrality, but to change them in their favor. In similar circumstances in the past they have sold munitions to belligerents. From a legalistic point of view their protest is unfounded. It is merely sentimental and moral. They appeal not to law but to equity.

Thirdly,—and this is probably the argument which appeals most strongly to our government—the sudden development of the war industries greatly strengthens our military position. If we should become involved in war today we could equip a respectably sized army in half the time it would have taken a year ago. Our General Staff can be counted on to oppose any measure which would tend to discourage the industries which are producing military supplies.

But of course the overwhelming argument against an embargo on the export of munitions is that most of us want the Entente Powers to win.

However, the agitation in favor of the embargo will probably continue. It will be supported not only by the German sympathizers and the Tolstoians but also by those friends of the Entente group, who believe that even in the midst of a great war our voice ought to be raised in favor of law and the rights of neutrals.

The situation of the British public in regard to the legality or illegality of their Orders in Council is peculiar. They know very little about it. The press censorship has prevented discussion. The great mass of the people believe that they are fighting in the cause of international law. Any newspaper which published the facts would be, if not suppressed by the government, accused of German sympathies and wrecked by the mob. Their papers are allowed to publish news to the effect that the Dutch are trading with the Germans, but a calm statement of the fact that the Dutch have the same right to trade with Germany that the English had to trade with both sides in the Russo-Japanese War, that we have to trade with England and France and Russia, would be regarded as seditious.

This fact cannot be too strongly emphasized. Our controversy is really with a small group of naval officers. The sea lords are sailors, not international lawyers. They want to do Germany as much harm as possible, and the fact that it is rankly illegal for them to blockade Holland, rankly in conflict with the stand taken by their government before, does not appeal to them as important. It is rumored that there have been serious disputes in the British Cabinet over this matter. It is probable that Sir Edward Grey was personally opposed to the policy of blockade which has thrown Sweden onto the German side and has alienated the sympathy of almost all the neutral nations.

The British public knows nothing about these questions: they do not believe that their government would give any honorable person a cause to protest. The majority of them believe that the German ambassador intimidates Mr. Wilson into writing his notes of protest.

In a state of war the military element always comes into power. Just as von Tirpitz seems to have imposed his submarine policy on the civilian chancellor, Bethmann-Hollweg, so it is probable that the British admiralty has forced on their government a policy of illegality which the public opinion of England would condemn as much as we.

An embargo on the export of munitions—or even a serious threat—would probably bring the sea lords to a juster appreciation of the situation.

Mr. Wilson's attitude in the German controversy resulted—temporarily at least—in the victory of the more moderate and law-abiding element in the governing circles of Berlin. If he can succeed in reëstablishing a reign of law on the seas by continued pressure on Germany and by an equally firm attitude in the British controversy it will be a great triumph for the cause of human progress.

The War has also forced upon us a consideration of our military situation. It is bad. Our army and navy appropriations have not been wisely spent and we have very little to show for the money. There seems a very general will to put through serious reforms in these departments.

Here again, before anything profitable can be done, we must first of all answer the question proposed in the last chapter: Are we or are we not a World Power? It is evident that our military needs in defence of our "traditional policy" are quite different from those we will have if we set out to reform the world. If we are going to declare war every time any nation tears up a scrap of paper we will need—at the very least—the largest army the world has ever seen.

Let us face that problem frankly. It would be frightfully expensive, but we are very rich. If we adopted the

Swiss militia system we could mobilize ten million men within forty-eight hours. The per capita burden—in taxes and time lost from productive industry—would be no heavier than in Switzerland, and the Swiss manage to carry it and prosper. No nation but Russia could hope to rival us.

If we decided to devote a large share of this money and energy to the navy we could dominate the seas. The German rivalry with England is illuminating. Single-handed they came near to reaching a par with Britain. We are much richer than the Germans.

However, not even our armament manufacturers advocate so extravagant a program. The practical question raised by this War is: What could we do if we were forced to enter it? The answer depends very largely on the unforeseeable action of popular psychology. If the nation was as deeply interested as it was in the Civil War—and public interest was often very slack in those four years—if we were prepared to face an equal sacrifice, we could recruit, drill and equip at least half a million men in the first year and could put a million new soldiers in the field annually as long as the bellicose spirit lasted. Such a calculation depends entirely on the material elements of the problem.

It is quite impossible to tell whether we would want to send an army over seas. It would be difficult to recruit an army corps for an unpopular war. But if as a nation we made up our mind to enter this War with our entire power we could—while being slow to start—in all probability be the determining factor if the present approximate equilibrium of forces remained the same for a couple of years.

But such a military effort would require for its success some motive of sufficient force to completely revolutionize our habits and our attitude towards life. The English intention to carry on "business as usual" has failed. The French ambition to maintain "democracy as usual" is threatened. We would have to give up all thought of progress at home and subordinate everything to the grim business of war. It might conceivably be necessary, but it would be desperately distasteful.

Nothing could be more disastrous for us—morally or materially—than a half-hearted war. Nothing would be more out of keeping with all that is good in our traditions. The issue should be put clearly before us. We should choose fairly; keep the peace, or fight to the limit. No halfway warfare could be dignified. An American army of a few hundred thousand men and a half dozen battleships would be a disgrace. We should all go—or keep the peace.

Sane statesmanship will bend every effort to maintain our neutrality.

CHAPTER XXV

NATIONAL DEFENCE

The European War has not altered our problem of national defence—it has only brought it more vividly to our attention. As there can be none of the "life, liberty and pursuit of happiness" which our Constitution intends, if foreign armies are to overrun our soil, it is manifestly the first duty of our government to protect us from such a fate.

It is possible that we may decide to send an expeditionary force to overrun some of Europe, but this evidently is not a matter of national defence.

Many of our "patriots" are using this War as a text to remind us that our navy is not so strong as that of Great Britain, that our coast defences are illogical and under-manned, that our army is small and ill-equipped. This, although it is quite true, does not meet the question of national defence. The assumption that the army and navy is our only hope of security is entirely unfounded. It is a tradition with us to maintain a military establishment but it is childish, or worse, to pretend that it is our soldiers and sailors alone who, these hundred years, have protected our frontiers.

With the exception of a short period after the Civil War, when our army and navy was exceptionally large, there has been no time when the British Empire was not strong enough at sea to have sent to Canada a much larger force than our army. From a purely military point of view they could easily have invaded us. We have not been prepared to prevent it. In time we could have gathered strength to drive them out, but what we have had in the past, and want for the future, is security from initial invasion. Driving the Germans out of Belgium will not bring Louvain to life again.

Our northern frontier has been safe, not because of our military strength, but because of the mass of common interests between us and England. To a large extent, we understand each other. We have had our bellicose spasms —"Fifty-four forty or fight" and all that. But we didn't fight. Now and then the English have been mightily vexed at us, sometimes without reason. But we speak the same language and to a large extent wear the same cut of clothes. This has given us, if not a thick and thin friendship, at least a mutual confidence which renders war improbable. The English knew that they could strip Canada of troops without fear of our trying to annex it.

It is entirely possible to stimulate such "defensive" understandings between nations. This is the key-note of the foreign policy of M. Delcassé. When he entered the Quai d'Orsay, France was on exceedingly bad terms with Italy and England. He made friends.

Sir Harry Johnson's "Commonsense in Foreign Policy" and Georges Bourdon's "The German Enigma" were efforts to lay the foundations of such an Entente with Germany. Neither of these men were "pacifists" but both dreaded the horror we now witness. Patriots, they foresaw the frightful cost of even a victorious war. They set to work earnestly to understand and to explain to their countrymen what the different nations of Europe wanted, wherein their aspirations conflicted, how their points of dispute could be compromised. Both believed that this war, which has been so long foreseen, might with better understanding be avoided.

If the British and French and German governments had been truly enlightened and really pacific, they would have circulated these and similar books by the hundreds of thousands. Such a campaign of education would have had more "defensive" value than a score of army corps. But it is the hoary tradition of Europe that the only way for a nation to protect its citizens from war is to make them more war-like than their neighbors.

But it is obviously more civilized to prevent war than to win at it. In the last few decades a noticeable start has been made in applying this very modern idea. The Rhodes scholarships, exchange professorships, the Interparliamentary Union, all such movements tend to facilitate protective understandings. They threaten the vested interests of militarists, diplomats, and armament makers and of course meet with small encouragement in countries where these classes rule. But in spite of much discouragement, some progress has been made.

The United States has, I believe, the honor of being the first nation to give official sanction to this form of national defence. The Bureau of American Republics was created to stimulate cordial relations with our neighbors to the south. It is a step in the right direction of which we may well be proud—but it is a pitifully small step. The amount we spend on it annually is little more than the cost of one broadside from a battle ship. But in spite of the niggardly appropriation, this effort to manufacture good will has proved its protective worth. The "A. B. C." mediation which for a time at least relieved the strain in Mexico and was of even greater value farther south, was its first fruits.

We ought to extend greatly the work and resources of this Bureau. It might well have branches in each of the Republics. Its personnel should not be confined to citizens of the United States, but every effort should be made to secure the collaboration of the Latin Americans. We have too often listened to the worst that could be said about them, too often we have shown them the worst of our life. The Bureau of American Republics, if properly encouraged, may become of great value in our scheme of national defence.

The only acute menace of war we have had in recent years has had to do with Mexico. It was not invasion by the Mexicans we had to fear. Here as elsewhere the danger is lack of understanding. We hope the Administration is well informed; the rest of us certainly are not. The newspapers contain absurdly contradictory statements, and we do not know which to believe.

But one thing we do know: there are too few schools in Mexico. An ignorant population is an easy prey to unscrupulous adventurers. It is the illiteracy of the Mexicans, not their army, which we have to fear.

Circumstances may arise which will persuade our government to conquer Mexico. The attempt will prove, if it comes, vastly more expensive than it would have been to have educated the country. But it is never too late to mend, and to allow the peons to remain longer illiterate is to invite the kind of complications most likely to lead to invasion. We do not have to fear that the Mexicans will sack St. Louis, but that we may be drawn into an aggression against a weaker power, a shameful war which foresight could have prevented. For every dollar we spend to put soldiers on our southern border, we should spend ten on the purely defensive work of building up an educated public across the frontier with whom we can be friends.

This is the logical work of the Bureau of American Republics. The results we could expect from it, given sufficient means, would be of lasting and immeasurable worth. The battle ships, which cost so much, very quickly become obsolete.

Since the Civil War no one has feared armed invasion from any country but Japan. This menace has been grossly exaggerated, not always from laudable motives. But there is no gain in the ostrich policy of refusing to look at what danger there is.

The thing which most sharply differentiates our relations with Japan from those with Great Britain is that while we are well acquainted with the English, the Japanese of all the great nations are the people we know least. The unknown is always fearsome. The English who have had the longest and closest contact with the Oriental races do not dread them. "The Yellow Peril" is a phrase attributed to the Kaiser, a man who has never been east of Suez. And we, who are woefully unacquainted with the Japanese, are unduly disposed to credit every sinister rumor.

This lack of understanding—and very dangerous it is—is not confined to us. The Japanese are as easily persuaded as we to believe fantastic and menacing stories from the other side of the Pacific. The day when Japan sent her ultimatum to Germany, the morning papers of Tokio contained what purported to be a despatch from Washington to the effect that President Wilson had read a special message to Congress about "our manifest destiny and predominant interests" in the Pacific, and that our Atlantic squadron was being rushed through the Panama Canal.

In a day or two this vicious canard was disproved. But for a day or two that kind of distrust which may so easily lead to worse was allowed free rein. If Japan ever does attack us, the chances are ten to one that the cause will be some such stupid misunderstanding. A government which does not strive earnestly to overcome such danger is wantonly neglecting the most obvious and simple form of defence.

Of course, if we wanted to, we could build a fleet so much larger than Japan could afford—it is merely a matter of dollars and cents—that they would be afraid to attack us single-handed and would be forced to seek new alliances with other naval powers. It was so that the German government understood the problem of national defence. But it would certainly be more civilized, less expensive, and very much safer, to establish a sound basis of mutual understanding, the foundation of a real friendship.

Any government of ours which allows us to be dragged into a war on a misunderstanding, no matter how effectively it has developed our army and navy, will deserve impeachment. Treitschke, a German professor of politics, has taught that there are inevitable conflicts between states which can be settled only by force. The people of the United States are loath to accept this theory, but they are determined not to go to war on any other basis. Few Americans are Tolstoians. But woe to any administration which involves us in an unnecessary war!

Before a new battle ship is built for our Pacific squadron, before a new gun is planted on our western coast, Congress ought to spend ten times as much to prevent the chance of having to use them. Every expense for war should be preceded by a more generous investment in peace. Chinese, Japanese, and Filipino students should be brought to America as the guests of our government. We cannot leave so important a matter to the chance generosity of private citizens. We should make them acquainted with our colleges and also with our politics and press and the other phases of our national life. They should be encouraged to tell their impressions, not only to their own people, but also to us. If we knew what the Japanese think of us, we would probably be less worried about them than we are; it would certainly make it easier to remove any offence we have unwittingly given them. And our young men and women should be sent to the Orient on the same mission.

Why not create a bureau of the Pacific, beside that of the American Republics? It was evident that our diplomatic corps, inevitably tied up with the red tape of their profession, could not do in Central or South America the things we wanted done. And there is no more reason to trust them across the Pacific—or the Atlantic.

Our General Staff is asking for an army of half a million men: 100,000 in active service; 400,000 in reserve. Their theory is that we should have immediately available a sufficient force to hold in check the first onslaught of any possible invader and to protect the vital part of the country while a volunteer army is being equipped and drilled. Besides this "standing" and "reserve" army, their scheme includes the encouragement of state militia and military schools, increased facilities for training officers and the accumulation of large stores of munitions.

It is the professional duty of Staff officers in times of peace to be excessively timid. They must plan to be on the safe side of the worst possible hard luck. Their scheme represents what they consider adequate protection against any threat of invasion which their imaginations—stimulated by their profession—can conjure up.

The obvious criticism of this program is the difficulty of recruitment. Soldiering has little attraction in times of peace. Garrison duty everywhere—here or in Europe—is the consummation of boredom. It is difficult to persuade the West Point graduates to stay in the army. It has always been hard to find volunteers for our former smaller establishment and the sheer tiresomeness of the life makes desertions frequent. The common sense of mankind makes it exceedingly difficult to arouse popular enthusiasm for military service when there is no war in sight. It is very doubtful if we can build up a professional army in time of peace as large as the General Staff asks for. No one has yet discovered a middle ground between an aggressive militarism and a policy of peace.

If we decide to accept the responsibilities of World Power, we will need a very much larger army than the General Staff asks for. The only way to make it popular and efficient is to keep it busy. And no one who is looking for a fight has to look far. But if we are to maintain our "traditional policy" there is no reason to be quite so timid as our General Staff. The army should be only one element—and by no means the most important—in our scheme of national defence.

We must state the issue clearly if we wish to meet it intelligently. Such activities as I have suggested for the Bureau of American Republics are purely defensive. They could not serve for aggression. Therefore they will not satisfy our imperialists. To educate the Mexicans, for instance, would be a fatal blunder, if it is our intention to subjugate them. If we want to crush all rivals in the Pacific we will need more of a navy. But if such is our ambition, let us be frank about it and not talk of "defence." It is a strangely perverted logic for people who plead for national security to urge us to spend all, or even a large part of, our defence fund on the forms of "protection" which have not saved our European friends from the horrors of war.

But our imperialists, despite their loud voices, are in a minority. On the whole, we are quite content with our present borders. The more the rest of the world is convinced that we have no aggressive designs, the greater will be our security.

CHAPTER XXVI

THE UNITED STATES AND PEACE

SINCE the War broke out, I have been collecting peace projects. The pile on my desk grows daily. The most remarkable thing about them is their lack of variety. Almost without exception, no matter what part of the world they come from—and most of them come from America—the authors agree in basing their arguments on what they call "the lesson of history."

Once upon a time men fought with teeth and claws whenever they disagreed. After a long lapse of time fighting became formalized—the duel. At last a stage of civilization was reached when men submitted their disputes to tribunals—which, in theory at least—based their judgments not on the might of the litigants, but on the rights of the case. This evolution is illustrated by diverse historic examples, but most generally by the unification of the French monarchy, the period when the lawlessness of the feudal lords was suppressed by the "king's justice."

Arguing by analogy from this "lesson of history," these advocates of peace foretell a time when the nations of the world will reason together about their disputes before some high court of justice. So will the epoch of might give place to the era of right. Every nation in its historic evolution achieved internal peace, so the world can win to international peace. As this argument seems eminently plausible, the peoples of Europe are asked to lay down their arms. It is manifestly, and shockingly, stupid to allow questions of moment to be decided by the irrational chance of arms when they might be so much more reasonably determined by arbitration. The variations from this argument among these peace proposals are slight.

Their authors are equally in accord in ignoring or glossing over the ugly side of their "lesson of history." The triumph of law in the various states of Europe grew out of violence and manifold injustices. Internal peace was established not by argument or reason or good will, but because one group in the community was able, *durch eisen und blut*, to impose *its* law on the rest. In France the court party won. The land was covered with gibbets on which outlaws, often better men than the kings, were hanged. In England, at Runnymede, it was the League of Barons; at Marston Moor it was the Parliament's army. More recently peace was brought to the German people by the mailed fist of Prussia. It was out of such desperate travail that law was born.

There are those who believe that the evolution toward world peace must follow the same violent course. Numerous efforts have been made in that direction. The Roman Empire was the most nearly successful. There have been few forces in the history of civilization more momentous than the *pax Romana*. Napoleon was always leading the French armies against those who disturbed *his* peace. If it had not been for the snows of Russia and the little island with too many ships, he might have imposed a long tranquillity on Europe. The British, after soaking India in blood, have brought to that unhappy land the first peace it has ever known. Our soldiers have suppressed tribal wars in the Philippines.

If the Germans win in this War, they promise to establish a compulsory peace. And no statesman of the Entente makes a speech without reaffirming that his country will fight it out until the bases of a permanent peace have been laid.

While the authors of the peace proposals that I have gathered very generally ignore the unpleasant aspect of their "lesson of history," we may be sure that they wish to improve on the historic method. It was not only unreasonably brutal, it was slow. It took the kings centuries to disband the private armies of their unruly subjects. If we leave the work of peace to natural evolution, the thirtieth century may possibly see its realization.

What we want to do—for I assume that all men, in their sane moments, hate war—is to speed up evolution and change its method. The "lesson of history" shows us what natural evolution accomplished between men in its slow, bungling, accidental way. We want to achieve the same thing between nations speedily, and with precision, by the conscious exercise of our will.

Most people could be divided into two classes on this issue. Some are fatalists in such matters; they think there is nothing we can do about it, they believe in "letting things take their course." The German chancellor, Herr Bethmann-Hollweg, is reported to have said that it was idle to talk of disarmament "as long as men are men and nations are nations." There are many like him, who say, "You can't change human nature." But there are others who believe that the will of man can influence his fate.

Almost everyone belongs to the second class in smaller issues. No one doubts that we can exercise our wills profitably on inert matter. We dig wells, build bridges, and every year plant the seeds of the harvest. A large majority of us believe that we can change human nature by exerting pressure on the minds and bodies of children. Our little red school-houses, our great universities, are nothing else but wilful efforts to improve on the happy-go-lucky scheme of evolution. We are not content to create the next generation after our own image; we are resolved to make it an improvement.

But for some reason there are more fatalists about these problems of foreign relations. Perhaps the reason why they are willing to let these things alone is that they do not see what can be done. Perhaps the projects they are asked to support seem too grandiose to promise success.

My criticism of these peace proposals is exactly that. They are dazzling—too dazzling. The substitution of reason for force, of right for might, throughout all the world seems an appallingly big undertaking to me. Personally I believe that we can change human nature. I am not interested in any reform which does not have this for its goal. But I doubt if we can do much to change other people's natures till we have succeeded in changing our own.

These American peace advocates ask the people of Europe to change their nations, gloriously, suddenly. They offer a wondrous picture of the commonwealth which is to come, but their propositions are too vague to take hold of. Archimedes was quite right when he said he could move the world if he could find a proper fulcrum on which to rest his lever. The peace movement needs a fulcrum.

Past efforts to bring the nations of the world together under a rule of law have not been very successful. A sincere desire for peace, a readiness for mutual sacrifice to the common good, have not been generally manifested. There can be no peace without justice, and justice means the renunciation by the strong of the privileges of their strength.

I do not wish to decry the work done at The Hague—at least some worthy ideals were given official sanction—but no real friend of peace can read the reports of the conventions without a heavy heart. The various nations were principally interested in getting or preserving advantages. The governments that had not begun to build air-craft wanted to prohibit, not war, but aerial warfare. The countries with weak navies tried, not to prevent war, but to put through an agreement by which the property of non-combatants would be protected on the sea as they were supposed to be in warfare on land. Our United States delegates made it clear at every opportunity that we would not even discuss the Monroe Doctrine. We were no more willing to submit that to an international court than Great Britain was willing to arbitrate the Boer War.

International law, just like civil law, will have to clip special privileges. The two ideas are mutually antagonistic. The concept of justice is a late achievement in the history of civilization. It is not yet fully realized in our internal relations. In international affairs the first step toward realization has hardly been taken. Justice does not happen; it is something which has to be created at the expense of immense and persistent effort.

Even in time of peace it was impossible to persuade the nations to give up their privileges—too often their plunder. They were not ready to put right above might. The War has rendered the situation vastly worse. A wave of rage is sweeping over Europe. This furor of hate is a matter of mob psychology: it is infectious. You can count on the fingers of one hand the men of note in any of the belligerent countries who are immune, who have kept their heads level through the crisis, who have preserved any objective sense of justice.

The situation of Holland gives a striking example. This little state is being ground between the upper and the lower millstone. The Dutch are a commercial people; their whole economic life depends on free communication with their distant colonies. Germany with her submarines, Great Britain with her battle cruisers, are both raining blows on Holland in the hope of indirectly hitting their enemy. Neither in the French nor the English papers have I seen any calm discussion of the rights of the case. The same statesmen who call down the wrath of Heaven on Germany because of her aggression on Belgium, find it quite natural to smother Holland. With naïve cynicism people who in normal times would be quick to champion the rights of the weak now discuss how to force the Dutch to declare war on Germany. It seems impossible to fight and to discuss ethics at the same time, and both sides believe that for them to stop fighting means destruction.

The pitiful spectacle of Europe gone mad is a very strong argument in favor of peace. When their blood cools, the combatants will see it themselves, and will doubtless repent of the extravagance of their hate. But to talk peace to them now, to urge them to the necessary mutual concessions, is the superlative of futility.

Imagine offering a peace prize to Cromwell and Charles I. if they would disarm! The Roundheads believed that they were fighting for the right, and knew they were strong enough to get what they wanted, whether it was right or wrong. The king also was fighting for what he thought was right—a divine right. He might have consented to arbitrate at the foot of the scaffold, but not while his army was afield.

It is just as futile to try to argue with the present belligerents. They believe very sincerely that their cause is sacred. Neither side will listen to mediation as long as they have a hope to win. And whichever side is defeated will find in its overthrow another proof that might triumphs over right.

Their ideals of justice are worlds apart. It is unfortunate that we use the same word to translate *droit* and *recht*. What they mean is not only different; it is antagonistic. The French Academy of Sciences—and the same thing is happening in all the countries at war—is expelling from its membership German scientists. There is small chance that these men, in their present frame of mind, would consent to sit on the same bench with a German jurist to determine some fine point of international law.

Among my pile of peace proposals there are a few, a very few, from the pens of men of the belligerent countries. They do not consider peace as possible or even desirable except on the basis of the defeat of the enemy. The Germans say that the disturbing element in Europe is the British naval supremacy. That destroyed, and there is a chance of peace. The pacifists of England are agreed that German militarism must be destroyed. I cannot see any reason to believe that one point of view is more sincere than the other.

Arbitration? Yes, between Liberia and Iceland. Perhaps even with the United States, *after the War*, over the commercial disputes arising from the various new brands of blockades each side is busily inventing. But arbitration over the Dutch complaints? Over the size of the German army or the British navy? Over France's interpretation of the *Acte d'Algésiras?* No; these are vital interests. "And, besides," say the belligerents on each side, "we are going to win; so why arbitrate?" There will be no chance to mediate in Europe till both sides are utterly exhausted or one side knows that it is defeated.

The only possible theater for a campaign of peace is the Western Hemisphere. And, after all, it would be quite as well, in fact, better, for us to make sure that we have healed ourselves before we set out to cure Europe.

The A. B. C. mediation in the Mexican embroglio was a step of the utmost importance. It did not solve the question at issue, but it planted a seed that, with proper culture, may grow into a Peace League of the American Republics.

There is no more promising field for peace work. Success—and if we resolve on success, we can find the means—would have immediate and tangible advantages. There is no excuse for pessimistic fatalism here. But it is not a matter which can be arranged by diplomats in conclave behind closed doors. Our institutions are in absolute opposition to such secret combinations. A democratic government cannot suddenly change the foreign policy of its people; it can only work fruitfully toward ends that are consciously desired by the nation. There is little to be gained by sending peace deputations to Washington. The work to be done must be done in every city and town and village from New York to Valparaiso. And we cannot rely on a sudden burst of enthusiasm to carry us through. What is needed is a wide-spread, intense, continuous campaign of education. Once the peoples of the two Americas really want a league of peace, their governments will have no trouble in solving the problems of detail.

There can be little doubt that a League of American Republics would mean peace for us, safety from outside aggression, and the chance to push on in our progress towards liberty and justice within. No matter who wins in this devastating European War, no one will lightly pick a quarrel with all the Americas united. Great oceans protect us from such sudden invasions as fell on Belgium and East Prussia. And within six months Great Britain was able to organize and equip a volunteer army which was bigger than any expeditionary force could be.

But despite its manifest advantages, wishing for such a league will do little good. Nothing worth having is won without effort. And it is well to realize some of the obstacles we must face. Most of the work would have to be done in the United States. The opposition to a peace league which would be encountered in Latin America would be real, but small in comparison to our reluctance to give up our position of predominance. Before we can establish the Peace of Justice on our hemisphere we must change the habits of thought—the human nature—of our people on a good many points. The South American republics are not going to ask us to establish a protectorate over them. They are ambitious to be something more than the tail of our kite. We shall have to outgrow a great deal of national egoism before we can accomplish any real work of peace.

A defensive League of American Republics would be more effective than any single-handed warning to Europe. To maintain the Monroe Doctrine unchanged is to needlessly and offensively assert our political supremacy in the New World. Our neighbors to the south very naturally hesitate to admit their hopeless inferiority. And no league worth the name is possible without their cordial coöperation.

It is true that we have more miles of railroads and more schools per hundred thousand inhabitants than Argentina. It is quite a different thing to insist on our political superiority. New Jersey has more schools and railroads in proportion to its population than Nevada, but both have two senators at Washington, and until we are willing to treat the Latin republics as our equals in this sense our peace efforts will be fruitless.

Secondly, no league of American republics is possible unless we widen our interests immensely. We must study and strive to understand our neighbors. Few of us ever think of Brazil except to wonder if there is by any chance some way in which we could make easy money down there. It hardly occurs to us that the Chilians have political problems—tariff questions, trusts and labor-unions. How many of us understand their struggle between church and state? We have been too busy with our own affairs to trouble about theirs. But it is hardly possible to be friends with complete strangers.

And thirdly, we must educate ourselves to the frame of mind in which we would consent to submit to the peace court of the League such disputes as our recent unpleasantness with Colombia. Unless we are willing to leave might out of such arguments, and reason them out on the sole basis of right, our peace talk is necessarily suspect.

The Colombian wrangle is a good example of the chief stumbling-block in the way of international law. Our government would not, I believe, have used its might—and of course Colombia yielded only to a show of force—if it had not been convinced that we also had right on our side.

The British government felt that it was armed with the sword of justice when it went to war with the Boer republics. The French government believed that it was justified in dethroning the Sultan of Morocco, in tearing up the Algeciras Treaty. As a general proposition, the statesmen of these countries would say, as ours say, that it is wrong for a great and powerful nation to add to its domains by picking a quarrel with a small and weaker people. But in these concrete instances there were special circumstances which justified a departure from the general rule; the Boers were impossibly irritating, the Sultan of Morocco was manifestly incompetent, our government believed, on very good evidence, that the politicians of Bogota were trying to blackmail us. And so the Dual Monarchy could find no end of special circumstances to salve its conscience in its stern demands on Servia.

But men are not permitted to determine for themselves when circumstances warrant a departure from the rules of law. They have to establish their rights in such cases before a competent tribunal. The frame of mind which recognizes and accepts this outside authority is what differentiates an outlaw from a citizen, a civilized man from a savage.

It is the same with nations. The states which have entered into federations have managed to climb this steep incline of progress. Bavaria does not determine for itself which are its rights in regard to Hesse. Texas takes its disputes with Delaware before the Supreme Court. We have refused to submit the Panama matter to a jury of our peers. And as long as we are determined to be the deciding judge in our own disputes, all talk of a civilized peace with our neighbors is a contradiction in terms. We may not have war. Nicaragua and Venezuela and Colombia may be afraid to fight us. They may sullenly prefer to accept what seems to them our injustice rather than risk the resort to arms. But such peace is not civilized.

We must make up our minds to it that a *régime* of international law requires that we, as well as our neighbors, shall submit to its discipline. This seems to me the nubbin of the peace problem. One school of philosophy—the pan-jingoists—has taught that the motor force of life was "the will to power" and that war is a normal activity. If this is true, we must change our natures and develop a will to justice. There is no other foundation for peace.

There is still another difficulty to be faced before we can establish closer relations with South America. Our public opinion must not only be educated to a new attitude in foreign affairs; we must also contrive the means to convince sceptics that the conversion is sincere. Our southern neighbors will be slow to put trust in our change of heart. According to a hoary tradition in the Latin republics, our ideals are far from those of peace.

It was a decided shock to me when I first visited Central America to find in one of the plazas of San José de Costa Rica, a monument in memory of the defeat of the filibuster Walker. An armed and beautiful lady—the spirit of Latin civilization—had her foot on the neck of a prostrate, but very villainous scoundrel, who represented us, the gringo aggressor. When I went to school I was not taught anything about that incident, but I found that in the history text-books in the Spanish-American schools there was a whole chapter devoted to the discreditable adventure. This traditional belief in our territorial greed will be hard to uproot. There is our Mexican War to support it, and of course it has been strengthened by our more recent annexations of Spanish speaking countries. It takes effort to overcome the inertia of such well-established ideas. We have a bad reputation to live down.

To prepare the ground for a League of American Republics will require great and persistent efforts. Such is the pioneer work, difficult, but necessary, which we must accomplish before we can expect others to take our peace talk seriously. But certainly anyone who is daunted by these difficulties has no right to urge the peoples of Europe to lay down their arms and to submit to an international court. It is decidedly insulting for us to assume that they are not intelligent enough to realize that our problems are child's play beside theirs. They are justified in sneering at our peace proposals so long as we have failed to put our own house in order.

But great as are the difficulties for us to overcome,—and there is no gain in minimizing them,—they are very small compared with the benefits of success. Do we in America really want peace—the Peace of Justice? If we do, the first concrete step is clearly indicated: the League of American Republics would give us peace. The effort would be richly repaid. And, granted a determined will, achievement would be assured.

The influence of the accomplishment would be vastly

greater than the security it would give us. Somewhat more than a century ago our fathers brought forth on this continent a new nation dedicated to the ideal of democratic liberty. Although we are still far short of realizing that ideal, it would be hardly possible to over-estimate the effect of our effort on Europe. If our form of government were to fail, no one of us would be more disheartened than the republican of the Old World. Every advance of ours is a new weapon for them in their long fight against tradition.

If our generation could establish the peace of justice and liberty in the Americas—and we can, if we resolve to—the effect around the world would be stupendous.

At last we should have a right to send peace proposals to Europe. The League of American Republics could most cordially urge other countries to similar action, could lend a powerful helping hand to every peace movement; and as soon as any new group became organized, a union would be possible. So might we reach the federation of the world.

It is certainly easier to advise Europe to lay down its arms than it is for us to educate and discipline ourselves to peace; but an ounce of example is worth many pounds of advice.

BIBLIOGRAPHY

The sources for a study of diplomatic history are of three kinds: official, semi-official, unofficial.

The official documents are the publications of the various foreign offices and the speeches of responsible ministers. This "source" is very limited. The "White Papers" and "Blue Books," etc., generally leave out the most interesting documents.

There has been, for instance, no official publication in France in regard to the secret annex to the *Entente Cordiale* of 1904. *Le Temps*, one of the most reputable papers of Paris, printed what purported to be the text of this agreement. The chances are that it was correct. But in reply to a question at the Quai d'Orsay, I was told that the French government had taken no cognizance of this publication and never admitted or denied its accuracy.

The student is continually faced by lacunæ and even rank contradiction in the "official documents." The case of the intrigues to gain railroad concessions in Asia Minor is typical. A certain amount of French "official" information is available on this subject. It is certain that their ambassador at Constantinople acted in a sense contrary to his instructions. There are two possible explanations. The French ambassador may have been working on a theory of his own and so ignored the orders of his chief, or secret instructions may have accompanied those meant for publication. The fact that the ambassador was not disgraced for insubordination lends color to the second hypothesis.

Another consideration which must always be borne in mind in studying these official documents is that a foreign office is rarely well organized. There is generally a struggle in progress between the permanent officials and the political appointees—transient chiefs. This is true in every country and not only in each foreign office, but in every embassy and legation.

A newly appointed ambassador arrives at Pekin. He finds himself surrounded by a permanent legation staff, who know—or at least think they know—a great deal more about the situation than he does. It is the same when a new minister of foreign affairs enters his office. The "appointed" policy and the "permanent" policy is almost always in conflict. It is often difficult to untangle them. And if anything goes wrong, the permanent officials—thanks to their *esprit de corps*—nearly always succeed in putting the blame on their transient chief.

Semi-official information reaches the public through the periodical press and books. It is always hard to distinguish it from the non-official which takes the same form.

It is necessary to know something of the personality of the writer of each book or article, his private interests, his political affiliations and his "standing" at the foreign office at the time of the writing.

For several years M. André Tardieu wrote the daily bulletins on foreign affairs for *Le Temps*. His first ambition had been towards diplomacy but after an apprenticeship at the Quai d'Orsay, he left the *carrière* to become a journalist. During the period of the Algeciras crisis he was very close to the foreign office. It was a personal rather than an official relationship. He had friends at the Quai d'Orsay. His writings on foreign relations—at this time—had a very real authority.

Later he became interested in the high finance of the Near East. He was connected with a group of bankers who were trying to persuade the French government to back up their railroad concessions—the Homs-Bagdad Line, a rival to the German Bagdadbahn. His writings on the diplomatic situation in the Near East during this phase of his career, have less authority, in my opinion.

The *London Times* has also had its ups and downs. For

years its correspondent has generally been *persona grata* at Downing Street. But now and then—frequently during this War—the relations between the great English daily and the government have been decidedly strained.

It is sometimes said that Maximilien Harden is the only independent journalist in Germany. He certainly cannot be suspected of being protected by the bureaucracy. But the very independence of his paper has made it a favorite medium for "indiscretions." Harden has the reputation of never betraying the source of his information. And many a disgruntled official has come to him with official secrets in the hope that their publication will injure a rival.

Uncertain and variable as is the value of the periodical press, its study is the only way to find flesh with which to clothe the dry bones of official documents. Although much of the newspaper comment on foreign affairs is ignorant, and some of it intentionally false, it cannot be ignored. More and more the foreign offices are developing their "press bureaux." As democracy develops in education and politics, it becomes necessary to know what the people at home were thinking in order to understand the actions of their far away ambassadors.

And all these considerations bear with equal weight on the more pretentious bound books on foreign affairs. Their value depends on that of their author.

Of the books published by Americans, the following have been very helpful to me:

1. Clapp: "The Economic Aspects of the War." It is primarily a statement of the diplomatic controversy between the United States and Great Britain during the first year of the War.
2. Dewey: "German Philosophy and Politics." The title is descriptive. It is perhaps the most profound book which the War has inspired in America.
3. Gibbons: "The New Map of Europe." A valuable study of the events which preceded the War, especially informing in regard to the problems of the Balkans.

4. Howe: "Socialized Germany." An American appreciation of the tangible results accomplished in internal affairs by the ideal of the Deutschtum.
5. Veblen: "Imperial Germany and the Industrial Revolution." A searching study of the economic foundations and structure of the German Empire. The author is not pro-German. His book gives the reverse of the medal of which Dr. Howe shows us the face.

Of the books which have appeared in England since the outbreak of the War, the following:

1. Fayle: "The Great Settlement." It is a serious effort to put before English readers the fundamental problems of the War and the Liberal attitude towards their settlement.
2. Forbes: "The Southern Slavs." This is one of the "Oxford Pamphlets," a series of university publications on different phases of the present crisis. They are all erudite but of varying worth. This is one of the best.
3. Morel: "Ten Years of Secret Diplomacy." This is a reprint of his "Morocco in Diplomacy" which was published in 1912. It is a vigorous attack on the British Foreign Office. It is one of the books circulated by The Union of Democratic Control. It is rather "heated" but most of its contentions are well founded. It is worth careful consideration. The defenders of Sir Edward Grey have failed to answer it satisfactorily. British patriots denounce it as pro-German.
4. Murray: "The Foreign Policy of Sir Edward Grey." A sincere but weak attempt to answer the criticism of Morel and his friends.
5. Toynbee: "Nationality and the War." A book similar in intent to Fayle's "The Great Settlement" but giving more special attention to the theory of the rights of nationalities.

The following books have been translated into English and are worth attention:

1. Anonymous: "J'accuse." It was first printed in Ger-

man by a respectable Swiss publisher who guaranteed its authenticity. The author claims to be a patriotic German. There is little else in the book of especial interest. It is a new statement in a ponderous German style of the familiar contentions of the orators of the Entente.
2. Bismarck: "His Reflections and Reminiscences." This book is full of interesting information on modern German and international affairs. The Iron Chancellor knew what he was talking about but did not always care to tell the truth.
3. Lipkowski: "The Polish Question." This is a pamphlet published under the auspices of "Polonia" a review printed in behalf of Polish interests in Paris. It presents the maximum claims of the Polish Nationalists.
4. Tardieu: "France and the Alliances." Published in New York in 1908. This book—a reprint of lectures given in America—is a statement of what the French wanted the rest of the world to think about their system of international relations. It is more persuasive than informing.
5. Von Bülow: "Imperial Germany." This is a broad presentation of the policies—internal and external—of the ex-Chancellor of the Empire. It does not have the form of Mémoires but it resembles such works in that it is to a certain extent "self-defensive." The Chancellor, having fallen from power, renders an account of his stewardship. It is of great value as a presentation of the psychology of the ruling class in the Germany of our day.

It is harder to recommend a few books in French, as there are so many of real value.
1. Albin: "Les grandes Traités Politiques. Depuis 1815 jusqu'à nos jours" contains the text of most of the diplomatic documents which have been published since the Napoleonic Era. The same author has written since the outbreak of the War "La guerre

Allemande. D'Agadir à Sarajevo—1911–1914." It is partisan but contains a great deal of information about the events of 1913 and 1914.

2. Andler: "Le Pangermanisme" also "Collection de Documents sur le pangermanisme—traduit de l'Allemand. Publiés sous la direction de M. Charles Andler." The first is a propaganda pamphlet. The second is the most sincere effort I have found in French to understand and state the ideals of the Deutschtum.

3. Bérard: "L'Angleterre et l'Impérialisme." A very good statement of what the French think of the British Tories.

4. Chéradame: (a) "La question d'Orient—La Macédoine—Le Chemin de Fer de Bagdad." (b) "L'Europe et la question d'Autriche au seuil du vingtième siécle." This author writes with special knowledge of the problems of the Near East. His discussion of the Bagdad Railway is especially interesting. His articles in the periodical press, too numerous to mention, are also worth attention.

5. Chervin: "L'Autriche et la Hongrie de demain. Les différentes Nationalités d'après les langues parlées." A valuable statistical study of the race problem in the Dual Monarchy.

6. Dupuis: "Le principe d'équilibre et le concert Européen de la paix de Westphalie à l'acte d'Algésiras." A scholarly study of the history of the ideas of "The Balance of Power" and "The Concert of Europe."

7. Gobineau: "Essai sur l'inégalité des races humaines." The second edition of this book was published in Paris in 1884. It has had small vogue in France but has been enthusiastically "accepted" in Germany. It is an argument in behalf of the theory of superior and inferior races.

8. Guéchoff: "L'Alliance Balkanique." Guéchoff was Prime Minister of Bulgaria during the period which saw the formation of the Alliance and the First Balkan

War. He writes from the inside. It is the most valuable book yet published on the subject.
9. Hanotaux: (*a*) "Histoire de la France Contemporaine" in four volumes. (*b*) "Études diplomatiques" in two volumes. The first is a presentation of the French Political Life from the founding of the Third Republic to the death of Gambetta, 1870 to 1883. M. Hanotaux is a "Moderate Republican" and this gives him a certain bias. His principal interest is in Foreign Affairs. His long ministry at the Quai d'Orsay gave him unusual facilities to have access to the Archives. His account of the Congress of Berlin has been especially valuable to me. The "Études Diplomatiques" are reprints of his articles in "La Revue Hebdomadaire."
10. Lair: "L'Impérialisme Allemand." A companion piece to Bérard, "L'Angleterre et l'Impérialisme."
11. Lémonon: "L'Europe et la Politique Britannique (1882–1909)." This is a very careful study of the change in British Foreign Policy from her former friendship towards the Germans to her entrance into the Entente.
12. Maurras: "Kiel et Tanger ou la troisième république devant l'Europe." Charles Maurras is the editor of "L'Action Française," the fighting paper of the Royalists. It is a bitter and clever attack on the Foreign Policy of the Republic.
13. Sembat: "Faites un Roi, sinon faites la paix." Marcel Sembat is one of the leading Socialists of France, and this book of his is a reply to the Royalist attacks on the Republic. It and the book by Maurras throw a high light on the internal affairs of modern France.
14. Tardieu: "La Conférence d'Algésiras." This is the most authoritative book by M. Tardieu and by far the best discussion in French of the Algeciras Crisis.

A selection from the mass of German books on European politics is also exceedingly difficult. I have found something of interest in the following:

1. Andrassy (the son): "Ungarns Augsleich mit Oesterreich." This gives the point of view of one of the Hungarian parties towards the problems of the Dual Monarchy.
2. Dehn: "Deutschland und der Orient" and "Deutschland nach Osten." The program of the Pan-Germanic League in the Near East.
3. Dernburg: "Zielpunkte des deutschen Kolonialwesens." Dr. Dernburg, well known in America, was for a while Minister of Colonies. This book is the fruit of that experience.
4. Franz: "Die Weltpolitik." Two volumes published in 1882-3. This is perhaps the most important work of this voluminous writer. During most of his life he was rather under a cloud as he was a bitter opponent of Bismarck. But of recent years pan-Germanic writers have borrowed heavily from his books. His theories were a strange mixture of Liberalism and World Domination. Virulent in his hostility to the Slavs, he was pro-English.
5. Goebel: "Das Deutschtum in den Vereintigten Staaten." An account of the progress of the German idea in the United States. A good presentation of the non-aggressive and unobjectionable phase of the Deutschtum.
6. Goette: "Deutscher Völkegeist." I have used quotations from this writer.
7. Lange: "Reines Deutschtum." Friedrich Lange has been one of the spokesmen of the more hectic pan-Germanism.
8. Naumann: "Asia." This writer is a protestant pastor. The book was inspired by the Kaiser's pilgrimage to the Holy Land. This pan-Germanist's comments on the Armenian massacres will shock all sincere Christians.
9. Popovici: "Die Vereintigten Staaten Oesterreichs." The author is a Roumanian of Bukovina. His book—

a plea for justice to the subject-races—is prohibited in Hungary.
10. Rohrbach. (*a*) "Die Bagdadbahn," (*b*) Der deutsche Gedanke in der Welt." Paul Rohrbach is one of the best known and widely respected writers on politics in modern Germany. His last book, "German Thought Throughout the World," has had an immense circulation. His point of view is moderate—one might almost say "modest"—pan-Germanism. His book on the Bagdad Railroad is specially interesting.
11. Sprenger. "Babylonien." Dr. Sprenger is one of the most erudite orientalists of our day. His studies on Islamic subjects—especially his Life of Mohammed—are authoritative. In this book he has turned aside from his scientific specialty and has adventured into Weltpolitik. He develops the "manifest destiny" of Germany in the Near East.
12. Springer: "Der Kampf der Oesterreichischen Nationen und den Staat." The author is a democrat and approaches the race problem in Austria from this point of view.
13. von Bülow (Joachim): "West-Morokko deutsche?" A pan-Germanic treatise on the Moroccan controversy.
14. von Halle: "Die volks- und Seevirtschaftlichen Beziehungen zwischen Deutschland und Holland." A discussion of the relations between Germany and the Netherlands.
15. Wagner: "Krieg." A treatise on war makes von Bernhardi's writings sound effeminate.
16. Wirth: "Volkstum und Weltmacht in der Geschite." An example of the pseudo-history on which the more inflated pan-Germanic dreams have been based.
17. Woltmann: (*a*) "Die Germanen und die Renaissance in Italien" (*b*) "Die Germanen in Frankreich." The first is the one in which he tries to prove that the real name of Leonardo di Vinci was Wincke.

INDEX

A

Africa, colonial ventures in, a cause of friction between Germany and England, 56–58; question of value of colonies in, to France, 203–204; division of colonial spoils in, if Allies win, 245–246; German claims in, in case of her victory, 260.

Agadir crisis, the, 118–122.

Algeciras Conference, events leading to the, 84–85; diplomatic defeat of Germany at, 93–95; War Party in Germany strengthened by, 99; participation of United States in, 99, 284, 287.

Allies, compared with Germany as to strength, 220; handicap to, of lack of centralized command, 220–221; lack of coördination among, shown by fiascos of fall of 1915, 221; improbability of breaking up of, 221–222; potential strength in field, compared with Germany, 222–223; good outlook for, from military point of view, 224; military outcome of War in case of victory by, 224–227; diplomatic tactics to be brought against, by Germany, in case of defeat of latter, 228; obvious joints in armor of, 229 ff.; demands of, in case of victory, 235–240; division of spoils by, 241–247; apportionment of Turkey and Asia Minor among, 248–253.

Alsace-Lorraine, application of theory of nationalities to, 171; prosperity under German rule, 171–172; independence or a union with Switzerland among propositions for eventual disposition of, 172; plans of Allies as to, in case of German defeat, 235.

Army, attitude of Germans toward their, 33.

Army increase law passed by Germans (June, 1913), 148.

Asia Minor, reapportionment of, if Allies win, 248–253.

Austria-Hungary, alliance between France and, feared by Bismarck, 13; formation of alliance between Germany and, 14; part taken by, in Bosnia and Herzegovina affair, 113–118; course of, in Balkan wars of 1912, 143–146; confusion of ethnological map of, and resulting difficulty of application of rights of nations theory, 168; three groups of population in, and numbers in each group, 169; project to transform into a Triple State, 169; favored position of section of Poles under rule of, 174–175; position as to trade routes, 183; crude methods of influencing public opinion in, 207; territorial demands on, in case Allies win, 237.

B

Bagdad railroad, German project for a, 65–68; bitterness caused by English opposition to, 68; interest of cotton interests in, owing to future plantations along route, 196; oil-bearing district to be opened up by, 196; differing opinions among different interests in England concerning, if Allies win, 250–251.

Balkans, alliance of powers in, declares war on Turkey, 124; historical development of states in, 124–139; question of origin of alliance of 1912, 140; secret treaties previous to breaking out of war, 141; course of the war, and results, 142–145; war between states in, resulting from disposition of spoils, 145–146; effects on Germany of the wars in, 148.

Belgium, treatment of, by Allies if they win, 235, 241; fate of, if Germany wins, 258; effect on American opinion of German treatment of, 297–298.

Bessarabia, taken from Roumania by Russia, 133; difficulty raised by applying rights of nations theory to, 166; slight chance of relinquishment by Russia, 168.

Birth rate, fluctuations in, and relation to colonial enterprise of different nations, 191–193.

Bismarck, policy of, at time of Congress of Berlin, 6, 7, 8 ff., 13; "coalition nightmare" of, 13, 17; forms alliance between Germany and Austria, 14; assertion by, of German supremacy on continent of Europe, 14; as an idealist, 15–16; supremacy of Germany in Europe apparently established by, 16; draws Italy into Triple Alliance, 18–19; forms the Dreikaisersbund, 20; policy of eliminating France, 21; policy of encouraging France in colonial adventure, 22; dropping of, by Kaiser Wilhelm II., 22; disadvantages attached to heritage left German nation by, 22–23; French colonial adventures encouraged by, 38; causes of rupture between Kaiser Wilhelm II. and, 39; question of postponement of dual alliance by, 42–43; responsible for German lack of colonies, 200; may have been right in not wanting colonies, 205; manipulation of public opinion by, 207.

Boer War, effect of, on British life, 69; demonstrates to English the danger of their position, 70.

Books, comparative difficulty of censoring, 210.

Bosnia and Herzegovina, affair of, 113–118.

Boulanger, General, doctrines of, 16.

Bucarest, treaty of, 146.

Bulgaria, creation of principality of, 5; beginnings of, as a national unit, 127–128; progress under dictatorship of Stamboulov, 128; political and educational conditions in, 128–129; interest in liberation of Macedonians, 129; defeat of, in second Balkan war, 145–146; question of responsibility of, for second Balkan war, 146; penalizing of, in case of Allies' victory, 237; claims of, if Germany wins, 259.

Bureau of American Republics, a step toward the right form of national defence, 307; establishment of schools in Mexico the logical work of, in interests of international peace, 308.

C

Casablanca crisis, the, 107.

Censorship of the press by governments, 206–211.

Chamberlain, Professor, apostle of religion of the "Deutschtum," 31–32.

Chervin, Arthur, definition of principle of rights of nations by, 165.

Clapp, discussion of British naval war against neutrals in book by, 295.

Coalitions, drawbacks to, 220–221.

Colonial expansion, European attitude toward, 80–82.

Colonies, importance of question of, in European diplomacy, 190–191; three main causes for desire for, 191; effect of surplus population on desire for, 191–195; value as a source of raw material, 195–196; importance as sales-markets, 197–199; points to consider in judging value of, 199; reasons for Germany's increasing interest in, 199–201; two systems of colonization, monopoly and free trade, 201–202; arguments of economic writers against the rage for, 202–205.

Commerce, rivalry between England and Germany in field of, 62–63; questions of, which enter into modern diplomacy, 178–189.

Congress of Berlin, monarchical character of, 3; marks the end of an epoch, 3–4; events leading to, 4–6; brilliancy of, 6–7; account of intrigues and diplomatic double-dealings at, 7–12; regarded as the starting point for modern diplomacy, 12; ideal of the "Deutschtum" nearly realized at, 16.

Constantinople, Russian claim to, if Allies win, 254; Bulgaria's claim to, in case of German victory, 258.

Cotton, importance of supply of, to European countries, 195–196; future plantations along route of Bagdad railroad, 196.

D

Dardanelles, effect of closing of, on Russian trade, 183; seriousness of closing of, to Allies, 252; military and economic importance of, 253–254; desirability of free trade over, 255; lack of development of great natural wealth about, 255–256.

Delbruck Law, the, 292.

Delcassé, Théophile, succeeds to French foreign office, 48; outstanding personality of, 49; question of attitude toward Germany, 49–50; quarrel of France with Italy smoothed out by, 51; charged with foreseeing and preparing for the war, 52; reported anti-English negotiations with Germany, 52; visit to Saint Petersburg, 52–53; arranges "l'Entente Cordiale" with England, in 1904, 71; resignation demanded by Germany, and downfall of, 88–90; blunders of, in running foreign office single-handed, 90.

Democratic control over foreign affairs, hope for a better Europe in, 270; arguments pro and con, 271–276; risks of war reduced though not eliminated by, 277.

"Deutschtum," the mystic ideal of the Germans, 15; significance of this ideal, 15; seeming realization of, at Congress of Berlin, 16; discussion of meaning of, to Germans and to others, 24; tracing genealogy of the, 25–26; achievements of Germans under ideal of, 28; grouping of the nations to resist development of, 83; non-German Europeans frightened by, 151.

Dewey, John, the "German Philosophy and Politics" of, 25; quoted, 30.

Disraeli, Benjamin, at Congress of Berlin, 3, 6; the "Peace, with honor" of, 3, 12.

"Dollar diplomacy," meaning of, 178.

Dreikaisersbund, formation of, 20; lapsing of, 39.

Dreyfus affair, account of, and results, 44–46.

Dual alliance, formation of, and reasons for, 39–41; significance of, to different nations, 41–42; doubtful if Bismarck could have postponed, 42–43.

E

Economic considerations of modern diplomacy, 178–189.

Education, superiority of Germany over England in, 63; as a remedy for the Mexican menace, 308.

Edward VII., rôle played by, in arrangement of "l'Entente Cordiale" of 1904, 71–72.

Egypt, provisions of "l'Entente Cordiale" concerning, 73–75.

England, relations of Germany and, during Bismarck's régime, 17; disputes with France over Egypt and colonial ventures, 46–48;

date of development of ill-feeling between Germany and, 54; economic growth of Germany largely at expense of, 56; friction with Germany over colonial interests, 56–57; Wilhelm II.'s efforts to reëstablish cordial relations, 57–58; disturbance over growth of German sea power, 58–61; outdone in overseas trade by Germany, 62–63; superiority of German methods in the sea-trade, 64–65; opposition of, to German Bagdad railway project, 65–68; effect on, of war in South Africa, 69; open to French approaches in 1901, 71; signing of "l'Entente Cordiale," 71; provisions of "l'Entente Cordiale," 72 ff.; apparent diplomatic insincerity of, in period after Algeciras Conference, 102; insincerity of, in preachments about preserving the status quo, 102–103; *entente* signed with Russia in 1907, 106–107; loss of prestige in Near East by, owing to *entente* with Russia, 113; unwillingness to fight for Serbia in Bosnian affair, 116; supports France in Agadir crisis, 121–122; disinclination to aid Russia against Germany and Austria in Balkan crisis, 147; reluctance to be drawn into Balkan dispute may have governed Germany in choice of pretence for war, 158; show of German friendliness toward, on eve of War, 158–159; significance of sea-rule by, to other nations, 184–185; question of value of colonies to, 203; government control of public opinion in, 208–209; percentage of potential strength of, in the field, 223; objections of other nations to sea-rule of, 229–230; claims of, in Africa if Allies win, 246; troops of, at work in Asia Minor, 249; question raised by denial of trading rights to neutrals by, 295–297.

Entente Cordiale, steps leading up to, and signing of, 69–71; question of part taken by Edward VII. in, 71–72; discussion of provisions of, and their significance, 72 ff.; secret clauses in the, 77–80; generally favorable reception of, in England and France, 80; opposition of French Socialists, 82; German opposition to, 82–83; action resulting from, by Germany, leading to downfall of Delcassé, 84–91.

F

Fashoda affair, the, 47–48.
Fez, French expedition to, resulting in Agadir crisis, 119–121.
Fichte, German ideals established by, 26.
France, alliance between Austria and, feared by Napoleon, 13; Bismarck's efforts to prevent union of Russia and, 20–21; Bismarck's policy of elimination of, 21; saved by Russia and England from a second invasion in 1875, 21; the Schnaebelé incident, 21–22; encouraged in colonial adventure by Bismarck, 22; rebirth of, after 1870, 36 ff.; steps in creation of present wealth of, 37–38; colonial expansion of, 38; alliance formed between Russia and, 39; reasons for Franco-Russian alliance, 39–40; the question of revenge, and of fear of fresh German aggressions, 40–41; "*l'affaire Dreyfus*," 44–46; bad state of relations between England and, 46; disputes with England over Egypt and colonial ventures, 46–48; the Fashoda affair, 47–48; Delcassé's policy as Foreign Minister, 49–53; first *entente* signed with Italy, 51; England ready to receive friendly approaches of, in 1901, 71; signing of "l'Entente Cordiale" with England, in 1904, 71; significance of "l'Entente Cordiale," 72–80; humiliation of, by Germany in forcing resignation of Delcassé,

88–90; failure of German plans for further humiliation of, at Algeciras, 92–94; Conference of Algeciras a diplomatic victory for, 95–96; question of sincerity of, in signing agreement of Algeciras, 97–98; expedition to Fez and the Agadir crisis, 118–122; position of, viewed from an economic standpoint, 179; question of value of colonies to, 203–204; percentage of potential force in field, as compared with Germany, 222; claims of, in Asia Minor if Allies win, 251.

Frankfort, treaty of, 3.

Free trade, solution of modern economic problems offered by, 186–187, 189; system of, in colonization, 202.

G

German East Africa, treatment to be accorded, if Allies win, 246.

Germany, delicate situation of, at time of Congress of Berlin, 6; mystic ideal expressed in word "Deutschtum," 15; national pride in superiority and preëminence of German race, 16–17; disadvantages of heritage left to, by Bismarck, 22–23; analysis of "das Deutschtum," and achievements under, 24–35; attitude of nation toward the army and war, 33, 34; essential difference between beliefs of, and beliefs of rest of world, 35; foundation of French fears of fresh aggressions by, 40–41; attitude toward dual alliance, 41; date of development of ill-feeling between England and, 54; marvellous advance of, and question of influence of Wilhelm II. in this growth, 54–56; development of colonial policy and resulting friction with England, 56–58; growth of sea power, 58–61; excels England in overseas trade, 62–63; superiority of methods of, in the sea-trade, 64–65; increased bad feeling toward England caused by Bagdad railroad project, and English opposition to, 65–68; sides with Boers in war in South Africa, 69–70; opposition of, to "l'Entente Cordiale," 82–83; the Algeciras crisis, 84 ff.; resignation of Delcassé forced by, 88–90; failure of plan to humiliate France at Algeciras, 92–93; attitude of smaller states shown toward, 93–95; War Party in, strengthened by results of Conference of Algeciras, 99–100; lost opportunity for successful crusade by, at time of Algeciras crisis, 100–101; diplomatic defeat of, in Casablanca crisis, 107–108; wins friendship of Young Turks, 112; diplomatic victory over Russia in Bosnia-Herzegovina affair, 113–117; yields to Anglo-French combination in Agadir affair, 121–122; deprives Serbia of fruits of victory in Balkan war, 147–148; detrimental effect on, of Balkan wars, 148; passes army increase law, 148; ideals of, a cause of joint fear among non-Germans, resulting in their union, 151 ff.; limited influence of pan-Germanists, 152; claim of a divine mission, 154; the claim that she is fighting a defensive war, 156; not German soil but the German ideal that is being defended, 157; reasons governing choice of time and manner of going to war, 157–159; problems of national unity in, 170–176; unsatisfactoriness of rule in Poland, 174; economic situation of, from viewpoint of "dollar diplomacy," 178–179; political motive of high tariff in, 180; question of trade routes, 181–183; relative poverty of, in colonies, 199–200; manipulation of public opinion in, 207–208; outcome of War in case of definite defeat of, 224 ff.; territorial demands on, in case Allies win, 237; diplomatic tactics in case of defeat of, 228–234; militarism of, to be destroyed, 237–238; blows to economic life that may be inflicted, 239–240; results in case of victory of, 257–261; possible Europeanization of, 261.

Gibraltar, comparative importance of Gallipoli and, 253.

Götte, Rudolf, "Deutscher Volkgeist" by, 32.

Great Britain. *See* England.

Greece, modern political history of, 134–137; possible gains to, in case of Allies' victory, 237; claims of, in Asia Minor, 251–252.

H

Hague Conference, attitude of American representatives at first, 285; position of United States at second, 286.

Hanotaux, Gabriel, French foreign minister, 41, 46; criticism of policy of, 48; resigns after Fashoda incident, 48.

Heligoland, cession of, to Germany by England, 57; Gallipoli more important than, 253.

Holland, fate of, if Germany wins, 258.

Honesty in state affairs, advantages of, 270–271.

Hyphenated Americans, problem of, 291–292.

I

Italy, position of, after 1878, 18; reasons for joining Triple Alliance, 19; first *entente* between France and, 51; declares war on Turkey in 1911, 122; ethnological problems raised by application of theory of rights of nations to, 168; situation of, from an economic viewpoint, 179; mystery surrounding entrance into War, 232; results to, of Allies' victory, 237; problems raised by territorial claims of, 242–244; claims of, in southern Asia Minor if Allies win, 251; results to, if Germany wins, 259.

J

Japan, danger of American invasion by, 308–309; how best to plan to insure peace with, 310.

Joffre, General, first appearance in French military history, 39.

K

Karageorovitch dynasty in Bulgaria, pro-Russian sympathies of, 130–131.

Kitchener, General, at Fashoda, 48.

L

League of American Republics, great advantages to be derived from a, 319–320; difficulties to be overcome before establishing, 320–322; persistent efforts necessary to prepare ground for, 323; the benefits of success, 323–324.

Lusitania, effect of sinking of, on American feeling toward Germany, 298.

M

Macedonia, interest of Bulgarians in liberation of, 129; location of, and description, 137–138; quarrels of different claimants to, 138; people and language of, 138–139; the cause of the Balkan alliance of 1912 and war on Turkey, 139–140; disposition of, by secret treaties prior to war with Turkey, 141; difficulty of applying rights of nations theory to, 166; Bulgaria's claim to, if Germany wins, 259.

Marchand, Colonel, at Fashoda, 47–48.

INDEX

Maurras, Charles, arguments of, against Republican form of government, 271.

Mesopotamia, British troops already conquering, 249; differing opinions in England as to best policy in, 250.

Mexico, spread of education in, advocated as a defensive step, 308; importance of the A. B. C. mediation in, as a step in right direction, 319.

Monroe Doctrine, the, 281; remarkable vitality of, 282; attitude of European statesmen toward, 282; corollary of, is Europe for the Europeans, 283; loss of meaning with shrinking of the earth, 285; still in force, though modified, 287; American traditional policy is to keep alive, 288.

Morocco, provisions of "l'Entente Cordiale" concerning, 73–76; attitude of different classes in France concerning, 81–82; affairs of, under discussion at Conference of Algeciras, 93–95; means used by France to overthrow independence of, 98; Franco-German agreement concerning, especially regarding railroads, 109–110; the Agadir crisis, 118–122.

Munitions of war, controversy over export of, 299–301.

N

National defence, American problem of, 305; friendly understandings between nations the best form of, 305–307; value of Bureau of American Republics in American scheme of, 307; spread of education in Mexico one means of, 307–308; establishing a friendly footing with Japan, 308–309; creation of a Bureau of the Pacific, 310; increased army called for by the General Staff not the most important element, 311–312.

Nationalities, theory of. *See* Rights of nations.

Navy, dependence of England upon her, 59; steps in development of German, 59–61.

Newspapers, governmental influence exercised on public opinion through, 206–209.

O

O'Farrell, book by, cited on cause of growth of Germany, 55.

Overproduction, need for foreign markets signified by, 197.

P

Pan-Germanists, limited influence of, in regard to the War, 152.

Pan-Slavism, history of expression, 163.

Peace, public opinion preoccupied with problem of, 211–213; relation of diplomats to question of, 213; two conceptions of, the "pax Romana" and a peace based on mutual justice, 213; why it is fantastic to expect peace to grow out of war, 214; basis of a permanent, dependent upon public opinion, 215–216; what United States may do to preserve, 319–324.

Peace conference, choice of a place for holding, 226–227.

Persia, partition of, by England and Russia, 102, 107.

Petroleum supply, rivalry of nations for control of, 196.

Philippines, question of value of, as a colony, 204.

Poland, difficulty of applying theory of rights of nations to, 167, 175; unsatisfactoriness of German rule in, 172–174; easier fate of Russian section, 174; favored position of Austrian section, 174–175; possibility of autonomy for, in case of German defeat, 177; plans of Allies as to, in case of German

defeat, 235–236; results to, if Germany wins, 259.
Population, relation of, to colonial enterprise, 191–195.
Portugal, British diplomatic controversy with (1915), 232; treatment of colonial holdings of, if Allies win, 246.
Press censorship, 207–211.
Prussia, special hatred for, felt by Germany's enemies, 237–238; treatment of, by Allies if they win, 238.
Public opinion, growth of, and its force, 206–207; methods of manipulation of, by governments, 207; governmental control of, in Austria, Germany, England, and France, 207–210; difficulty of censoring newspapers and books, 210; governmental effort to direct, an admission of force of, 211; preoccupation of, with problem of a permanent peace, 211–213; real decisions as to basis of permanent peace will depend upon, 215–216.

R

Raw material, value of colonies as a source of, 195–196.
Reichstadt, treaty of, 5.
Rights of nations, theory of the, 163; English, Russians, and French favorable to, 165; only white men included in theory, 165; not accepted by Germans, 166; difficulty of applying in cases like Bessarabia, Macedonia, Poland, the Tyrol, etc., 166–168; applied to Slav population of Austria-Hungary, 168–170; difficulties presented by Poland, 172–175; extent of application dependent on outcome of War, 176–177.
Rivers, not good frontiers, 172.
Roosevelt, Theodore, and the Algeciras crisis, 99, 284; effect on American foreign policy of belief in United States as a World Power, 286; great body of Americans not converted by, 287; opposed to United States neutrality in the War, 291, 292–293.
Roumania, coöperates with Russia in war against Turkey, 5; historical development of, 131–132; modern conditions in, 132–133; despoiled of Bessarabia by Russia, 133; neutrality of, in present War, 134; Roumanian peasants in Austro-Hungarian provinces, 168–169; probable results to, of Allies' victory over Germans, 236–237; territorial claims of, 244–245.
Russia, successful campaign of, against Turkey, prior to Congress of Berlin, 4–6; alliance of 1879 between Austria and Germany directed against, 14; reasons for joining the Dreikaisersbund, 20; kept from uniting with France, by Bismarck, 20–21; German alliance with, not favored by Kaiser Wilhelm II., 39; alliance formed between France and, 39; reasons for Franco-Russian alliance, 39–40; Delcassé's visit to, in 1901, 52–53; *entente* signed in 1907 with England, 106–107; forced to yield in Bosnia-Herzegovina affair, 115–118; satisfaction over downfall of Bulgaria in second Balkan war, 146; forced to sacrifice interests of Serbia by Germany, 148; favorable economic situation of, 178; growing importance of foreign trade, 179; disadvantages to, of insufficient access to ice-free seas, 181; effect on trade of, of closing of Dardanelles, 183; percentage of potential force of, in field, 222–223; treatment of Poland by, in case of Allies' victory, 235–236; claims of, in Asia Minor, 253; English and French promise of Constantinople to, 254; dependence of future of Europe on internal politics of, 264; chances of a successful revolution in, 265.

S

San Stefano, treaty of, 5.
Schleswig-Holstein, application of theory of nationalities to, 170–171.
Schnaebelé incident, the, 21–22.
Secrecy, arguments for and against diplomatic, 231–232, 270 ff.
Sembat, Marcel, defence of Republican form of government by, 271, 272.
Serbia, clashes with Austria in Bosnia-Herzegovina affair, 113–118; disgust of, over Russian concessions, 118; beginnings of, as a national unit, 129; struggles of, against Austria-Hungary resulting in pro-Russian sympathies, 130–131; bullying of, by Austria and Germany after war of 1912, 143–145; victory over Bulgaria in second Balkan war, 145–146; gains prestige in second Balkan war, 148; treatment of, by Allies in case of their victory, 236; territorial claims of, 244; fate of, if Germany wins, 259.
Slavs, first appearance of, in Balkans, 125; great population of, in Austria-Hungary, and disposition under theory of nationalities, 169; effect on, of Italy's territorial claims, 243.
Socialists, opposition of, in France, to the Moroccan adventure, 82.
Spain, share of, in secret agreement between France and England, 87, 88; *entente* between France and, 88; marriage of king to an English princess, 95.
Suez Canal, threatened competition of Bagdad railroad with, 250.
Sweden, angering of, by British naval policy, 221.

T

Talleyrand, tactics of, at Congress of Vienna, 228.
Tardieu, André, as spokesman of French foreign office, 209.
Tariffs, as an economic consideration of diplomacy, 178–181.
Theory of nationalities, the, 163.
Toynbee, Arnold, "Nationality and the War" by, 210, 267.
Trade routes, as an economic consideration of diplomacy, 181–189.
Trading rights of neutrals, 295–297.
Trieste, conflict of Italian, Slav, and German interests in, 243.
Triple Alliance, formation of, 19.
Turkey, Russia's victorious war against, 4–6; delegates of, at Congress of Berlin, 7, 8; existence of, at stake, 9; Young Turk revolution, 110; diplomatic intrigues in, in period following 1906, 110–112; Italy declares war on, in 1911, 122; war of Balkan alliance against, 124, 140–142; the fate of, in case of Allies' victory, 237, 246–247, 248–256; possible arrangements with, if Germany wins, 258–259.
Tyrol, difficulty of applying theory of nationalities to, 167–168.

U

United States, Wilhelm II.'s policy toward, 34; participation in Algeciras Conference, 99, 284, 287; question of part taken by, in Agadir affair, 121; growing importance of foreign trade, 179; as a place for holding Peace Conference, 226–227; objections of, to sea-rule of England, 229–230; traditional foreign policy of, 281 ff.; the Monroe Doctrine, 281–283; not expected to intervene in European affairs, 283–284; representatives of, at first Hague Conference, 285; effect of President Roosevelt's view of, as a World Power, 286; at second Hague Conference, 286; question of influence to be exerted on Europe by, 286–287; not pledged not to go to war with European powers, 288–289; revolution in our concept of life necessary if we would be a World Power, 290; problems brought by the War to, 291 ff.; sources of opposition to neutrality of, in the War, 291; shock from development of hyphenated American, 291–292; problem of attack on neutral policy of, led by Mr. Roosevelt, 292; majority of citizens hardly in favor of *Weltpolitik*, 293; question of what to do to protect American interests, 295; British infraction of trading rights of, as a neutral, 295–297; anger roused against Germany by outraging of Belgium and sinking of *Lusitania*, 297–298; consideration of our military situation forced upon us by the War, 302–304; sane statesmanship would adhere to maintenance of neutrality, 304; problem of national defence, 305 ff.; establishment of friendly relations with other powers, 306–307; means of bettering relations with Mexico, 307–308; investments in peace with Japan, 308–310; an increased army not the most important element in scheme of national defence, 311; Peace League of American Republics a promising field for work by, 319–324.

V

Veblen, book by, cited on cause of growth of German economic strength, 55.

W

Walfish Bay, clashing of English and Germans at, 56, 57.

War, attitude of mass of German people toward, 34.

Wilhelm II., Bismarck dropped by, 22; policy of, toward United States, 34; causes of rupture between Bismarck and, 39; reason for acceptance of dual alliance by, 43; attitude toward peace and war, 43–44; in his own way has tried to live on good terms with his neighbors, 44; beginning of ill-feeling between Germany and England coincident with advent of, 54; extent of influence of, on advance of Germany since his accession, 54–55; development of German sea power by, 58–61; address to Sultan of Morocco at Tangier, 86; worsted at Algeciras Conference, 93–95; qualified peace doctrines of, 152.

Wilson, President, opponents of neutral policy of, 291; effect of policy, if successful, 302.

Y

Yellow Peril, misconceptions concerning, 308–310.

Young Turks, question as to who financed revolution of, 110–112; won over by Germany, 112.

Z

Zanzibar, Anglo-German friction over, 56, 57.

Printed in the United States of America.

THE following pages contain advertisements of books by the same author.

BY THE SAME AUTHOR

The Barbary Coast

By ARTHUR BULLARD ("ALBERT EDWARDS")
Author of "Panama," "Comrade Yetta," etc.

Illustrated, 12°, $2.00

Arthur Bullard's "Panama: The Canal, the Country and the People" has gone into many editions and received wide and favorable comment. In this new volume Mr. Bullard relates some of his remarkable and always interesting experiences in the states of northern Africa. Mr. Bullard does not write with a history or a book at his elbow; what he says does not come to the reader from a second-hand knowledge. He has been in Africa himself and he writes out of his own life. "The Barbary Coast" has freshness and vigor, newness in point of view and a wealth of adventure. Beginning with Algiers, Mr. Bullard's book contains chapters as follows: The Sirocco, Bedouins, Spaniards, Arabs, The Shareef of Makainfain, Hadje Mohmed of Luna Park, Asmassian — Apostle of Civilization, The Best Story I Ever Heard, The Magic Carpet, Housekeeping in Mogador, The Beggars of Mogador, The Religion of Muley Khamedo, The Song of Muley Khamedo, and The Perfumes of Araby.

"Unless our critical judgment errs exceedingly, the author has caught the romance and atmosphere of Algiers and all the Barbary Coast as have very few other writers. There is character, there is reflection, and there is human interest throughout. The book is literature or it is nothing; and . . . we venture to assert that these sketch-stories are truly literature. They have charm, they have color, and they have reality."— *The Outlook*.

THE MACMILLAN COMPANY
Publishers   64-66 Fifth Avenue   New York

BY THE SAME AUTHOR

A NOVEL OF GREAT SOCIAL SIGNIFICANCE

Comrade Yetta
By ARTHUR BULLARD ("ALBERT EDWARDS")
Author of "A Man's World"

Cloth, 12mo, $1.35

"Comrade Yetta" is the story of a young Jewess, — *Yetta* — a girl typical of thousands who fill our factories and sweat shops. It tells of her evolution from a worker at the machine to a leader among her people.

As in "A Man's World" Mr. Bullard has written fearlessly and vividly out of an intimate knowledge of the New York City underworld.

He has painted in bold realism the tragic picture of the east side and laid bare the industrial shame of a great city in a novel that is powerful in its truth and sincerity.

"We welcome this novel for its truth, for its nobility of purpose, for its fearlessness," says Milton Bronner of Arthur Bullard's "Comrade Yetta." "Its people are live people. Their actions are those of flesh and blood beings. They become part of the reader's world. Read the novel and you will understand something about certain New York strikes. You will understand the spirit that animates the propagandists. You will know how Tammany works in the dark. And best of all, you will renew your faith in mankind and believe that, after all, these things that outrage your sensibilities so are part of the evolutionary ferment that will eventually lead to a cleaner, better civilization."

THE MACMILLAN COMPANY
Publishers   64-66 Fifth Avenue   New York

BY THE SAME AUTHOR

A Man's World

BY ARTHUR BULLARD ("ALBERT EDWARDS")

Cloth, 12mo, $1.25

"A striking book that should attract wide attention." — *New York Tribune.*

"There never has been a book like 'A Man's World.' . . . A novelist of skill and power. . . . His greatest gift is his power of creating the illusion of reality. . . . Vividness and conviction unite in the wonderful portrait of Nina. . . . There never has been such a character in American fiction before. . . . Nina will be one of the famous twentieth century heroines." — *Brooklyn Eagle.*

"It is a great book, full of the real things of life. . . . Zola might have written such a book had he lived in New York and not in Paris. Yet, it is doubtful if he could have told a better tale in a better way, for Nina and Ann are just as true to life as Nana and Ninon." — *Chicago Record-Herald.*

"The book is far from ordinary and its philosophy is extraordinary." — *New York Times Book Review.*

"A new type of human document — written in all sincerity and honesty." — *New York Herald.*

THE MACMILLAN COMPANY
Publishers   64–66 Fifth Avenue   New York

BY THE SAME AUTHOR

PANAMA, the Canal, the Country, and the People

By ARTHUR BULLARD ("ALBERT EDWARDS")

Illustrated, new edition, 8°, $2.00

"A thoroughly satisfactory book for one who is looking for solid information." — *Boston Globe*.

"A most interesting picture of the country as it is to-day." — *San Francisco Chronicle*.

"One of the very few books on any Latin-American country that gives any idea of the whole land and people." — *Los Angeles Times*.

"One of the very best of travel books." — *Continent*.

"Lively and readable, containing the real atmosphere of the tropics." — *Minneapolis Tribune*.

"A book which every American ought to read, both for pleasure and profit." — *New York Herald*.

THE MACMILLAN COMPANY
Publishers   64–66 Fifth Avenue   New York